The Invisible
Empire in
the West

The Invisible Empire in the West

Toward a New
Historical Appraisal
of the Ku Klux Klan
of the 1920s

Edited by Shawn Lay

University of Illinois Press

URBANA AND CHICAGO

First paperback edition, 2004
© 1992, 2004 by the Board of Trustees
of the University of Illinois
All rights reserved
Manufactured in the United States of America
P 5 4 3 2 1

♾ This book is printed on acid-free paper.

The Library of Congress cataloged the hardcover
edition as follows:
The Invisible empire in the West : toward a new
historical appraisal of the Ku Klux Klan of the 1920s /
edited by Shawn Lay.
p.   cm.
Includes index.
ISBN 0-252-01832-X
1. Ku Klux Klan (1915–)—West—History.
I. Lay, Shawn.
HS2330.K63158   1992
322.4'2'0978—dc20   91–2081
Paperback ISBN 0-252-07272-9

Contents

Preface

Like many other people who delve into the history of their local communities, I was shocked to learn that a large and thriving chapter of the Ku Klux Klan had existed in my hometown during the 1920s. This was particularly unsettling because I had believed that El Paso, Texas, the city where my family and I had resided for more than twenty years, had always been a remarkably tolerant and peaceful community. Located hundreds of miles from other large Texas cities, El Paso has historically been much more of a western community than a southern one, a city distinguished by a unique border culture based on considerable ethnic and cultural accommodation. How could the Knights of the Ku Klux Klan, a secret society that espoused white Protestant supremacy and engaged in acts of brutal terror, ever have recruited thousands of El Pasoans to its sinister cause?

In the early 1980s, as a graduate student working on my master's thesis at the University of Texas at El Paso, I began to piece together the story of the local Klan. That required more than two years of combing through microfilm copies of newspapers and other sources, engaging in the type of pick-and-spade research that most scholars prefer to relegate to poorly paid assistants, but the results were both rewarding and, to me at least, surprising. Rather than being composed of unrestrained racists and bigots from the lower reaches of the socioeconomic order, the El Paso Klan clearly drew the bulk of its membership from the local middle class. Although the hooded order ardently proclaimed the superiority of white Protestant Americans, it cleverly subsumed its bigotry within a number of important and legitimate local issues, and as a result it became a powerful political force in El Paso for a period. The Klan was without doubt disruptive and did much to poison community relations, but I found no evidence that the group engaged in the violent vigilantism and racial terror the KKK used in eastern and southern parts of Texas. Indeed, minus their white robes and hoods, Klansmen appeared to be quite similar to other politically active middle-class citizens concerned about the course of local society.

When my thesis was published as *War, Revolution, and the Ku Klux Klan: A Study of Intolerance in a Border City* in 1985, I doubted whether my conclusions concerning the El Paso Klan would hold true for KKK chapters elsewhere. El Paso is, after all, a unique city, located on the Mexican border and possessed of a population that in the early 1920s was more than 60 percent Hispanic and Roman Catholic. The local Klan had clearly been forced to adapt to unusual circumstances. After entering the graduate program in history at Vanderbilt University, however, I began for the first time to thoroughly explore Klan historiography and encountered detailed examinations of the Klan that had arrived at conclusions very similar to mine. One of the most important, Robert A. Goldberg's *Hooded Empire: The Ku Klux Klan in Colorado* (1981), was based on his 1977 doctoral dissertation that focused on the Klan in five Colorado communities. Using rare Klan membership data, Goldberg demonstrated that members of the hooded order were drawn from a balanced cross-section of the white Protestant population. He further observed that local conditions profoundly shaped the Klan's program and activities and varied from community to community. Another work that placed the Klan in a detailed local context was Christopher N. Cocoltchos's 1979 doctoral dissertation on the KKK in Orange County, California, a study that made extensive use of a comprehensive Klan membership list. As had Goldberg, Cocoltchos concluded that "the way in which the hooded order grew, the activities in which it engaged, and the reasons for its demise were all locally generated." Composed of average citizens drawn from the broader middle class, the Orange County Klan had been not a form of racial and religious terror but rather a means of mainstream political activism. Similarly, a third important work, Larry R. Gerlach's *Blazing Crosses in Zion: The Ku Klux Klan in Utah* (1982), argued that the KKK in Utah had demonstrated significant local variety and had for the most part attracted ordinary, middle-class residents.

In 1988, while still working on my Ph.D., I contacted Goldberg,

Cocoltchos, and Gerlach about the possibility of putting together an edited volume that would consolidate and distill recent scholarship on Klan chapters in the West. To my great pleasure they responded positively, although they made clear that the project would go nowhere until I had secured a publication contract from a suitable academic press. Fortunately, the University of Illinois Press was willing to take a chance on a book edited by a graduate student, by which time I had secured three more contributors: Oregon Klan experts Eckard V. Toy and David A. Horowitz, and Leonard J. Moore, an authority on the Klan in Indiana, who agreed to write a historiographical essay.

The composition of *The Invisible Empire in the West: Toward a New Historical Appraisal of the Ku Klux Klan of the 1920s* proceeded smoothly for the most part, but there was a significant amount of scholarly debate and discussion. Moore had characterized some of the other contributors' work as being part of a "populist revision," a term that was strongly rejected by Robert Goldberg, who argued that in many places the Klan was far from populistic; some changes were accordingly made to Moore's essay. Goldberg also objected to my initial draft of the volume's introduction, which had emphasized the "anti-elite" nature of early Klan recruiting. "The Klan and elites interacted in a variety of ways," he wrote to me. "The Klan recruited among elites. The Klan opposed elites. The Klan supported some elite groups over other elite groups. Elite groups used the Klan. In many communities elite power was never questioned." Convinced that Goldberg was correct, I modified both the introduction and conclusion to indicate the diverse manner in which the Klan had insinuated itself into particular communities.

In early 1992 *The Invisible Empire in the West* was released. As anyone who has brought a scholarly book to publication knows, there is initially great elation, and relief, but then there is growing worry about the reviews in academic journals. I was particularly concerned because the Ku Klux Klan is a topic that almost inevitably arouses strong emotions and heated discussion, and I feared that reviewers might feel that the volume's commitment to "neutral and sober reasoning" constituted an effort to downplay the more sinister aspects of Klan activity. The culture wars between conservatives and liberals were intensifying during the early 1990s, and there was always the possibility our book would get caught, however unfairly, in the crossfire.

As things turned out, my fears were probably unjustified. Reviews of *The Invisible Empire in the West* were overwhelmingly favorable and indicated that fellow academics of all political persuasions appreciated both the book's approach and general conclusions. Particularly gratifying was a review by Glen Jeansonne, a leading scholar of twentieth-century social and political movements, who described the book as a "valuable corrective grounded in substantial primary research that provides [a] more realistic interpretation." Moreover, Jeansonne noted, "The fact that the Klan was relatively mainstream makes it all the more disturbing; it would have been less dangerous if it had been an aberration." The reviewer for the *Journal of the West* similarly observed, "In seeking a more accurate picture [of the KKK] the authors are certainly not apologists for the Klan. To indicate that the members were mainstream says as much about the mainstream as about Klan members." Assessments such as these provided welcome confirmation that the book's challenge to traditional thinking about the Klan would enable readers to perceive more clearly the complex and subtle ways that intolerance has influenced U.S. society.

Favorable reviews notwithstanding, I have over the years developed some regrets about *The Invisible Empire in the West.* In the spirited effort to counter earlier scholarship on the KKK, the volume probably did not extend sufficient credit to the previous generation of Klan scholars, most notably David M. Chalmers, Kenneth T. Jackson, and Charles C. Alexander. Chalmers's *Hooded Americanism: The First Century of the Ku Klux Klan, 1865–1965* (1965) was characterized by a number of the same deficiencies that had marred earlier work on the KKK, but it also effectively countered the unsubstantiated claim that the Invisible Empire's appeal was confined to America's small towns and declining rural hinterland. Jackson's *The Ku Klux Klan in the City, 1915–1930* (1967) went even further in challenging traditional thinking, emphasizing the predominant role of urban residents in the Klan movement, the rationality of most Klansmen, and the importance of the local case study in assessing the hooded order. Alexander's *The Ku Klux Klan in the Southwest* (1965) likewise argued that the Klan was strongest in urban communities and recruited ordinary citizens who were reacting to very real social problems. As careful readers of *The Invisible Empire in the West* will recognize, the book rests in no small measure on the foundation laid by these senior scholars; indeed, their work can still be consulted to great benefit.

I also have come to regret that the anthology does not provide a better sense of the Klan's adverse impact on community relations. *The Invisible Empire in the West* focuses, as Leonard Moore notes in his essay, on "Klansmen themselves, the communities in which they lived, and the activities in which they engaged." This approach constitutes a revisionist effort to counter earlier work on the Klan that was plagued by, as contributor David Horowitz has observed, "unthinking predispositions, stale formulations, and unwarranted stereotypes." In other words, the priority has been to understand, not to denounce and engage in emotional grandstanding.

A problem with this more objective and dispassionate type of scholarship, however, is that it may fail to provide readers with a full appreciation of how inherently mean-spirited the Klan movement was and thus why it was so ardently opposed. Although Klansmen may have attempted to address legitimate problems and many were sincerely striving to create a better community for their families and fellow citizens, they also knew full well that they belonged to an organization that conspired, spied, lied, and deliberately provoked fear among innocent people. That Klansmen were largely rational and well-established citizens makes their decision to affiliate with the Invisible Empire all the more reprehensible. Although we may increasingly understand why Americans of the 1920s decided to embrace the Klan, it is not a decision that we are obligated in any way to respect.

As I note in the conclusion of *The Invisible Empire in the West,* one of the book's major goals was to assist and encourage additional scholarly work on the Klan of the 1920s. It is unclear how successful the book has been in this regard, but the 1990s did witness the publication of a number of works that presented similar themes and conclusions. Shortly before the anthology's release, two major studies that examined the Klan in the Midwest—William D. Jenkins's *Steel Valley Klan: The Ku Klux Klan in Ohio's Mahoning Valley* and Leonard Moore's *Citizen Klansmen: The Ku Klux Klan in Indiana, 1921–1928*— appeared and largely supported the assessment of the second Invisible Empire presented here. Moore's book was particularly persuasive because it was informed by an unprecedented wealth of Klan membership data and sophisticated statistical analysis. The revisionist assessment of the 1920s' Klan was also strongly endorsed in my book *Hooded Knights on the Niagara: The Ku Klux Klan in Buffalo, New York* (1995). Based on intensive work in local sources, including a comprehensive KKK membership list and dozens of undercover reports on Klan gatherings, I argued that the Buffalo Klan primarily served as a form of mainstream political activism, which suggested that the conclusions of *The Invisible Empire in the West* could be applied to KKK chapters in the industrial Northeast. The anthology's findings were also endorsed by Chris Rhomberg's article on the Oakland, California, KKK in the winter 1998 issue of the *Journal of American Ethnic History* and by David Horowitz's insightful analysis of rare Oregon Klan documents in *Inside the Klavern: The Secret History of a Ku Klux Klan of the 1920s* (1999).

In 1994 Nancy K. MacLean's provocative study *Behind the Mask of Chivalry: The Making of the Second Ku Klux Klan,* which focused on the Klan in Athens, Georgia, was released. Like scholars who have investigated the KKK in other communities, she found that Athens Klansmen were largely middle class, committed to moral reform and strict prohibition enforcement, and politically active, even sweeping the city elections of 1924. MacLean argued, however, that in contrast to most KKK members outside the South, Klansmen in Athens and other parts of northern Georgia often engaged in violent vigilantism. Widespread Klan-sponsored violence in the South has also been detailed in another important study, Glenn Feldman's *Politics, Society, and the Klan in Alabama, 1915–1949* (1999). The conclusions of *The Invisible Empire in the West* and other revisionist scholarship may therefore not fully apply in the South, a region long plagued by exceptional violence. As Feldman's book emphasizes, however, Alabama Klansmen in the 1920s were also ardent proponents of better public schools, expanded road construction, honest elections, improved public health, and other "progressive" initiatives. In fact, the leading progressive figure in the state, Gov. Bibb Graves, served as the Exalted Cyclops (chapter president) of the Klan in Montgomery. Thus, in the South as elsewhere, the more intolerant and dangerous aspects of the Klan movement were often interwoven with mainstream political and social concerns.

Much scholarly work on the Ku Klux Klan of the 1920s remains to be done. The Klan experiences of only a relatively few communities have been examined in detail, and many basic questions about the KKK's membership and activities across the nation are still the subject of academic debate. Nonetheless, scholarship concerning the second Klan has significantly improved in recent years, both in terms of quantity and of quality. Such progress has been the result of diligent research, the careful analysis of rare Klan records, and the determination of scholars not to be restrained by stale and uncritical thinking concerning this notorious organization. This meticulous and objective approach is well displayed in *The Invisible Empire in the West,* and thus the anthology continues to be a valuable resource for those who wish to understand more about the complex, and often surprising, ways that intolerance has shaped the course of American society. During the current acrimonious debate over foreign immigration, affirmative action, the erosion of traditional morality, and other controversial issues, such historical understanding is sorely needed.

The Invisible
Empire in
the West

Introduction:
The Second Invisible Empire

Even in our time of apparent widespread historical illiteracy, few Americans have not heard of the Ku Klux Klan and formed strong opinions about this controversial organization. Many would agree that no single group more starkly demonstrates the endurance of dark social forces in the United States—racism, religious bigotry, extralegal vigilantism, moral authoritarianism—than the Klan, a hooded secret order now well into its second century of existence. As one popular writer has termed it, the KKK is commonly viewed as "America's recurring nightmare," a persistent social virus thriving during periods of exceptional discord, tension, and intolerance.[1] This appraisal, however, obscures the fact that the Klan has not been a monolithic movement throughout its history. Although linked by a common name and a commitment to secrecy, the major episodes of mass Klan activity have been characterized by distinctive organizational features, recruiting patterns, and sociopolitical agendas.

The unsettled conditions of the post–Civil War South fueled the rise of the first Ku Klux Klan, a group Confederate veterans originally formed as a secret social club in Pulaski, Tennessee, in 1866. Throughout the late 1860s, as opposition to federal Reconstruction policies intensified, southerners seized upon the Klan as a promising agency with which to insure the continued dominance of the Democratic party and the white race. Eventually this self-proclaimed "Invisible Empire" spread to every former state of the Confederacy and inaugurated a program of terror against blacks and white Republicans, engaging in what has accurately been described as "one of the most far-flung and persistent crime waves in American history." At first the numerous state, county, and local units of the KKK (which were never truly bound into a centralized regional organization) attracted the support and participation of prominent southerners, especially Democratic politicians, but this backing waned as Klan-sponsored violence became more difficult to control. The withdrawal of elite support coincided with belated federal efforts to restore order in the South under the terms of the Enforcement Acts (1870–71), resulting in the precipitous decline and eventual fading away of the order.[2]

Eight decades later, national policies produced another upsurge in Klan activity in the South, during the civil rights struggle of the 1950s and 1960s, the so-called Second Reconstruction. Outraged by the *Brown* v. *Board of Education of Topeka* decision, growing black political activism, and the use of federal troops during the Little Rock school desegregation crisis, nearly forty thousand southerners had joined some type of Klan group by 1958 in a last-ditch effort to preserve white supremacy. Severe organizational fragmentation, however, undermined the KKK's utility in the resistance movement, with more than two dozen factions–such as Jesse B. Stoner's Christian Knights of the Ku Klux Klan and the Georgia-based U.S. Klans–competing for power and members. Moreover, the Klan held little appeal for middle- and upper-class southerners, most of whom preferred to express their social views through participation in the more genteel White Citizens Councils or by voting for segregationist political candidates. This left control of the Klan in cruder hands, a development well demonstrated by the hundreds of violent acts perpetrated by the various branches of the Invisible Empire throughout the late 1950s and 1960s. Eventually these outrages–most notably the execution-style murders of three civil rights workers in Mississippi in the summer of 1964–forced federal authorities to take strong action against the KKK. The government jailed outspoken leaders such as Robert M. Shelton, head of the powerful United Klans of America, on various charges; and the Federal Bureau of Investigation, utilizing an extensive network of informers, systematically disrupted Klan activities. These efforts proved very effective: by 1968 the FBI estimated that the order's total strength had dwindled to fourteen thousand; by the early 1970s it was less than two thousand.[3]

The Klan, however, soon proved it resilience, Beginning in 1974, an independent KKK faction in Louisiana under the direction of David Duke skillfully exploited the media to spearhead a revival of the Invisible Empire, attracting over three thousand members across the nation.

Duke's group eventually split apart as the result of internecine squabbling, but sizeable pockets of Klansmen persisted in various locales. For the most part, these Klan members were diehard racists and vehement anti-Semites. They also possessed a tendency toward violence, as was revealed by a bloody confrontation with Communist activists in Greensboro, North Carolina, in 1979; the setting up of Klan-sponsored military training camps; and numerous random attacks on individual blacks. By the mid-1980s this violent militancy had led the KKK into a close relationship with other fanatically racist organizations such as the Aryan Nations, the Order, and certain neo-Nazi factions. At present, the KKK remains a militant fringe group, despised by the vast majority of Americans and closely monitored by governmental authorities.[4]

More than seventy years ago, between the eras of the Klans of the first and second Reconstructions, an even more distinctive, and histori-cally significant, Invisible Empire appeared—the Knights of the Ku Klux Klan (Inc.). While its earlier and later namesakes were either confined almost exclusively to the South or were relatively small in size, this organization demonstrated great appeal among mainstream elements across the nation, attracting millions of members at the height of its power in the 1920s. Simultaneously a vast social, political, and folk movement, the Klan of the twenties, more than any other manifestation of the hooded order, succeeded in significantly influencing national life for a period, establishing the white-robed Klansman as one of the enduring symbols of a critical decade in American development. The central mission of this book will be to further our understanding of this important yet elusive secret society.

The reemergence and spread of the Ku Klux Klan in the 1920s can in part be attributed to an earlier process of scholarly and popular cultural revisionism, which changed the way Americans viewed the post–Civil War Klan. According to the "tragic legend of Reconstruction" developed at the turn of the century by prominent northern scholars such as William A. Dunning, John W. Burgess, and John Ford Rhodes, unrelieved corruption and social disorder had characterized the years of Radical rule in the South, with carpetbaggers, scalawags, and semisavage blacks viciously trampling on the rights of the native white population. Given the general chaos and injustice of this dark chapter in American history, white resistance to Radical rule seemed in retro-spect to be understandable, even admirable. While academic authors commonly noted in passing that the Ku Klux Klan had committed some brutal crimes, most would have concurred with future president Woodrow Wilson's assessment that the "white men of the South were aroused by the mere instinct of self-preservation to rid themselves, by fair means or foul, of the intolerable burden of governments sustained by the votes of ignorant negroes [sic] and conducted in the interests of adventurers."[5]

The new view of Reconstruction that emerged in the 1890s and early 1900s remained virtually unchallenged for decades and quickly insinuated itself into mainstream popular thought. The legend of an imperiled Anglo-Saxon people valiantly struggling against the forces of barbarism and corruption conformed well with the aggressive nationalistic and imperialistic sentiments that pervaded early twentieth-century America; it also complemented the emerging theories of inherent racial differences and black inferiority that an influential generation of sociologists and anthropologists were formulating.

Considering these overall trends, it was perhaps not too surprising that the Invisible Empire underwent a popular historical rehabilitation in the decade preceding World War I, most notably in Thomas Dixon's best-selling novel, *The Clansman* (1905), which portrayed the KKK as a noble order that had preserved southern "Civilization" during a dangerous period. In retrospect, Dixon's work seems little more than a self-indulgent exercise in racist paranoia, filled with repulsive descriptions of blacks and an unconvincing idealization of southern whites and the Klan, but the book at the time masterfully pandered to a Victorian and evangelical Protestant mindset that tended to view events and issues in terms of good versus evil.[6] Moreover, the impact of *The Clansman's* Manichaean depiction of the Reconstruction South was not to be confined to the reading public. In the spring of 1914, Dixon sold the screen rights to his novel to the brilliant filmmaker David Wark Griffith. The end result was the appearance the following year of the most artistically ambitious and commercially successful motion picture produced up to that time, *The Birth of a Nation.*

Griffith's cinematic masterpiece constituted a major milestone in the development of mass popular culture and established moviemaking as one of the most powerful forms of artistic expression. It also completed the process of rationalizing and romanticizing the activities of the original Klan. For millions of Americans who viewed *The Birth of a Nation* (many of whom were attending their first motion picture) the enduring image of the Invisible Empire would be of the robed and hooded Klansmen who ride to the rescue of the imperiled white heroine at the film's climax. "It is like writing history with lightning," commented President Wilson after viewing a private screening, "and my only regret is that it is so terribly true." Although civil rights groups such as the National Association for the Advancement of Colored People bitterly protested the film's blatant racism and historical inaccuracies, the public's enthusiasm for Griffith's spectacle swept aside these objections.[7] As the *New York Times* would favorably note in 1916, "This generation is being taught to idealize the Klan. . . . It was the uprising of Confederate soldiers against an intolerable tyranny."[8]

The widespread success of *The Birth of a Nation* offered a promising opportunity for a revival of the Invisible Empire in one form or another. Apparently a short-lived Klan appeared in San Francisco soon after the film's California premiere, but the great KKK movement of the twenties originated in Georgia, founded by William Joseph Simmons, a thirty-five-year-old Spanish-American War veteran and former Methodist circuit rider. Simmons, as historians of the Klan have been fond of pointing out, hardly seemed a likely candidate to head a successful enterprise of any type. Chronic ineptitude had characterized his career as a minister, resulting in a formal suspension by Methodist church authorities in 1912, and a drinking problem undermined what little ability he possessed for long-term planning. Yet, Simmons did have certain assets, including an impressive physical appearance, an ability for effective public speaking, and an amiable personality. After his dismissal from the clergy, Simmons embarked on a career as a professional "fraternalist," soliciting recruits for men's societies such as the Woodmen of the World (which assigned him the honorary rank of "Colonel," a title he would proudly use the rest of his life). The former minister's personal skills served him well in the fraternal world of the South and he eventually rose to the position of district manager for the Woodmen in Atlanta. This moderate bout of success encouraged Simmons in a longstanding ambition to found a men's order of his own. As he envisioned it, the organization would be the grandest of patriotic fraternities, a banding together of true Americans that would "destroy from the hearts of men the Mason and Dixon line and build thereupon a great American solidarity."[9]

After an accident placed him in the hospital for a three-month stay, Colonel Simmons had time to develop detailed plans for his fraternal society. Drawing upon the colorful tales he had heard about the Reconstruction Klan, and recognizing that the public mood was auspicious, Simmons decided to create a Klan of his own, albeit an essentially fraternal one. In the days that followed, the Colonel devised an elaborate Masonically inspired ritual for the order and designed the eerie hoods and robes that would become so notorious; he also laid out an elaborate chain of command for the new Invisible Empire, ranging from an Imperial Wizard at the top of the hierarchy to the various klaliffs, kludds, kligrapps, klabees, kladds, and klexters who would manage the affairs of the organization's various local chapters (dubbed klaverns).[10] By the time of his release from the hospital, all that remained for Simmons to do was to persuade others to join the revived Klan, a task for which his earlier fraternal work had left him well prepared.

The Colonel energetically applied himself to finding members for his new order and by October 1915 had recruited thirty-four Georgians, who successfully petitioned their state for an official charter. On a cold and windy Thanksgiving evening a month later, Simmons and fifteen others of the group ascended Stone Mountain outside Atlanta, ignited a large cross at the peak's summit, and declared the rebirth of the Invisible Empire. This and similar publicity efforts, often in association with Atlanta showings of *The Birth of a Nation,* intensified local interest in the Klan and by the end of the year Atlanta Klan No. 1 was in operation. During the first months of its existence, the new KKK scarcely resembled the original order. Although formally committed to the principles of Protestantism, Americanism, and white supremacy, Klansmen demonstrated little interest in social or political affairs, preferring to occupy their time with fraternal ritualism. The advent of American participation in World War I thrust the Klan into a broader role, however, as the organization became involved with the Citizens' Bureau of Investigation, a volunteer home-front vigilante group. Appointed as "secret-service men" by Imperial Wizard Simmons, Klansmen harassed those they perceived to be slackers, enemy aliens, or immoral women.[11] As spirited as these activities were, they nevertheless drew little special attention to the Klan during a period when many of the nation's citizens were participating in vigilantism of one kind or another. As a southwestern newspaper editor observed in 1918, "In a hundred American communities the Ku Klux Klan is riding again . . . , not by that name, but in that spirit."[12]

Despite its increased activity during the war, the Klan's membership remained small, numbering only a few thousand by the end of 1919, almost all of whom resided in Georgia and Alabama. Chronic financial problems threatened even this modest growth, particularly after a leading Klan officer embezzled several thousand dollars in precious initiation fees. In 1920, however, the KKK's fortunes improved dramatically, following Colonel Simmon's decision to acquire the services of the Southern Publicity Association, a small advertising agency headed by Edward Young Clarke and Elizabeth Tyler. Efficient business managers who realized the Klan's potential had barely been exploited, Clarke and Tyler completely reorganized the secret society's finances and membership procurement procedures, floating large new loans and hiring hundreds of full-time recruiters (kleagles). In short order, Klan representatives were visiting communities across the South, touting the order's commitment to pure Americanism and the defense of traditional standards of law, order, and social morality.[13]

Relatively little is known about the precise manner in which these professional organizers went about setting up fledgling klaverns, but evidently the majority of initial contacts took place in fraternal lodges, particularly those of the various Masonic orders. Fraternal connections gave the kleagles valuable access to prominent men, including elected officials, whose recruitment enhanced the organization's prestige and general appeal. But the Invisible Empire's interaction with leading civic elements was exceedingly complex and varied from community to community. Depending on the local set of circumstances, the Klan might support, oppose, or ignore a particular group. Essentially the Klan was a chameleon during this early organizational stage, adjusting its sales pitch in light of the local context and the dictates of opportunism.[14]

Benefiting from its adaptability, the revitalized Ku Klux Klan dramatically demonstrated its popular appeal throughout vast regions of the southern United States in 1920 and early 1921, garnering tens of thousands of eager recruits, mostly in Texas, Louisiana, and Oklahoma. The KKK simultaneously provided evidence of some of the darker impulses of its members, as an outbreak of violent extralegal vigilantism accompanied the spread of the Invisible Empire. While blacks did not escape the secret order's ire, the bulk of the violence focused upon perceived moral offenders who were white.[15]

This upsurge in vigilante activity soon attracted the attention of the national press, which began to detail alleged Klan outrages in an attempt to alert the country to a mounting danger. Leading the way was the Pulitzer-owned *New York World,* which extensively investigated the organization in mid-1921 and then released a sensational exposé of Klan-sponsored violence. At the same time, major publications such as *Literary Digest, Outlook,* and *Independent* started to feature numerous articles dedicated to uncovering the pernicious appeal and activities of the revived KKK. The alarm generated by this media coverage prodded the Congressional House Rules Committee into holding hearings in October 1921 to determine whether there were grounds for a federal investigation. While evidence presented in the hearings indicated that the Invisible Empire was far from the pristine group it claimed to be, no major irregularities came to light, and Imperial Wizard Simmons emerged from hostile questioning in surprisingly good form. In subsequent months, Congress failed to take any further action concerning the Klan, and to many Americans it appeared that the order had received at least a degree of official approval.[16] Apparently among those convinced was President Warren G. Harding, who entered the ranks of the Invisible Empire in a special ceremony held in the Green Room of the White House.[17]

The publicity produced by the *World*'s widely syndicated exposé and the subsequent Klan hearings assisted the Invisible Empire in escaping its sectional confines and becoming a bonafide national movement. By early 1922, local Klan chapters—which would include tens of thousands in Chicago alone—were gathering strength in the Midwest, and Ku Kluxing continued at a furious pace up and down the Pacific coast; the order likewise began to make impressive inroads in Pennsylvania and parts of New York and New England, even setting up a klavern at Harvard University.[18] It now appeared a definite possibility that the Ku Klux Klan might establish itself as a major and enduring influence in American society.

This tremendous and sudden success naturally delighted Imperial officials but also fostered a belief within the upper echelons of the hierarchy that the Klan required better leadership. Gradually, throughout 1922, a politically ambitious coeterie of prominent Klansmen wrested control of the order from Colonel Simmons, who was being variously condemned for heavy drinking, financial ineptitude, and an unswerving defense of Edward Young Clarke and Elizabeth Tyler in the aftermath of a morals scandal. Replacing Simmons as Imperial Wizard was Hiram Wesley Evans, a successful Dallas dentist who would head the KKK for the remainder of the 1920s. Evans's ascendency signaled the advent of intensive Klan involvement in politics, and he dreamed of forging the hooded order into "a great militant political organization."[19] Such an aspiration, however, had to contend with the relative independence of the Klan's hundreds of widely scattered local chapters. Although on paper the Invisible Empire seemed tightly structured along quasi-military lines, the chain of command served little purpose other than to funnel funds back to Imperial headquarters in Atlanta. Once established, klaverns received only minimal central direction. Most of the national Klan experience, therefore, would be played out in numerous community-level KKK episodes, in which local conditions would profoundly shape the goals, activities, and membership of the Invisible Empire.

A central core of beliefs, of course, held the Klan together. As the organization's constitution and other Imperial documents indicate, Klansmen advocated "pure Americanism" and "the faithful mainte-nance of White Supremacy." The Klan viewed with suspicion those who owed "allegience of any nature or degree to any foreign Government, nation, institution, sect, ruler, person, or people," and proudly asserted that Anglo-Saxons were "the only race that has ever proved its ability and supremacy and its determination to progress under any and all conditions and handicaps." The order also advocated strict enforce-ment of the law, particularly the various prohibition statutes.[20] Yet, the appeal of this program—which was well-grounded in mainstream views that the vast majority of white Protestants probably shared to one degree or another—did not insure a uniform level of success for the Klan across the nation. In neither Mississippi nor South Carolina, overwhelmingly Protestant states with powerful racist and vigilante traditions, did the Klan establish itself as a major force, while the order thrived in more "progressive" locales such as Oregon, Michigan, and Ohio. In Tennessee, the KKK prospered in Memphis and Knoxville but quickly died in Nashville, surely not an exceptional bastion of liberal enlightenment in the 1920s. In Orange County, California, the communi-ties of Anaheim, Fullerton, Brea, and La Habra proved very receptive to the Invisible Empire's appeal, but the hooded order never developed an enduring following in the nearby towns of Orange and Santa Ana.[21] Thus, almost inevitably, one is drawn to the community level in order to assess the sources of the Klan's popularity or lack thereof. Indeed, few topics in the American past more clearly demonstrate the validity of the famous dictum that "all history is ultimately local history" than the Ku Klux Klan of the 1920s.

Until relatively recently, the complex manner in which the rise and fall of the second Klan was connected to specific local circumstances remained largely uninvestigated. For decades, in fact, very little Klan scholarship of *any* type appeared, prompting Charles C. Alexander to observe in 1965 that the state of KKK studies could best be characterized as "a hiatus in the historiography of the twenties."[22] This situation resulted from a number of factors, including a shortage of cooperative oral history sources and the scarcity of official Klan records and membership lists, but probably an even more important reason was that by the end of the 1920s journalists, academics, and intellectuals in general had formulated an enduring consensus of opinion concerning the nature and appeal of the Invisible Empire. This consensus received its most influential expression in John Moffatt Mecklin's *The Ku Klux Klan: A Study of the American Mind* (1924), which appeared while the Klan was still a powerful force throughout much of the United States. Based primarily on a selective examination of government documents and newspaper reports, Mecklin determined that the typical Klansman came from the "well-meaning but more or less ignorant and unthinking middle class" that resided in the nation's declining villages and small towns. Characterized by a "beautiful but unreasoning loyalty to orthodox Protestantism" and a "provincial fear of all things foreign," the average knight had joined the hooded order to escape the drabness of small-town life and also because KKK leaders skillfully played on his "stubborn, uncritical mental stereotypes of Catholics, Jews, and foreigners."[23]

In retrospect, it can readily be seen that this portrait of the Klan's rank and file—a description based on very limited research—itself constituted an "uncritical mental stereotype," one popular among the intellectual and literary elite of the twenties. Yet, despite its transparent bias and scholarly weaknesses, the Mecklin thesis and its variants dominated Klan historiography for nearly forty years, and elements of this assessment persist to the present. Only very gradually have historians recognized that the Klan resists easy stereotyping. In work at the state level conducted over a period of thirty years, Emerson H. Loucks, Norman Weaver, and Kenneth E. Harrell found considerable variation among local klaverns in Pennsylvania, Indiana, Ohio, Wisconsin, Michigan, and Louisiana. Major regional and national studies produced in the mid-1960s by David M. Chalmers, Charles Alexander, and Kenneth T. Jackson likewise revealed the numerous types of environments in which the Invisible Empire thrived.[24] Unfortunately, however, these authors often sought to replace the Mecklin stereotype with unifying theories of their own that obscured the complex sources of the Klan's appeal.

Over the past decade, a time when the historical profession has become increasingly receptive to the case-study approach, scholars have finally begun to conduct detailed examinations of individual klaverns. Much of this work has focused on Klan chapters in the western United States. The West, it must be confessed, is not the ideal region in which to appraise the Ku Klux Klan. Although the Invisible Empire became very powerful in certain states–Oregon and Colorado being two of the more prominent jewels in the Imperial crown–KKK activity was minimal in many areas, and western Klansmen probably never constituted more than 7 percent of the organization's total membership. This volume's contributors suspect, nevertheless, that western Klans did not differ radically from klaverns in other regions (primarily because westerners shared many of the same community problems that confronted Americans elsewhere) and therefore can serve as the initial basis of a new general synthesis; indeed, recent research on the KKK in Indiana, Ohio, and New York conforms well with the overall conclusions that appear here.[25]

As a means of distilling and focusing the work that has been done on the Klan in the West and of demonstrating the importance of examining the Invisible Empire in its local context, this volume will present essays assessing the KKK experiences of six western communities: Denver, Colorado; El Paso, Texas; Anaheim, California; Salt Lake City, Utah; and Eugene and La Grande, Oregon. While these essays obviously do not constitute a systematic survey of the entire West, they do look at the Klan in a variety of diverse settings in a number of states, including those where the order achieved the greatest success. So that the case studies could be more easily compared, the contributors were asked to focus on a set of basic questions:

1. What was the community under consideration like in the 1920s? What major social and economic factors shaped local community life? What distinctive social traditions influenced local affairs?

2. Why did the Klan develop a following in the community? What specific local conditions, if any, gave rise to the Klan?

3. Who joined the Klan? What was the social and economic status of most Klansmen?

4. What was the program of the local klavern? How did Klansmen propose to remedy local problems? Did the Klan resort to violence or other forms of illegal activity?

5. What were the reasons for the local klavern's decline?

The essayists were free to explore additional lines of inquiry and to utilize any method of historical investigation, provided their final product reflected a thorough mining of local sources. Naturally, because of the considerable variation in the quantity and quality of research materials available to individual authors (Klan membership rolls, for example), not all of the core questions could be addressed with the same degree of comprehensiveness for each community; but this is probably inevitable when examining a secret society for which official records are often no longer extant.

In addition to its emphasis on the importance of studying the Klan in its community context, this volume will stress a second major theme: the need to evaluate the Invisible Empire in as objective and sensitive a manner as possible. It should never be forgotten that beneath the threatening white robes and hoods walked millions of otherwise respectable Americans, many of them earnestly striving to forge a better life for themselves and their families. We hope through this book to align Klan studies with the dominant trend in United States social history, that of compassionately and nonjudgmentally assessing the lives and activities of ordinary citizens. Admittedly, it has at times been difficult for this particular group of contributors to keep our personal biases in check: we include two Roman Catholics, two Jews, a Greek American, and two ardent proponents of liberal causes—hardly the type of jury the Klan would choose to stand in historical judgment. Yet, we feel that our assessment of the KKK has for the most part been based on neutral and sober reasoning. So that readers will further understand our orientation and can place our work in its appropriate context, our book begins with a concise survey of the major contours of Klan historiography.

NOTES

1. Fred J. Cook, *The Ku Klux Klan: America's Recurring Nightmare* (New York, 1980).

2. Allen W. Trelease, *White Terror: The Ku Klux Klan Conspiracy and Southern Reconstruction* (Westport, Connecticut, 1971), 418. Trelease's volume is

---

the best study of the Reconstruction Klan to date, but much supplemental information can be found in Stanley F. Horn, *Invisible Empire: The Story of the Ku Klux Klan* (Boston, 1939); David M. Chalmers, *Hooded Americanism: The History of the Ku Klux Klan* (New York, 1981); and Wyn Craig Wade, *The Fiery Cross: The Ku Klux Klan in America* (New York, 1987).

3. Wade, *The Fiery Cross,* 276–367. Much work remains to be done on the various Klan groups of the 1950s and 1960s. For an insightful criticism of the popular stereotypes undermining an accurate evaluation of this tense era of race relations, see Harvard Sitkoff's review of the film *Mississippi Burning* in *Journal of American History* 76 (December 1989): 1019-20.

4. The best sources for the Klan activity of the past decade are the various newsletters and "intelligence reports" of the National Anti-Klan Network, a group based in Atlanta; and the Klanwatch Project of the Southern Poverty Law Center, headquartered in Montgomery, Alabama. See also Wade, *Fiery Cross,* 368–403.

5. Woodrow Wilson, *A History of the American People,* vol. 5 (New York, 1902), 58. For surveys of the scholarship that shaped the popular view of Reconstruction, see Vernon L. Wharton, "Reconstruction," in Arthur S. Link and Rembert W. Patrick, eds., *Writing Southern History: Essays in Historiography in Honor of Fletcher M. Green* (Baton Rouge, 1965), 295–315, and Kenneth M. Stampp, *The Era of Reconstruction, 1865-1877* (New York, 1966), 3–23.

6. Thomas Dixon, *The Clansman* (New York, 1905). For more on Dixon and his work, see Raymond Allen Cook, *Thomas Dixon* (New York, 1974).

7. *The Birth of a Nation* is now widely available on videotape. For more on the making of the film, see Wade, *Fiery Cross,* 119–39.

8. *New York Times,* September 26, 1916.

9. William G. Shepherd, "How I Put Over the Klan," *Collier's* 82 (July 14, 1928): 7, 32; Charles O. Jackson, "William J. Simmons: A Career in Ku Kluxism," *Georgia Historical Quarterly* 50 (December 1966): 351–54; U.S., Congress, House, Committee on Rules, *Hearings on the Ku Klux Klan,* 67th Cong., 1st sess., 1921, 67–68.

10. Shepherd, "How I Put Over the Klan," 6, 32. The term "klavern" can be used interchangably to refer to either a Klan meeting hall or the group of Klansmen making use of such facility.

11. Ibid., 34–35; *Hearings on the Ku Klux Klan,* 69; William G. Shepherd, "Ku Klux Koin," *Collier's* 82 (July 21, 1928): 8–9, 38–39; *New York Times,* September 1, 1918.

12. *El Paso Times,* May 6, 1918.

13. Shepherd, "Ku Klux Koin," 38–39; Robert L. Duffus, "Salesmen of Hate: The Ku Klux Klan," *World's Work* 46 (May 1923): 33–36; Charles C. Alexander, "Kleagles and Cash: The Ku Klux Klan as a Business Organization, 1915-1930," *Business History Review* 39 (Autumn 1965): 351–53.

14. Although much work remains to be done on the KKK in southern communities, it appears that *in general* dominant political and business elements looked askance at the Klan. One might well appreciate how certain influential groups preoccupied with ordering local society would quickly realize the dangers posed by the existence of a hooded, secret society. Indeed, by 1922 almost all major southern urban dailies, which typically served as the spokespieces of entrenched political and economic interests, openly opposed the Klan. See George B. Tindall, *The Emergence of the New South, 1913–1945* (Baton Rouge, 1967), 195.

15. Charles C. Alexander, *The Ku Klux Klan In the Southwest* (Lexington, Kentucky, 1965).

16. *Hearings on the Ku Klux Klan,* 1–184. Most of the popular press's major anti-Klan articles and reports have been cataloged in Lenwood G. Davis and Janet L. Sims-Wood, *The Ku Klux Klan: A Bibliography* (Westport, Connecticut, 1984).

17. Wade, *The Fiery Cross,* 165. Wade cites as his sources Case File 28, Calvin Coolidge Papers, Manuscript Division, Library of Congress, and an interview with a member of the Klan's "Presidential Induction Team."

18. Kenneth T. Jackson, *The Ku Klux Klan in the City, 1915–1930* (New York, 1967), 93–126, 161–214.

19. William G. Shepherd, "The Fiery Double-Cross," *Collier's* 82 (July 28, 1928): 8–9, 47; Charles C. Alexander, "Secrecy Bids for Power: The Ku Klux Klan in Texas Politics in the 1920s," *Mid-America* 46 (January 1964): 7–8.

20. *Hearings on the Ku Klux Klan,* 114–26.

21. Jackson, *Klan in the City,* 45–65, 237; Don H. Doyle, *Nashville Since the 1920s* (Knoxville, 1985), p. 307, n. 32; Christopher N. Cocoltchos, "The Invisible Government and the Viable Community: The Ku Klux Klan in Orange County, California During the 1920's" (Ph.D. dissertation, University of California, Los Angeles, 1979).

22. Alexander, *Klan in the Southwest,* vii.

23. John Moffatt Mecklin, *The Ku Klux Klan: A Study of the American Mind* (New York, 1924), 99, 101 103.

24. Emerson H. Loucks, *The Ku Klux Klan in Pennsylvania: A Study in Nativism* (Harrisburg, Pennsylvania, 1936); Norman F. Weaver, "The Knights of the Ku Klux Klan in Wisconsin, Indiana, Ohio, and Michigan" (Ph.D. dissertation, University of Wisconsin, 1954); Kenneth E. Harrell, "The Ku Klux Klan in Louisiana, 1920–1930" (Ph.D. dissertation, Louisiana State University, 1966); Chalmers, *Hooded Americanism;* Alexander, *Klan in the Southwest;* Jackson, *Klan in the City.*

25. See Leonard J. Moore, "White Protestant Nationalism in the 1920's: The Ku Klux Klan in Indiana" (Ph.D. dissertation, University of California,

Los Angeles, 1985); William D. Jenkins, *Steel Valley Klan: The Ku Klux Klan in Ohio's Mahoning Valley* (Kent, Ohio, 1990); and Shawn Lay, "Cultural Pluralism Confronts the Invisible Empire: The Ku Klux Klan in Buffalo, New York, 1921–1926," study in progress.

1

Historical Interpretations of the 1920s Klan: The Traditional View and Recent Revisions

LEONARD J. MOORE

Two recent books, one a study of "right-wing political extremism" in American history, the other a popular history of the Ku Klux Klan, tell a familiar story about the Klan movement of the 1920s. It is the story of a backward segment of American society, one trapped by economic insecurity, dying small-town ways, and an inability to adjust psychologically to the "modern age," which seemed to emerge so clearly in the decade before the Great Depression.[1]

In *The Party of Fear*, David Bennett places the 1920s Klan in the context of what he calls America's right-wing "subculture," that portion of society that responded to the changing social conditions of the nineteenth and twentieth centuries by attacking un-American citizens (the foreign-born) and in more recent decades, an un-American ideology (communism). Bennett argues that the Klan of the twenties contained both of these elements, but that primarily it was "traditional nativism's last stand," the final appearance of the type of extremism that had been responsible for the Know-Nothing movement of the 1850s and the American Protective Association of the 1890s.[2]

Bennett explains the massive Klan movement of the twenties as a product of that decade's impressive economic expansion and accompanying social and cultural changes. The economic boom brought higher wages, automobiles, radios, and other new consumer goods. It produced more leisure time for the worship of movie stars and sports heroes, and it enshrined new values built around personal freedom and cosmopolitan sophistication. At the same time, however, the boom years also created a population of "new outsiders" and "losers." These were the "small-town folk in the South, West, and lower Midwest" who had been "left behind" economically, and also the "many who felt a terrible loss in the displacement of traditional values no matter what their personal economic or social situations." Filled with anger and resentment over their exclusion, and perhaps even "furious at being denied access" to "the fabled world of jazz age swingers" and "sexual and social freedom," the new outsiders turned to "repressive movements" such as Prohibition, fundamentalism, and the Ku Klux Klan. Through the Klan, Bennett contends, disgruntled defenders of tradition could recover a measure of their lost status by doing what other nativists had done: define themselves as America's saviors and blame Catholics, Jews, and other "un-American" ethnic groups for all the problems of modern society.[3]

Wyn Craig Wade's *The Fiery Cross: The Ku Klux Klan in America* differs in many ways from Bennett's work. It is directed at a general rather than scholarly audience, and its style is strongly narrative, not analytical. On the subject of the 1920s Klan, Wade places more emphasis than Bennett on racism, lawlessness, and the tradition of the Reconstruction-era Klan popularized in the film *The Birth of a Nation.* Wade, much more than Bennett, sees fundamentalism as a driving force behind the Klan's popularity.[4] Still, the two works have much in common. Like Bennett, Wade argues that the Klan appealed primarily to the unwashed residents of America's hinterlands, those who felt threatened by urban-industrial society and wanted to lash back at ethnic minorities and the wicked ways of the city. Wade's chapter on Indiana, the state with the largest and politically most powerful Klan organization of the period, makes this argument in its most basic form. The Klan achieved its greatest success in Indiana, he argues, because of the tradition of "clannishness and backwardness" in the state. Indiana had been settled by the "displaced, uneducated Southern rustic," and its people had come to relish their reputation for being "insulated, proud, and belligerent." By the 1920s the ingrained "simplicity" and "narrow-minded arrogance" of Indiana's people had become "the weakness that the Ku Klux Klan would exploit to the hilt."[5]

In many ways it is remarkable that two books published in the late 1980s would make such an argument. The concept of "status anxiety" on which this interpretation is based has been roundly criticized for quite some time. Recent research on such related topics as early twentieth-century reform, Prohibition, fundamentalism, and antebellum nativism indicates that the idea continues to be rejected.[6] Historians have also attempted in recent years to avoid descriptions of the "urban-rural conflict" of the 1920s that read as if they might have come from the pen of H. L. Mencken. The argument that the Klan movement can be explained primarily by the "backwardness" of the Klansmen seems extraordinarily condescending and out of step with the dominant trend in social and political history: to approach the lives of ordinary people—whether they lived in cities, towns, or the countryside—with seriousness and respect.[7]

The argument put forward in these two works also seems surprising in light of recent research on the Klan movement. Since 1979, a series of studies on the Klan in Colorado; Indiana; Utah; El Paso, Texas; and Orange County, California, have each challenged the traditional interpretation.[8] These studies demonstrate that the Klan served different purposes in different communities, but that in general, it represented mainstream social and political concerns, not those of a disaffected fringe group. Prohibition enforcement, crime, and a variety of other community issues seemed most responsible for the Klan's great popularity in these states and communities. Each of the studies de-emphasized the role of ethnic conflict in the Klan movement. To varying degrees, each found that the Klan focused a good deal of energy on community business elites who stood in the way of popular social and political reforms. These studies suggest that the Klan of the twenties might be best understood as a populist organization rather than a nativist one, as least as nativism is usually defined.[9]

Clearly, Wade and Bennett would have made more convincing arguments had they at least acknowledged the existence of this new interpretation and avoided terms like "losers" and "narrow-minded arrogance" in describing a huge portion of society perceived to be representative of rural and small-town America. At the same time, however, it must be remembered that this view of the 1920s Klan has been set in concrete for many years, so much so that few historians have thought to challenge it. Therefore, relatively little research has been done; the revisionist works that have appeared are not well known; and most American historians, like Bennett and Wade, remain content with the idea that there is little new that can be learned about the Ku Klux Klan.

Scholars and journalists who observed the Klan movement as it unfolded were the first to conclude that it sprang from backward elements in society. The most influential assessment came in 1924 in a book by Dartmouth sociologist John Moffatt Mecklin, *The Ku Klux Klan:*

A Study of the American Mind. Mecklin was convinced that the Klan emanated from America's small towns and villages, particularly, but not exclusively, those of the South. In contrast to those who did not join the Klan–farmers, because they were too difficult to organize, and both industrial workers and businessmen, because they were inoculated by the constant change and diversity of urban life–the "well-meaning but more or less ignorant and unthinking middle class" of the small town was ripe for recruitment. Their isolation and lack of sophistication made small-town residents "prone to accept uncritically all forms of half-baked radicalism in politics" (Populism, for example), and led to a "provincial fear of all things foreign" and an affinity for the "crude ejaculations of Mr. Bryan and the Fundamentalists." The "petty impotence of the small-town mind" created a need for conformity and made it difficult to view members of other ethnic groups in any way other than by gross stereotypes. The Klan, Mecklin concluded, "offered some relief from the deadly monotony of small town life" and gave the villager, with his "dwarfed and starved personality," a means of escaping his own "mediocrity."[10]

Frank Tannenbaum made a similar assessment in his *Darker Phases of the South,* which, like Mecklin's book, appeared just as the Klan was reaching the peak of its popularity in 1924. Tannenbaum also placed the center of the Klan movement in the small southern town. The white citizens of these communities, he argued, were especially susceptible to the Klan because of the high incidence of illiteracy, the "pure and simple boredom" that characterized small towns, and the tradition of vigilantism, which kept irrational passions close to the surface of everyday life, especially in matters concerning the issue of interracial sex. These and other conditions imprisoned the small-town southerner in a state of "emotional infanthood," unable to cope with his "unconscious fear of changing status" caused by "the forces of modern industrialism."[11]

Robert and Helen Lynd used much less disparaging language to describe the citizens of Muncie, Indiana, but they too saw the Klan as an irrational response to powerful, increasingly complex forces working on traditional community life. The Klan, the Lynds observed, came into Middletown like a "tornado" and "blew off the cylinder head of the humdrum. It afforded an outlet for many of the frustrations of life, economic tensions and social insecurity, by providing a wealth of scapegoats against whom wrath might be vented." Those most attracted to the Klan were members of Middletown's beleaguered working class.

With a passion that seemed almost to baffle the Lynds, these workers were drawn to wild-eyed warnings about Catholic and Jewish threats to America. Ultimately, the Lynds concluded, the movement dissolved as quickly as it appeared, and had no real impact other than to contribute while it lasted to the general disintegration of cohesiveness in the community.[12]

The Lynds' brief analysis of the Muncie Klan underlined a theme journalists had begun to explore after 1923: that the Klan appeared to be particularly powerful in the Midwest. Unlike Mecklin and Tannenbaum, who strongly emphasized the Klan's southern roots, writers such as R. L. Duffus and Stanley Frost pointed out that the Klan had become extremely popular in Indiana, Illinois, Michigan, Ohio, Kansas, and even farther west in Colorado, California, and Oregon. Duffus used the same theme as other writers to explain the Klan's success in these areas. Frost, however, distanced himself from the prevailing belief that the Klan was a product of ignorant small-town hysteria. He explained the Klan's national popularity as an expression of patriotic idealism, a continuation of the recent wartime nationalism. Duffus, Mecklin, and Tannenbaum saw a more negative connection between the Klan movement and the World War. They believed the Klan's popularity could be attributed in part to the war's unspent passions and to a profound disappointment with the state of the postwar world.[13]

These and other accounts by contemporary observers played a vital part in later analyses of the Klan movement. Between 1955 and 1960, books by Richard Hofstadter, John Higham, William Leuchtenburg, and John Hicks adopted the themes first outlined in these earlier works and placed them in the context of sophisticated arguments about the "cultural conflict" of the 1920s and the nature of political extremism in America.[14]

Each of these authors agreed that the Klan represented an explosion of resentment from America's countryside. Higham attributed the hostility primarily to the postwar economic crisis, especially as it affected agriculture, and to renewed large-scale immigration from southern and eastern Europe. These forces, combined with the problems of Prohibition and the drift toward isolationism, touched off the latent "Anglo-Saxonism" of American small towns and villages, transforming the "one hundred percent Americanism" of the war years into a more blatant form of old-fashioned nativism. The Klan, according to Higham, represented the locus of the new anti-Catholic, anti-Jewish hostility, a "litmus-paper test of rural nativism."[15] Hofstadter, Leuchtenburg, and

Hicks gave a somewhat different explanation for the Klan's sudden popularity in the 1920s. In their view it was not so much a consequence of the brief postwar economic crisis or renewed immigration as it was a result of the decade's prosperity. Economic advancement, technological change, and the growing domination of the city had undermined the place of the small town and the rural village at the center of American life, according to these authors. By the 1920s, the "modern age" had established itself to a point where native white Protestants who identified with the traditions of the nation's rural and small-town past could express their displeasure only through extreme and futile movements such as Prohibition, fundamentalism, and the Klan. By joining the Klan, defenders of America's lost Arcadia could heap their anger on two closely related symbols of modernity: the city and the urban immigrant.[16]

Whether support for the Klan had been sparked more by postwar turbulence or prosperity and "advancement," there was little disagreement about the nature of the Klan movement and the people who joined it. Like Mecklin, Tannenbaum, and other writers of the 1920s, Higham, Hofstadter, Leuchtenburg, and Hicks all agreed that Klan radicalism could be traced to the benighted culture of rural, small-town America. Hofstadter declared that the Klan gained its greatest support "in the small towns, where gullible nativists gathered," and where "the spirit of country Protestantism was still strong." Higham indicated that through the Klan, "small-town America turned inward, in a final effort to preserve the values of the community against change and against every external influence."[17] All of these authors believed that the Klan was inherently violent. "Wherever the Klan entered," Leuchtenburg claimed, "in its wake came floggings, kidnappings, branding with acid, mutilations, church burnings, and even murder."[18] Each also associated the Klan's perceived small-town roots with ignorance and economic marginality. Hofstadter linked the Klan to "the shabbiness of the evangelical mind," and noted that the movement "appealed to relatively unprosperous and uncultivated native white Protestants." Leuchtenburg claimed that the Klan "recruited the poorer and less educated."[19] Hicks's observation that "fundamentalists provided the backbone for the Ku Klux Klan" represented another common theme, and further evidence, in the view of these authors, of the Klansman's pitiful desire to keep the modern world at bay.[20]

During the early 1960s several book-length treatments of the Klan appeared, all adopting the same basic themes present in earlier works. One, by William P. Randel, concentrated mainly on the Reconstruction-era Klan, dealing in only one chapter with the Klan of the twenties, and then only as part of a superficial attempt to demonstrate the continuity of Klan racial violence between 1865 and 1965. Another study, *The Ku Klux Klan in American Politics,* by Arnold S. Rice, examined the 1920s movement more seriously, focusing on the Klan's considerable influence over state and national party politics. While superior to Randel's book in many ways, Rice's study offered the same basic view of the Klan as a pathological movement by social deviants.[21] To a large degree, the same can be said of David Chalmers's *Hooded Americanism,* which first appeared at this same time and remains the most comprehensive history of the Klan. Relying primarily on journalist's accounts and state histories, Chalmers presented a state-by-state report of Klan activities and political influence during the 1920s. Status anxiety motivated the Klansmen, Chalmers argued, not only in the 1920s, but also in the Reconstruction era, the 1950s, 1960s, and after. For more than one hundred years, he concluded, the Klan has been "a secret terrorist society dedicated to maintaining white rule in the United States."[22]

It is not surprising that interest in the history of the Ku Klux Klan increased during the 1950s and early 1960s, nor that historians viewed the Klan and the social groups perceived to support it with such obvious contempt. These historians had witnessed the results of European fascism, the frightening power of Joseph McCarthy, entrenched resistance to the civil rights movement, and the appearance of new, extremely violent Klan organizations. The Klan of any era understandably inspired little sympathy, and perhaps at this time in particular, it is less than surprising that historians made the condemnation of bigotry a first priority.

Still, the interpretation contained fundamental problems. The first and most significant was the problem of evidence, or more precisely, the lack of it. Any historian who has attempted to explain the Klan of the twenties has had to contend with the reality that secret organizations leave few records. For the most part, the authors of the traditional interpretation relied on surviving Klan recruiting literature, articles and speeches by Klan leaders, newspaper accounts of Klan activities, and, as mentioned, observations by scholars and other writers of that era. As a result, the traditional view focuses almost exclusively on ideology and leaders. Certainly, these are important parts of any social movement, but at the same time insufficient by themselves as explanations for the social basis of the Klan's membership and the activities in which Klansmen typically engaged. Essentially, the traditional conclusion that Klansmen came from small towns and villages, that they were violent, uneducated, poor, and subscribers of religious fundamentalism would be more properly described as an assumption, one based as much on a transparent cosmopolitan bias as on anything else.

There is also ample reason to question the traditional view of the Klan as an extremist organization devoted almost exclusively to the persecution of Catholics, Jews, immigrants, and blacks. There can be no argument that the Klan's racist, anti-Catholic, anti-Semitic ideology was offensive and threatening to many Americans during the 1920s. To describe such ideas as extremist and pathological, however, is to paint a rather distorted picture of mainstream racial and ethnic attitudes. Blatantly discriminatory immigration restrictions were enacted during this time not by the Ku Klux Klan, but by a bipartisan coalition in the United States Congress. And if anti-Catholicism was the code of a radical fringe group, it was also the most important single factor in Herbert Hoover's victory in the presidential election of 1928.[23] The idea that the Klan existed primarily to supress ethnic minorities fails to explain why the Klan became most popular in states where members of these groups lived in the smallest numbers, and why, when the Klan gained political power in these states, it all but ignored the local populations of ethnic minorities that did exist. The argument that the Klansmen in these areas were concerned primarily with the distant urban immigrant and all that he symbolized is unconvincing. It precludes the possibility that local events and circumstances played any important part in the Klan's popularity.

A related problem with the traditional interpretation is that it cannot account for any amount of diversity within the Klan movement. In the traditional view, all Klansmen had the same background and joined the Klan for the same reason. Klansmen may, in fact, have come from a variety of social groups and been drawn to the Klan for a variety of reasons. Klan organizations in different communities may have responded also to a wide range of state and local social, cultural, economic, or political conditions. Regional differences may have existed as well. Why should one assume that the Klan was exactly the same kind of organization in Michigan as it was in Georgia, Texas, Montana, New York, Indiana, or Oregon? And other than suggesting that some regions of the country seemed to have high concentrations of "mediocre" men, how does the traditional interpretation explain varying levels of Klan popularity and political success?

Even as the traditional view was becoming doctrine among American historians, some scholars did see the Klan in a somewhat different light. One study, a 1954 doctoral dissertation by Norman Weaver, disagreed with the idea that the Klan was innately violent and that it existed primarily to persecute ethnic minorities. Weaver asserted that in Wisconsin, Indiana, Ohio, and Michigan, the Klan attracted average, seemingly harmless citizens, and that they seemed to be motivated primarily by a desire to defend traditional white Protestant values and to support liquor and other vice laws.[24]

Two books published in the mid-1960s also offered challenges to the traditional interpretation. In *The Ku Klux Klan in the Southwest,* Charles Alexander argued that much of the Klan's popularity in Texas, Oklahoma, Arkansas, and Louisiana could be explained by widespread interest in upholding the "moral status quo," law and order, and traditional Victorian values. Klans in these states engaged in a great deal of vigilante violence, Alexander found, perhaps more than in any other region of the country. The violence, however, was not directed against Catholics, Jews, Mexican immigrants, or blacks, but against white Prohibition violators, gamblers, wife beaters, and others who broke traditional moral codes.[25] Alexander also pointed out that except for the controversy surrounding these vigilante activities, the Klan appeared to be widely accepted, even welcomed by the social mainstream, especially for its devotion to Protestantism and its many philanthropic, social, and civic activities.[26]

Kenneth Jackson's *The Ku Klux Klan in the City* attacked one of the cardinal assumptions of the traditional interpretation by arguing that the Klan movement was centered in large cities, not in small towns or rural areas. Jackson estimated that many of America's cities contained huge numbers of Klansmen: fifty thousand in Chicago; thirty-five thousand in Detroit; thirty-eight thousand in Indianapolis; thirty-five thousand in Philadelphia; and twenty thousand in Atlanta, just to cite a few examples. The overall membership, Jackson believed, was probably divided equally between city and country, but the Klan's state organizations were always located in major cities; and in many states, especially those where the Klan was only moderately popular, the large urban chapters made up a great percentage of the total membership and exercised dominant influence over the rest of the state. Jackson described the urban Klansmen as lower middle-class white- and blue-collar workers who belonged to Baptist, Methodist, and Christian churches. Badly paid and barely educated, these men on the economic margin were unable to flee older city neighborhoods and came to feel overwhelmed during the 1920s by "residential competition" with expanding, adjacent populations of immigrants and blacks. Jackson also concluded that previous accounts had greatly exaggerated the level of violence in the Klan movement.[27]

These works by Weaver, Alexander, and Jackson were far superior to previous studies. Each began with the realization that an organization such as the Klan, with millions of members spread throughout the country, had to have roots in the social mainstream, and had to be responding in some way to conditions in the cities, towns, and neigh-borhoods where the Klansmen actually lived. Each examined the Klan closely within a particular geographic setting rather than attempting to make broad generalizations about the entire national movement based on little more than scattered events and newspaper stories. These studies found that those drawn to the Klan appeared to be average citizens, not social deviants, and that their motives and activities could not be explained simply by an examination of the writings of a handful of Klan ideologues. Weaver and Alexander demonstrated that the defense of traditional values played a large part in the Klan's success in the two regions of the country where the movement may have been most popular. Jackson's urban thesis, of course, added a whole new dimen-sion to historians' understanding of the movement. Jackson did some-thing else that had not been done by other historians: he made use of several Klan membership lists in an attempt to discover, where he could, religious, occupational, and residential patterns.[28] In general, these works demonstrated that the Klan movement was more complex than previously thought. They showed that the Klan seemed to appeal to a wide array of social groups; that Klans in different communities spoke to a variety of concerns; and that, for the most part, the Klan appeared to respond to real social problems, not symbolic or imagi-nary fears.

At the same time, however, these new insights into the Klan move-ment left many of the components of the traditional interpretation intact, and in some ways made them stronger. Alexander and Jackson still interpreted the Klan as a radical organization and the Klansmen as

26

rather pathetic figures who had been overwhelmed by the modern world. Alexander's Klansmen of the Southwest were devoted to traditional values, but their program amounted to a violent campaign of "moral authoritarianism." The Klan in his view "became a device for the ruthless dictation of community morals and ethics," and engaged in "direct, often violent, attempts to force conformity."[29] While Alexander's work could be interpreted as proof that the Klan was basically violent, Jackson's refocused attention on the idea that the Klan grew primarily in response to the expanding influence of ethnic minorities in American society. By arguing that the Klan movement was centered in the cities, and that those who joined generally did so in response to a battle for control of urban neighborhoods, Jackson gave new life to the part of the traditional view that Weaver and Alexander had worked to dismantle. The Klansman, in Jackson's view, was something other than Mecklin's simple-minded village bigot, and he was not particularly violent. But he was still an angry white Protestant who had been displaced—perhaps literally—by urban immigrants and blacks.

From the late 1960s to the present, most historians have continued to adhere to the traditional interpretation of the 1920s Klan. At times they have incorporated the works of Weaver, Alexander, and Jackson into their view, and in other instances discounted the challenges these studies represented to accepted thinking about the Klan. One essay appearing in a widely read volume on the 1920s seems in many ways typical of the continued attachment to the traditional interpretation. Robert Moats Miller's "The Ku Klux Klan" described the hooded order as an American version of European fascism, the product of a decade of turmoil that brought to the surface the worst aspects of the American character. According to Miller, the Klan was "first, if not foremost, a movement to keep the black man in his place." Anti-Catholicism, Anglo-Saxon racism, and fundamentalism, he claimed, were also driving forces behind the Klan's popularity. Miller recognized that the defense of traditional values played a part in the movement and admitted that "thousands of good, decent citizens" welcomed the Klan as a positive force in dealing with moral decay and civic corruption. This, however, had not been the movement's main purpose, and those average citizens who joined had simply failed to discern the Klan's true nature.[30]

Seymour M. Lipset and Earl Raab reiterated the traditional interpretation in their 1970 book, *The Politics of Unreason.* According to Lipset and Raab, the Klan of the twenties was a "low-status backlash" against the forces of modernity symbolized by urban immigrants, Catholics, Jews, political radicals, and social elites. Drawing heavily on Jackson's work, Lipset and Raab located the Klan's status anxiety in the city as well as in the countryside, claiming that resentment of urban industrial society and its new values could be felt not only by those who still resided in small towns, but also by those who had been forced to leave rural areas to make a living in the city.[31] These recent migrants tended to hold blue-collar and unprestigious white-collar jobs, Lipset and Raab contended. They were "less educated" and "adhered to the more fundamentalist denominations." Like their equally unprivileged country cousins, these urban white Protestants craved a sense of moral superiority to make up for their low social status, and were drawn, therefore, to the Klan's bigotry and its vigilante campaigns against sexual sinners, bootleggers, and "un-American" ethnic and political groups.[32]

Several histories of 1920s America that appeared in the 1970s and early 1980s made similar arguments about the Klan movement. In his *The Great War and the Search for a Modern Order,* Ellis Hawley described the Klan as that era's "most prominent manifestation of the traditionalist counterattack against modern ways." Appearing at times to be something akin to European fascism, Hawley claimed, the Klan combined "middle-class rightism" with "traditional bigotry and war-fostered vigilanteism." Hawley did not indicate whether the Klan movement had urban or rural roots or if it had any purpose other than terrorism. He concluded that the Klan came and went quickly because at base it was a "temporary emotionalism incapable of sustaining itself."[33] David Shannon depicted the Klan as a "hate organization" that became popular by appealing to "whatever prejudice was popular" in different regions of the country: white supremacy in the South, anti-Catholicism in the Midwest, and anti-Semitism in the East. The Klan's main purpose, Shannon suggested, was to force society to accept rural and small-town values (Prohibition, sexual purity, and fundamentalism) by political means if possible or by violent means if necessary.[34] Geoffrey Perrett's popular history of the twenties contained all the major tenets of the traditional interpretation of the Klan. The secret order, in his view, was primarily a vigilante organization, especially prone to violence outside urban areas. It appealed to regional prejudices, focusing its hatred on Mexicans in Texas, the Japanese in California, and blacks and Catholics in the South. Whether Klansmen lived in cities or in the country, Perrett claimed, they were the product of the provincial small-town mind and the victims of their own "inferiority and impotence."[35]

Despite the continued dominance of the traditional view, several historians during this time appeared convinced that Weaver, Alexander, and Jackson had been right to question the conventional wisdom, and suggested that perhaps these challenges had not gone far enough. In two essays, Stanley Coben described the Klan as a movement dedicated primarily to the defense of twentieth-century versions of American Victorianism, "though a rather simple version of it and a rather sour defense." Coben downplayed violence, economic insecurity, small-town ignorance, or religious radicalism as important reasons for the Klan's popularity. Instead, he suggested that white Protestants from many walks of life seemed to have been drawn to the Klan because it represented the most organized means of resisting the many forces that were undermining white Protestant culture.[36]

An article by William D. Jenkins on the Klan in Youngstown, Ohio, made a similar argument. While resentment toward this steel town's many Catholic and Jewish immigrants explained part of the Klan's popularity, the local movement directed itself primarily at the failure of politicians to enforce prohibition, vice, and other laws regulating moral behavior. In its successful bid to elect a new city administration, Jenkins found, the Klan proved quite willing to downplay ethnic prejudices that might distract from its main goal—moral reform.[37] Kenneth D. Wald, in an article examining the Klan's political influence in Memphis, Tennessee, found that for the most part, the Klan acted as an "interest group peacefully pursuing its goals through conventional political activity." Using regression analysis to uncover the social basis of support for the Klan's unsuccessful mayoral candidate in 1923, Wald discovered that the Klan electorate was not strikingly different from the rest of the city's voters, and did not appear to hold exotic or extreme attitudes. In communities around the country, he concluded, "the shape of the Klan electorate may have depended greatly upon the local context."[38]

These works offered new ideas and methods for understanding the Klan movement and strongly suggested the need for extensive new research. Rather than seeing the Klan as a radical organization dedicated almost exclusively to the persecution of perceived enemies, these works made it seem that the Klan may have been a relatively conventional social movement appealing to a wide cross section of

America's white Protestant society, and addressing a broad spectrum of interests and concerns. These works also demonstrated that it was not enough to paint horns and tails on the Klansmen and dismiss them to their small-town or low-status hell. To understand the Klan movement, historians would have to investigate more closely the Klansmen themselves, the communities in which they lived, and the activities in which they engaged.

Five studies appearing from 1979 to 1985 adopted this more intensive approach to the Klan movement and with their similar findings advanced a whole new interpretation. Three of these works—by Christopher Cocoltchos, Robert Goldberg, and Leonard Moore—made extensive use of rare Klan membership documents and therefore were able to combine their close examinations of Klan activities and local conditions with well-documented evidence of the Klan's social composition and political influence.

In his study of the Klan in Orange County, California, Cocoltchos presented a wealth of information gleaned from a Klan membership list, local public records, and church rolls. He discovered that the Klansmen represented a wide cross section of the population in the county's overwhelmingly white Protestant communities. Like other local citizens, many of the Klansmen were migrants from Midwestern states; they attended mainstream Protestant churches; and they were employed at a large variety of white- and blue-collar occupations. If Orange County Klansmen stood apart from their neighbors in any significant way, it was not due to economic marginality or status anxiety but because they were particularly involved in community affairs. Cocoltchos found that Klansmen joined social and civic organizations and participated in elections at higher rates than other citizens. He further determined that the Klan ignored the county's considerable population of Mexican and Mexican-American farm workers. Instead, the Klan focused its energies on the local economic elite, which it held responsible for poor prohibition enforcement, other crime problems, and disruptions to community life caused by aggressive boosterism and economic growth. As the Klan grew and eventually gained control of county government, its main enemy turned out to be the Chamber of Commerce.[39]

Goldberg's *Hooded Empire: The Ku Klux Klan in Colorado* made use of membership lists for the largest Klan chapter in the state (Denver) and rural Fremont County. Like Cocoltchos, Goldberg found that the Klan's membership could not be described as a low-status, socially isolated fringe group. For the most part, Goldberg found Denver and Fremont County Klansmen to be highly representative of the larger populations from which they came.[40] Like the Orange County Klansmen, Colorado members tended to be civic activists dedicated to a variety of social and political issues. The focus of the Klan's activities, Goldberg argued, shifted from community to community depending on the nature of local problems. Prohibition and related vice law violations, again, appeared to be of primary concern, especially in the cities of Denver and Pueblo. In Fremont County, the Klan was more disturbed over the power of Canon City's economic elite. These business leaders had succeeded in the years before the Klan's arrival at blocking popular demands for higher taxes to finance modern roads, a sewage system, and new school buildings. Local Klansmen championed a successful political attack on the fiscally conservative establishment. The Colorado Klan did appear to be motivated in part by hostility toward ethnic minorities, and there were instances of Klan violence in the state. Goldberg contended, however, that ethnic hostilities played a part in the Klan only in those communities (Denver primarily) where non-white Protestants could be found in significant numbers, and that isolated vigilante episodes did not change the fact that the Klan was generally oriented toward peaceful political reform. The strongest support for Goldberg's conclusion could be seen in 1924 when Klan political candidates made a clean sweep in the state election.[41]

Moore's study of the Indiana Klan involved a unique set of Klan membership documents that allowed him to go further than either Cocoltchos or Goldberg in estimating the social basis of the Klan movement. Moore not only made use of several membership rosters for Indianapolis and other communities but he also uncovered a Klan document listing a membership figure for all but three counties in the state in 1925. Using quantitative methods, census data, a variety of other public records, and church membership lists, he established that Cocoltchos's and Goldberg's conclusions about the Klan's composition could be applied on a statewide basis to the most important Klan organization of the period. Indiana's Klansmen generally made up an occupational and religious cross section of white Protestant society. They came in large numbers from all types of communities throughout the state and gathered in the highest concentrations not, as traditionally assumed, in southern Indiana, but in central and northern counties. In 1925, when the movement was in decline, more than 20 percent of

Indiana's native-born white men were still members of the Klan. This and other evidence leads to a conservative estimate that between one quarter and one third of Indiana's native white men had been members of the movement at its zenith.[42]

The case of Indiana gives powerful support to the idea that the Klan was a popular social movement, not an extremist organization. Despite acrid rhetoric about the threat that Catholics, Jews, and blacks posed to America, social or political conflict with the state's tiny population of ethnic minorities played a small, relatively insignificant part in the Klan's activities. Nor could the Indiana Klan accurately be described as a violent vigilante organization or a movement dedicated to Protestant fundamentalism. Typically, the Klan acted as a social and civic organization, reinvigorating a sense of unity and cohesiveness in community life with its spectacular social events, civic activities, and philanthropic works. Even more important, it became a means through which average citizens could express their dissatisfaction with the political establishment, which had failed to enforce Prohibition and had ignored or contested a variety of other popular interests. The Indiana Klan not only took over state government, it overturned local political organizations in both parties throughout the state.[43]

Larry Gerlach's study of the Utah Klan, and Shawn Lay's assessment of the secret order in El Paso, Texas, were not able to make use of rank-and-file Klan membership lists. Their detailed investigations of local events and the Klan's influence in social and political affairs, however, produced findings consistent with those of Cocoltchos, Goldberg, and Moore.

In Utah, the Klan probably enrolled no more than five thousand members, and never achieved anything approaching the kind of political power it enjoyed elsewhere. Still, the movement was significant due to the setting in which it occurred and the unique form it took. Essentially, the Utah Klan was an organization of non-Mormon white Protestants protesting Mormon social, economic, and political domination. Gerlach estimated that the great majority of Utah's Klansmen lived in Salt Lake City and Ogden, the only communities in the state with significant non-Mormon populations. He discovered that the Salt Lake Klan leadership was made up of disgruntled non-Mormon businessmen who hoped the secret society could be used as "an economic combine to challenge Mormon mercantile power." Klan demonstrations became vehicles for the expression of anti-Mormon attitudes.

Speakers charged, among other things, that the church used public schools for religious purposes and employed "ecclesiastical influence" to control politics. In 1923, Klan-backed political candidates demanding the "complete and absolute separation of church and state" precipitated "one of the nastiest municipal elections in Salt Lake history." Gerlach also found instances of social conflict between Klansmen and the small groups of Greek and Italian immigrants working in the state's railroad and mining operations. The divisions between Utah's Mormon majority and its non-Mormon minority, however, explained more than any other factor the reasons for the Klan's rise and ultimate decline.[44]

The El Paso Klan enjoyed more success, at least for a time, but like the Utah Klan, it too faced a unique set of circumstances. El Paso's social, economic, and political life was dominated to a large degree by its proximity to the Mexican city of Juárez. Mexican and Mexican-American workers virtually monopolized El Paso's blue-collar labor force. Illegal liquor, drugs, a great deal of violent crime, and large numbers of American tourists all flowed freely between the border cities. Lay argues that the Klan drew its support from El Paso's overwhelmingly middle-class Anglo population, which had come to hold the city's business leaders responsible for these undesirable conditions. He found no evidence that the El Paso Klan was violent. Instead, the order shared many of the same concerns as the city's reformers, and quietly lent them political support as they attempted to force El Paso's economic elite to clean up the city, slow down the growth of the tourist trade, and stop supporting its political machine with the purchase of illegal Mexican votes.[45]

Together, these recent works make it nearly impossible to interpret the 1920s Klan as an aberrant fringe group motivated primarily by its overwhelming hatred of ethnic minorities. Certainly the Klan attracted its share of "low status" individuals, men prone to violence, and many thousands from rural communities and small towns who felt threatened by urban America and might have wished for nothing better than to see the great cities and their "un-American" inhabitants disappear from the landscape. In-depth analysis of state and community Klans from different regions of the country make it clear, however, that the Klan was composed primarily of average citizens representing nearly all parts of America's white Protestant society. These studies also demonstrate that local conditions and circumstances played a large part in shaping Klan activities, and that those conditions were not necessarily linked to a sense of conflict between urban and rural America or between white Protestant and other ethnic groups. The Klan, it seems, could direct itself to popular desires for new school buildings, clean government, and crime-free streets as easily as it could represent popular prejudices.

A single term may not be adequate as a label for the 1920s Klan; the authors of the new Klan studies have certainly not agreed on one. If a label is needed, however, as a means of identifying the common ground on which these works appear to stand, "populist" seems best. Certainly it is better than "extremist," "terrorist," "nativist," or the other terms historians have traditionally employed. The Klan appears to have acted as a kind of interest group for the average white Protestant who believed that his values should be dominant in American society. Prohibition represented the great symbol of that desire, and support for Prohibition seemed to bond together the nation's Klansmen more tightly than any other single issue. The crisis of Prohibition enforcement, in fact, may have been the most powerful catalyst of the Klan movement and during the early 1920s the Klan may have been the most popular means of expressing support for the Noble Experiment. The reformist attacks on political and economic elites detailed in each of the recent works make the term "populist" appear particularly credible. In each of these instances, the Klan became a means through which average citizens could resist elite political domination and attempt to make local and even state governments more responsive to popular interests. Further investigation of this type may add other dimensions to the Klan movement of the twenties and create a need for an even more precise label. It seems unlikely, however, that any new research would justify a return to the traditional view. The Klansmen were too much a part of America's social mainstream to be dismissed as an extremist aberration. Their movement spoke to too many social and political concerns to be understood through ideology alone.

NOTES

A slightly different version of this essay appeared, by permission of the Press, in the *Journal of Social History* (Winter 1990).

1. David H. Bennett, *The Party of Fear: From Nativist Movements to the New Right in American History* (Chapel Hill, 1988); Wyn Craig Wade, *The Fiery Cross: The Ku Klux Klan in America* (New York, 1987).

---

2. Bennett, 1–14.

3. Ibid., 199–237.

4. Wade, 140–60, 167–78.

5. Ibid., 219–21.

6. On recent trends in the historiography of Progressive-era reform, see Daniel T. Rodgers, "In Search of Progressivism," *Reviews in American History* 10 (December 1982): 113–32; Richard L. McCormick, *The Party Period and Public Policy: American Politics from the Age of Jackson to the Progressive Era* (New York, 1986), 263–88; Jack F. Reynolds, *Testing Democracy: Electoral Behavior and Progressive Reform in New Jersey, 1880–1920* (Chapel Hill, 1988), 1–6. On Prohibition as a reform movement in the Progressive tradition, see K. Austin Kerr, *Organized for Prohibition: A New History of the Anti-Saloon League* (New Haven, 1985), 1–11. Literature on fundamentalism is discussed in George M. Marsden, *Fundamentalism in American Culture: The Shaping of Twentieth-Century Evangelism, 1870–1925* (New York, 1980), 1–8. See also, Edward J. Larson, *Trial and Error: The American Controversy Over Creation and Evolution* (New York, 1985), 28–57. On the close relationship between the Know-Nothing party and social and political reform, see William E. Gienapp, *The Origins of the Republican Party, 1852–1856* (New York, 1987) and Dale Baum, *The Civil War Party System: The Case of Massachusetts, 1848–1876* (Chapel Hill, 1984).

7. For a discussion of recent attacks on the urban-rural thesis, see Charles W. Eagles, "Urban-Rural Conflict in the 1920's: A Historiographic Assessment," *Historian* 49 (November 1986): 41–48. An examination of the concept of a "new rural history" is in Steven Hahn and Jonathan Prude, eds., *The Country-in the Age of Capitalist Transformation* (Chapel Hill, 1985), 3–21. See also I. A. Newby, "Introduction: Plain Folk, 'Poor Whites,' and 'White Trash,'" in his *Plain Folk in the New South* (Baton Rouge, 1989), 1–19.

8. Robert Alan Goldberg, *Hooded Empire: The Ku Klux Klan in Colorado* (Urbana, 1981); Leonard J. Moore, "White Protestant Nationalism in the 1920's: The Ku Klux Klan in Indiana" (Ph.D. dissertation, University of California, Los Angeles, 1985); Larry R. Gerlach, *Blazing Crosses in Zion: The Ku Klux Klan in Utah* (Logan, Utah, 1982); Shawn Lay, *War, Revolution, and the Ku Klux Klan: A Study of Intolerance in a Border City* (El Paso, 1985); Christopher N. Cocoltchos, "The Invisible Government and the Viable Community: The Ku Klux Klan in Orange County, California, during the 1920's" (Ph.D. dissertation, University of California, Los Angeles, 1979).

9. Bennett cites none of these works. Wade makes brief reference to factual information in the studies by Goldberg and Gerlach without mentioning their revisionist themes. The term "populist" is used here to describe the Klan's interest in exerting a greater measure of popular control over social and political affairs in the states and communities in which it flourished.

It is not meant to suggest any connection to the People's party or agrarian radicalism in the 1890s but is employed by the author alone and has not been used or agreed upon by the other authors of these revisionist works.

10. John Moffatt Mecklin, *The Ku Klux Klan: A Study of the American Mind* (New York, 1924), 95–125. Another book-length treatment appeared in the early phase of the movement, shortly after the congressional investigation of the Klan in the fall of 1921. The basic theme was similar to Mecklin's, although it emphasized even more the idea of the KKK as a violent vigilante organization. See Henry Peck Fry, *The Modern Ku Klux Klan* (Boston, 1922). For another sociological analysis that paralleled Mecklin's, see Frank Bohn, "The Ku Klux Klan Interpreted," *American Journal of Sociology* 30 (January 1925): 385–407. Another notable account appeared during the 1930s stressing similar themes. See Emerson H. Loucks, *The Ku Klux Klan in Pennsylvania* (Harrisburg, 1936).

11. Frank Tannenbaum, *Darker Phases of the South* (New York, 1924), 3–38.

12. Robert S. and Helen Merrell Lynd, *Middletown: A Study in Modern American Culture* (New York, 1929), 481–84.

13. Robert L. Duffus, "The Ku Klux Klan in the Middle West," *World's Work* 46 (August 1923): 363–72; Stanley Frost, *The Challenge of the Klan* (Indianapolis, 1924); Mecklin, 120–25; Tannenbaum, 3–26. Frederick Lewis Allen's *Only Yesterday: An Informal History of the Nineteen-Twenties* (New York, 1931) also draws a straight line from the war, through the Bolshevik Revolution and the Red Scare to the Klan, and accepts, too, the idea that the KKK was a product of small-town ignorance.

14. Richard Hofstadter, *The Age of Reform: From Bryan to F.D.R.* (New York, 1955); John Higham, *Strangers in the Land: Patterns of American Nativism, 1860–1925* (New Brunswick, 1955; second edition, New York, 1975); William E. Leuchtenburg, *The Perils of Prosperity, 1914–32* (Chicago, 1958); John D. Hicks, *Republican Ascendency, 1921–1933* (New York, 1960).

15. Higham, 285–99.

16. Hofstadter, 288–301; Leuchtenburg, 204–24; Hicks, 167–86. For a full explanation of the theory of status anxiety and its application to the Klan of the twenties and "right wing extremism" in modern American society, see Daniel Bell, ed., *The New American Right* (New York, 1955) and *The Radical Right* (New York, 1963), particularly the essays by Richard Hofstadter, Seymour Martin Lipset, and Daniel Bell. See also, Seymour Martin Lipset and Earl Raab, *The Politics of Unreason: Right Wing Extremism in America, 1790–1970* (New York, 1970).

17. Hofstadter, 293; Higham, 286, 295. See also Leuchtenburg, 209, and Hicks, 94–96.

18. Leuchtenburg, 211. See also Hicks, 95; Higham, 295–96; Hofstadter, 299.

19. Hofstadter, 288, 293; Leuchtenburg, 209. Also, Hicks, 182–83; Higham, 289–90.

20. Hicks, 182–83; Leuchtenburg, 223; Hofstadter, 288–89; Higham, 293.

21. William Peirce Randel, *The Ku Klux Klan: A Century of Infamy* (London, 1965); Arnold S. Rice, *The Ku Klux Klan in American Politics* (Washington, D.C., 1962).

22. David M. Chalmers, *Hooded Americanism: The First Century of the Ku Klux Klan* (New York, 1965). See the third edition of this volume, retitled *Hooded Americanism: The History of the Ku Klux Klan* (New York, 1981), 424–26.

23. Robert A. Divine, *American Immigration Policy, 1924–1952* (New Haven, 1957), 20–25; Allan J. Lichtman, *Prejudice and the Old Politics: The Presidential Election of 1928* (Chapel Hill, 1979), 40–73, 231–39.

24. Norman Weaver, "The Knights of the Ku Klux Klan in Wisconsin, Indiana, Ohio, and Michigan" (Ph.D. dissertation, University of Wisconsin, 1954).

25. Charles C. Alexander, *The Ku Klux Klan in the Southwest* (Lexington, Kentucky, 1966), 23–24, 58–82.

26. Ibid., 83–100.

27. Kenneth T. Jackson, *The Ku Klux Klan in the City, 1915–1930* (New York, 1967), 235–49, 306–7.

28. Jackson presented occupational distributions for Knoxville, Tennessee, and Chicago, Aurora, and Winchester, Illinois (pp. 62, 108, 119–20); a religious distribution for Knoxville (p. 63); and geographic distributions for Chicago, Indianapolis, and Denver (pp. 114, 153, 225).

29. Alexander, 19, 21.

30. Robert Moats Miller, "The Ku Klux Klan," in John Braeman, Robert H. Bremner, and David Brody, eds., *Change and Continuity in Twentieth-Century America: The 1920's* (Columbus, Ohio, 1968), 215–55. Miller made use of the studies by Weaver and Alexander but saw them flawed in some respects. On Weaver's dissertation, Miller observed that "one is almost lulled into concluding that the Klan was harmless." Alexander's book, Miller concluded, overstressed the theme of moral authoritarianism. Miller suggested that these works might have been better had their authors kept in mind the "principle of Ockham's Razor": that "complex and refined explanations of observed phenomenon must not obscure the simple and the evident." See 217–18, 253–54.

31. Lipset and Raab, 110–49. It should be noted that Jackson rejected the idea that urban Klansmen were composed primarily of recent migrants from rural areas. See Jackson, 241.

32. Lipset and Raab, 132–33, argue that in American history, "Status backlash, especially low-status backlash, has been the chief determinant and constituent of bigotry," and that the "less educated" have been the "least constrained by cross pressures against bigotry and the most vulnerable to bigotry."

33. Ellis W. Hawley, *The Great War and the Search for a Modern Order: A History of the American People and Their Institutions, 1917-1933* (New York, 1979), 128–29.

34. David A. Shannon, *Between the Wars: America, 1919-1941* (Boston, second edition, 1979), 89–91.

35. Geoffrey Perrett, *America in the Twenties: A History* (New York, 1982), 72–78.

36. Stanley Coben, "The Assault on Victorianism in the Twentieth Century," *American Quarterly* 27 (December 1975): 604–25; and "The First Years of Modern America, 1918-1933," in William E. Leuchtenburg, ed., *The Unfinished Century: America Since 1900* (Boston, 1972), 281–85.

37. William D. Jenkins, "The Ku Klux Klan in Youngstown, Ohio: Moral Reform in the Twenties," *Historian* 41 (November 1978): 76–93. For another local study that lends support to the idea of the Klan as an organization concerned primarily with traditional morals, see William Toll, "Progress and Piety: The Ku Klux Klan and Social Change in Tillamook, Oregon," *Pacific Northwest Quarterly* 69 (April 1978): 75–85. See also Robert A. Goldberg, "The Ku Klux Klan in Madison, 1922-1927," *Wisconsin Magazine of History* 58 (Autumn 1974): 31–44.

38. Kenneth D. Wald, "The Visible Empire: The Ku Klux Klan as an Electoral Movement," *Journal of Interdisciplinary History* 11 (Autumn 1980): 217–34. Wald estimated that Klan voters were slightly more likely to be of low economic status and to reside in racially mixed political wards. He found no relationship between support for the Klan mayoral candidate and anti-Catholic attitudes measured by the vote for Al Smith in 1928.

39. Cocoltchos, 611–47.

40. Goldberg, *Hooded Empire,* 35–48, 132–35. Goldberg's book is based on his University of Wisconsin dissertation of the same title, which was completed in 1977, two years before Cocoltchos's study. While Goldberg's findings for Canon City (and Colorado Springs as well) are quite similar to Cocoltchos's for Orange County, Goldberg sees different forces at work in other communities, and his main theme focuses on the diverse interests of the various Klan chapters in the state.

41. Ibid., 12–35, 59–83, 118–48, 166–69.

42. Moore, 61–123.

43. Ibid., 124–272.

44. Gerlach, 23–53, 136–37. Gerlach identified the Mormon church as "the single greatest obstacle to the development of the Klan" in the state. In nearly every community Gerlach investigated, the KKK's success appeared to depend largely on the number of white Protestants available for recruitment. See 36, 63–101.

45. Lay, 49–124.

2

Denver: Queen City
of the Colorado Realm

ROBERT A. GOLDBERG

In the spring of 1921, William Joseph Simmons stepped from a train at Denver's Union Station. Dressed in a well-fitted suit emblazoned with lodge buttons, this tall, heavy-set man attracted little notice from the crowd. Few Denverites realized that on the train platform stood the self-proclaimed Imperial Wizard of the Knights of the Ku Klux Klan.[1]

Peering through his pince-nez glasses, Simmons immediately spotted his old friend Leo Kennedy. Kennedy, a Mason and former member of the anti-Catholic American Protective Association, hurriedly greeted Simmons and quickly led him from the station. Simmons's visit to Denver was part of a national recruiting drive. At Kennedy's request, the Imperial Wizard had scheduled a private meeting at the Brown Palace Hotel to explain the Klan message. The select group of prominent Denverites had already formed when Simmons and Kennedy arrived. With the fervor of a revivalist, Simmons extolled the virtues and principles of his new secret society. The men were convinced and he promptly initiated them. The Ku Klux Klan had arrived in Colorado and would soon spread to every county in the state.[2]

By train and automobile the kleagles scoured Colorado for prospective Klansmen. Topographic variations in the new sales territory influenced their efforts. In 1920, four of every ten Coloradans lived within a thirty-mile-wide strip running along the base of the foothills of the Rocky Mountains and extending the length of the state. Crowded into this band were all but one of Colorado's cities with a population of eight thousand or more. The urban centers were also physically close: Denver was only thirty miles from Boulder, fifty-four miles from Greeley, seventy miles from Colorado Springs, and 112 miles from Pueblo. Because they were so easily accessible, the people of this section experienced the most intensive Klan recruiting campaigns. Strong klaverns would soon appear in their midst able to exert great influence in decision making. The Rocky Mountains to the west slowed Klan expansion; klaverns were not organized in western Colorado until 1924, several years after similar efforts on the Eastern Slope. Important Klan units would arise from Grand Junction in the north to Durango in the south, but the sparsely populated Western Slope proved most resistant to the Klan onslaught. At its height, the Invisible Empire claimed the allegiance of thirty-five to forty thousand Coloradans.[3]

The Klan offered a program of Americanism, militant Protestantism, fraternity, order, religious intolerance, and racial purity—a plethora of causes from which to choose. But such abstract causes could not generate membership unless they drew meaning from the immediate environment. Real community tensions and neighborhood conflicts rather than distant dangers produced Colorado Klan growth. "You cannot put into effect any set program," insisted Hiram Wesley Evans, the Klan's second Imperial Wizard, "for there are different needs in the various localities. Your program must embrace the needs of the people it must serve."[4] Klan leaders thus molded the movement to the needs of their Protestant neighbors and made the hooded order's solutions to local problems appear reasonable and inexorable. Joining the Denver Klan, then, could mean something far different from membership in either the Pueblo or Grand Junction organizations.

The Colorado realm, moreover, was for several years immune from national Klan meddling. Distance, the distraction of the Imperial Wizard, and the personality of Colorado's Grand Dragon enabled state Klansmen to develop their organizations in relative isolation. As a Grand Junction Klansman recalled: "We knew that the Klan came out of Georgia, but we never thought of them being at the head of it. We knew that they probably got a dollar out of our ten dollars to join . . . and we knew our bed sheets came from there. As far as we were concerned Denver was the head of it."[5]

During the 1920s, Denver was the financial and commercial center of the Rocky Mountain West, unchallenged in a wide trade area extending for hundreds of miles in all directions. Primarily a distribution and collection point, the city never developed substantial heavy industry. Manufacturing was diversified, small scale, and oriented toward local and regional markets. Denver was also Colorado's capital and largest city, containing slightly more than one-fourth of the state's total population. The city's 256,000 inhabitants were predominantly white and Protestant. Only 6,175 blacks, 37,748 Catholics, and 17,000 Jews made their homes in the community. Aside from a few immigrant neighborhoods, the city was ethnically and culturally homogeneous.[6]

Soon after their initiation at the Brown Palace Hotel, the Ku Klux Klan's new recruits founded a klavern under the title "Denver Doers Club." The inspired initiates wasted no time in spreading the Klan message to friends and relatives. To coordinate recruiting efforts and direct the enlistment campaign, the Klan's Propagation Department in Atlanta quickly dispatched kleagles to the city. On June 17, 1921, after a few months of secret organizing, the Denver Klan was ready to announce its existence. The Klan boasted, in a letter to the *Denver Times,* of its ability and eagerness to suppress crime: "We are a law and order organization assisting at all time the authorities in every community in upholding law and order. Therefore we proclaim to the lawless element of the city and county of Denver and the state of Colorado that we are not only active now, but we were here yesterday, we are here today and we shall be here forever."[7]

In July, A. J. Padon, Jr., the Grand Goblin of Domain No. 7, which included Colorado, claimed that 175 Denver men had been recruited and promised 2,000 more members in ninety days. The Klan, he said, was ready to place these men at the disposal of the chief of police within three minutes whether day or night. Only with these additional forces could crime be driven from Denver. Americanism, relief of the poor, protection of the home, and brotherhood were also declared goals. The image-making process had only just begun.[8]

Anti-Klan sentiment quickly surfaced. Mayor Dewey C. Bailey condemned the Klan as a threat to lawful government and ordered an investigation. The city tax collector launched a probe into the local Klan's alleged failure to pay federal taxes on initiation fees and dues. Simultaneously, the Department of Justice sent agents to Denver to gather evidence for its investigation of the national Klan. In September the *Denver Express,* a liberal, labor-oriented newspaper, began the first of several exposés of Klan secrets.[9]

The Klan, partly in reaction to these moves, closed its recruiting office, and its kleagles left the city. Mention of the activities of the Denver Klan disappeared from the newspapers for the rest of the year. The Klan, however, had not surrendered; rather, a shift in tactics was needed. Responsibility fell into the hands of a nucleus of local men who chose to carry on their crusade underground. Klan leaders, now shielded from hostile opinion makers and authorities, guided their movement through its formative stage. Quickly they organized and the ranks swelled.[10]

The leader of this determined band was an enigmatic Denver physician, John Galen Locke. Born in New York City in 1873, he came to Denver twenty years later to complete his medical education. In appearance, Locke was hardly awesome or inspiring. He was a short, fat man, weighing 250 pounds, who wore a Vandyke beard and a carefully trimmed moustache. Yet underneath this deceptive exterior was a charismatic personality possessing the necessary traits of leadership. Locke's genius for organization, his eloquence, and ability to inspire fanatical loyalty made him one of the most important factors in the growth of the Denver and Colorado Klans. Under his astute direction as Exalted Cyclops and later Grand Dragon, the Invisible Empire came to dominate not only Denver but the state.[11]

Locke, despite his position as Klan leader, was rarely accused of bigotry. He had been married to a Catholic and paid the pew rents for his two Catholic secretaries. At Klan meetings Locke preached moderation and nonviolence; a Catholic priest credited him with preventing the bombing of Denver's Immaculate Conception Cathedral. For legal advice Locke turned to Catholics and Jews. It was neither prejudice nor money that lured Locke to the Klan; it was his lust for power. A close friend of the Grand Dragon declared: "He felt a sense of history and mission all of a sudden. Here, he, Dr. Locke, who had never done anything but work on this poor human carcass, was shaping the course of life of thousands of people. And he loved the power, he just loved it. No doubt about it."[12]

The Denver Klan reappeared in January 1922 with a donation to the Young Men's Christian Association. A month later Klansmen warned city health officials to take precautions against a threatened smallpox epidemic. Nine recent deaths attributed to the disease gave credence to Klan fears. In March a destitute widow received $200 from the Denver klavern. Klansmen trumpeted these acts of benevolence and public service as evidence of their sincere desire to aid their fellow citizens. Such activities were also effective public relations devices that lessened community resistance and attracted new members. Visitations and contributions to Protestant churches reinforced the Klan's image of piety. Thus did Klan power grow. It was reflected not only in a larger membership base but in informal alliances with other, more established community organizations.[13]

The Klan's benevolent activities only briefly masked a darker side. On January 27, 1922, black janitor Ward Gash received a letter from the Denver Klan charging him with "intimate relations with white women" and "abusive language to, and in the presence of white women." He was warned to leave town by February 1. "Nigger," the note concluded, "do not look lightly upon this. Your hide is worth less to us than it is to you."[14] Gash turned the letter over to District Attorney Philip Van Cise and promptly left Denver. Van Cise carefully investigated the Klan's charges and found them groundless, characterizing Gash as a "good boy." He then turned his anger against the Klan. A grand jury was called and began its probe of the Klan on March 10. A second Klan threat, sent this time to George Gross, the president of Denver's National Association for the Advancement of Colored People, made the grand jury's work more imperative. After a month, the grand jury issued a report returning no indictments but recommending further investigation. Van Cise decided against launching another formal inquiry and instead ordered five of his men to infiltrate the organization and spy on its activities. Van Cise's tactical decision helped guarantee Klan success. With Denver's publicity-minded mayor amenable merely to verbal anti-Klanism, the district attorney was the only city official in a position to exert the government's power against the secret order. When Van Cise opted for weekly spy reports and minimal infiltration, he removed the government as an effective obstacle to Klan ambitions.[15]

Denver's inability to generate an effective counterforce during the Klan's formative years, whether in the form of attitudes or an opposition organization, facilitated the movement's expansion. City officials underestimated their adversary and failed to pursue a policy of continual harassment and confrontation. Opinion makers—Protestant ministers, newspaper editors, and other leading community figures—emitted ambiguous signals; most were unable or perhaps unwilling to define the Klan as deviant. Rather than intimidating and exhausting the Klan, their silence created an atmosphere that allowed the secret society to gather resources—men, money, and goodwill—with only minor interference. The Klan easily defended itself against a confused and sporadic opposition composed mainly of minority group members. Protestant Denver accepted or at least tolerated the Klan and only occasionally questioned it as a legitimate response to community needs. It is not surprising, then, that within a year of its creation, the Denver Klan boasted 2,000 members.[16]

The Klan's most effective draw was its pledge to clean up Denver and rid the city of its criminal element. Police statistics revealed a significant rise in the crime rate during the early 1920s. "The wave of lawlessness sweeping Denver in 1921," reported the *Denver Express*, "exceeded all previous criminal reigns."[17] Police arrested an average of fifty-three persons per day for a total of 19,649, an increase of 28 percent over the 1920 figure and almost double the number apprehended in 1919. The crime rate continued upward in 1922, and, although more cases were filed than in 1921, convictions declined. Prohibition law violators accounted for much of the increase. Liquor was cheap and easily obtainable, and police raids failed to dam the city's supply. Prostitution also flourished in the city. Although Denver police had officially closed the red-light district, lax regulation after World War I had enabled sixty brothels to reopen and scores of prostitutes to work the streets. Denver's drug problem was less publicized, but equally alarming. To stimulate business, organizers of the traffic were reported to be visiting high schools and distributing free samples. Confiscations and arrests failed to check the trade or lessen parental concern. In addition to bootlegging, prostitution, and narcotics, the city reeled under frequent and intense epidemics of burglaries, holdups, and murders. Unsolved crimes proliferated and further compromised police, who already were indicted for inefficiency and corruption. Distrustful of their police force and impatient with the court system, many Denverites turned to the Klan as the only agency capable of driving crime and vice from the community.[18]

The Denver Klan raised the Catholic specter to garner members. The Klan excoriated Catholics for their devotion to a false church and "pagan" worship. More important, kleagles accused Catholics of placing their allegiance to the pope above loyalty to the United States. Ever ready to expand his power, the pope had long coveted Protestant America. With Catholic votes he would elect men to do his bidding. Catholics in control of government would destroy the separation of church and state, ban the Bible, and end the freedoms of press, speech, and religion. In fact, the Klan argued, there were signs that the conspiracy had reached Denver. In 1921, a Colorado chapter of the National Council of Catholic Men was organized. Its objectives were vague: to unite Catholic men all over the United States for "general welfare work." Also in 1921, Catholics established the Colorado Apostolate to wage a campaign for converts and to aid Protestant ministers in their "leap toward the light." Klansmen even spread rumors of a Knights of Columbus plot to arm the city's Catholics. For those alert to Catholic machinations, the news was ominous. Denver needed the Klan, said one early member, because "the Catholics and the Jews were taking over and we had to do something. So we went down to the Masonic Lodge and organized."[19] Kleagles also searched the rosters of the anti-Catholic Loyal Orange Society, Night Riders, and American Protective Association for recruits. The long-dreaded Catholic revolution, given credence by local, tangible evidence and Klan speakers, had begun. Protestant rule was being challenged. Denver and Colorado had to be defended.[20]

The kleagles did not create Denver's anti-Semitism; they merely exploited it. Denver's Jewish population had increased almost nine-fold between 1916 and 1926, to 17,000 persons. The Jews were primarily concentrated around West Colfax Avenue, an area derisively referred to as "Little Jerusalem" or "Jew Town." The compact settlement housed many immigrants and Orthodox Jews who maintained their traditional values and customs. Culturally, ethnically, and religiously distinct, the West Colfax Jewish community generated distrust and disgust among many Protestants. The inhabitants of the section, contended a former Klansman, were "cagy and aggressive, with Jew-stuff oozing out of every pore."[21] Denverites were suspicious for reasons other than the community's alien nature. The public linked the Jews to bootlegging and illicit gambling operations.[22]

The Italians of North Denver also incited Klan hostility. Little Italy was an enclave of old-world culture where Italian was spoken as often as English. The Klan's indictment, however, went beyond ethnicity and religion, for the colony was tagged as the source of Denver's supply of bootleg whiskey and wine and the center of the city drug traffic. The Italians, like the Jews, concentrated in a small but highly visible ethnic pocket, were an obvious fulcrum upon which to build the Klan.[23]

Black Denver was numerically smaller but in rebellion against its second-class status. In the 1920s, blacks attempted to integrate downtown movie theaters, school social events, and municipal recreational facilities. Meanwhile, blacks were escaping from their Five Points ghetto and buying homes in white neighborhoods. They received a hostile reception. Whites reacted with mob violence, bombings, and covenants prohibiting the sale of homes to blacks. Thus, black efforts to achieve equality posed an immediate threat to white control. White Denverites believed that racial mixing at school functions imperiled the chastity of their daughters. Property values, they feared, would surely plummet once blacks moved into all-white neighborhoods. It is not difficult to understand, then, why some Denverites looked to the Ku Klux Klan to preserve neighborhood homogeneity and restrain contentious blacks.[24]

The Klan appeal involved more than its issue-oriented campaign. The Invisible Empire offered an exotic fraternal life complete with ghostly costumes and eerie burning crosses. Regular lodge nights were supplemented with parades, outings, concerts, and picnics. Somewhat akin to the lodge men were those seeking fun, adventure, and a share of the secret. Membership for a time became faddish; "everyone wanted in the Ku Klux Klan because it was the thing to do."[25] But such ties were usually fragile and dissolved after only a few meetings. As the Klan grew it also wielded an economic club to convince the reluctant. Employees filled out application blanks to get or keep jobs. Scores enlisted to increase business or prevent a boycott.[26]

The multifaceted image and platform of the Ku Klux Klan offered something for everyone. The result was a loose coalition of diffuse, unorganized camps distinguished by their particular needs. Distinct groups are discernable, although the pattern is blurred, for few took out membership on the basis of a single feature of the Klan program. Aside from the opportunists, the coerced, and the faddists, whose influence was minimal, several salient groupings can be identified. The Klan contained a small hard core of true believers eager to save the community from marauding Catholics, Jews, and blacks. An allied bloc, less steeped in the rhetoric of prejudice, reacted to immediate threats to their homes and neighborhoods. The lodge men found the mysteries of Kloranic ritual more satisfying than minority baiting. Yet, none of these groups alone or combined was sufficient to propel the movement to power. Success came only when the Klan merged their grievances with demands to restore law and order to Denver. Many of those concerned about spreading lawlessness were not particularly bigoted. They tolerated the rabid passions of fellow Klansmen primarily because of a white Protestant heritage of distrust and the minority connection to crime. The Denver Klan's law and order emphasis reflected its drawing strength and the needs of its membership. Klan leaders representing the different interests guaranteed, however, that no issue was neglected.

A rough balance, through careful juggling, was thus affected under Dr. Locke's steadying hand, which precluded any major radical thrusts.[27]

The Denver environment proved congenial to Klan mobilization success. City government could not solve a stressful crime problem or suppress what appeared to be a coordinated minority uprising against Protestantism. Denverites who believed that local authorities had abandoned them could only look to the Ku Klux Klan for their salvation. Unfulfilled fellowship needs, too, sought an outlet. In John Galen Locke, the Klan found a charismatic leader who generated zealous enthusiasm among his followers. Locke, assisted by capable and energetic lieutenants, molded the Klan into a solution for almost every concern. In addition, the Klan encountered no substantial counterattack. A man did not fear his minister's censure or neighbor's scorn when he enlisted in the hooded society. The movement operated in an atmosphere devoid of widespread public hostility and a meaningful opposition. The risks were few, the rewards unlimited. With all variables tilted in the Klan's favor, it is not surprising that nearly seventeen thousand Denver men passed through the portals of the Invisible Empire. Klansmen also encouraged their wives, mothers, and sisters to form an auxiliary. Foreign-born Protestants enrolled in the Klan-sponsored Royal Riders of the Red Robe and the American Crusaders. Denver Klansmen even organized their children.

Still, the Klan had one hurdle to clear on the road to power. It had to attract the support of men and women whose needs or frustrations lacked the intensity to cause membership yet were sufficient to evoke sympathy for Klan aims. For this population, too, the interplay of Klan leadership, local tensions, governmental responsiveness, and community perceptions was crucial in confirming allegiance. Victory with these men and women would ensure Klan goals, for it would yield controlling influence over Denver's formal decision-making process.

The Denver Klan's program and growing strength dictated political action, and the first opportunity came in the Denver mayoral election of 1923. The hooded order secretly supported Benjamin F. Stapleton against the Republican incumbent Dewey Bailey. Stapleton, a former Denver judge, police magistrate, and postmaster, campaigned for office pledging a war on crime and vice, lower taxes, and efficient government. He counted among his allies the *Denver Post, Denver Express,* the Italian-American Social Club, and organized labor groups. Stapleton was the Klan's obvious choice; he was a close friend of Dr. Locke and

Klan member No. 1,128. Rumors of Stapleton's secret affiliations surfaced throughout the campaign, and he condemned the Klan to appease his Jewish and Catholic supporters. On election day, a coalition of Klan and anti-Klan forces swept him into office over an incumbent tainted with corruption and linked to organized crime.[28]

Mayor Stapleton quickly implemented many of his campaign promises. The new administration stressed economy, weeded out corrupt members of the police department, and intensified anticrime activities. Although Stapleton appointed a few Catholics and Jews to office, the Klan's mark was very much in evidence. The mayor named fellow Klansman Rice Means as manager of safety and later city attorney. Klansman Reuben Hershey succeeded Means as manager of safety after first serving as manager of revenue. Klansmen filled the offices of clerk and recorder, manager of improvements and parks, and city accountant, among others. The mayor named a Klansman as chief of police and the department was heavily infiltrated with seven sergeants and dozens of patrolmen, all card-carrying members. Secret influence on the municipal court system was readily apparent. Kluxers served as justices of the peace and district court judges. The threat of Klan justice emanated not only from the bench but also from juries drawn from Klan membership lists.[29]

Klan control encouraged militancy. Klansmen burned crosses at will throughout the city. The municipal auditorium was leased to the Klan for a recruiting lecture. Klansmen threatened to boycott businessmen advertising in the *Denver Express* and *Denver Catholic Register.* Mimeographed lists of proscribed Catholic merchants were circulated at Klan gatherings. Members routed their kavalkades past West Colfax synagogues and mocked worshipers. Jewish activists and Catholic priests were also subjected to physical harassment and death threats; "feeling ran so high that just the sight of a white collar set them off."[30] At least two Klan opponents were kidnapped and pistol whipped.[31]

While such acts are reprehensible and to be condemned, it is also necessary to consider them as tactics in a struggle for power. Klansmen, now protected from government retaliation, attempted to strengthen their position in the community. These incidents demonstrated to members and nonmembers that the Klan intended to carry out its pledge to shackle minorities. They also served to heighten movement unity and to hamper the mobilization of resources by anti-Klansmen.

Bigotry is thus only a partial answer. The quest for power also plays an explanatory role.

The Klan's domination of city hall prodded opponents to initiate a movement to recall Mayor Stapleton and they gathered sufficient signatures to force a special election in the summer, 1924. Anti-Klansmen selected former mayor Dewey Bailey as their candidate. The choice was unfortunate in light of the candidate's reputed underworld connections and earlier defeat by Stapleton. Bailey's antilabor record also dogged his efforts. Bailey based his campaign on one issue, Denver's invisible government. "If I am elected mayor of Denver," he promised, "there will be no nightgown tyranny in this town."[32] Throughout the summer, prorecall speakers such as Juvenile Court Judge Benjamin Lindsey and *Denver Express* editor Sidney Whipple assailed the Klan and Stapleton's secret ties. The *Denver Post,* in its first major confrontation with the Klan, reiterated the recall's theme: "SHALL THE KU KLUX KLAN, AN ANONYMOUS SECRET MASKED SOCIETY RULE DENVER, OR SHALL THE PEOPLE RULE DENVER? . . . ALL OTHER ISSUES, HOWEVER IMPORTANT THEY MAY SEEM, SINK INTO ABSOLUTE INSIGNIFICANCE."[33]

Arrayed against recall were organizations as formidable as they were diverse: the Anti-Saloon League, Denver Labor County Central Committee, Colored Citizens League, and the Denver Ministerial Alliance. The Stapleton campaign also drew strong support from the *Rocky Mountain News, Denver Democrat,* and the *Colorado Labor Advocate.* The antirecall forces contended that disgruntled political job seekers and bootleggers in league with yellow journalists had engineered the drive to seize power for their selfish ends. The Klan issue was merely a ruse to distract the voters.[34]

Despite other sources of support, however, Stapleton's most powerful ally was the Ku Klux Klan. The Klan dominated the Stapleton campaign, contributing more than fifteen thousand dollars and scores of election workers. On July 14, 1924, Mayor Stapleton addressed a Klan gathering and reaffirmed his commitment: "I have little to say, except that I will work with the Klan and for the Klan in the coming election, heart and soul. And if I am re-elected, I shall give the Klan the kind of administration it wants."[35] Police Chief William Candlish later clarified Stapleton's words: "Another term with the mayor and the red necks and slimy Jews would crawl into their holes and pull the holes in after them."[36]

Election day was peaceful as the city cast the heaviest vote in its history. Stapleton swamped Bailey at the polls, piling up 55,130 votes to

23,808 and winning all sixteen election districts. Stapleton was routed only in the West Colfax Jewish precincts. Noting the size of the Stapleton vote, the *Denver Post* remarked, *"The victory yesterday proves beyond any doubt that the Ku Klux Klan is the largest, most cohesive and most efficiently organized political force in the State of Colorado today."*[37] The Klan and its leaders had managed Stapleton to victory by refusing to do battle on the invisible government issue. By avoiding the subject, the winning coalition of strange bedfellows was forged. Moreover, Klan campaigners shrewdly capitalized on anti-Klan blunders, especially the naming of Bailey as the recall candidate. Many who opposed recall as a matter of principle or who detested Bailey chose Stapleton without regard to his position concerning the Klan. Thus enough indifferent or sympathetic non-Klansmen had voted with the minority to defeat the recall.[38]

"They came from City hall and from the suburbs," observed a *Denver Express* reporter stationed outside a Klan meeting. "Tall, short, young and old—some well dressed by tailors and some from Curtis Street second hand stores."[39] Who joined the Ku Klux Klan? The hood and robe concealed the identities of the Klan's rank and file. Membership lists were closely guarded, and rarely did the names of ordinary Klansmen appear in the newspapers. Were Klansmen the stereotypic "marginal men" of American society seeking shelter from failure in a mass organization? Was the Klan a movement of a particular social and economic class? Was the Klan a symptom of working-class authoritarianism? Or did the Klan's diverse appeal attract a cross section of the white, Protestant, male population?

Fortunately, Denver's Klansmen have not been lost, because the official Roster of Members as well as the 1924 Membership Applications Book have been preserved. A statistical investigation of the Denver Klan's 17,000 members offers key insights into the Invisible Empire. To test the long-held observation that early joining Klansmen differed in socioeconomic status from late joiners and to examine membership patterns over time, the Klan roster was divided into early and late joiner groups and random samples of 375 and 583 men, respectively, drawn from each for analysis. This division also mirrored the Klan's shift from its formative stage to a more aggressive and open involvement in the community.[40]

Few differences were detected between these two groups in terms of age, marital status, place of birth, or military service. The Denver Klan was a movement of mature men and not an uprising of callow, thrill-seeking youths. The overwhelming majority of members were thirty years of age or older when they entered the Invisible Empire. Teenage Klansmen represented just 1 percent of recruits. Stability and maturity are also reflected in marital status statistics. More than three-quarters of the men were married, with only 1 percent divorced. The Midwest, not the South, was the Klan's chief spawning ground. Illinois, Iowa, Kansas, Missouri, and the rest of the states of the east and west north-central regions furnished the bulk of Denver's Klan population. Although one-third of Denver men were native to the state, Colorado-born Klansmen comprised less than a fourth of the two sample groups. Fewer than one-fourth of the late joiners and one-fifth of the early joiners were born in cities of a hundred thousand or more and most members claimed a rural and small-town background. In Klan ranks, recently discharged veterans were noticeable by their absence. All but a fraction of the Klansmen had escaped service in any of America's wars. Missing past crusades to defend American freedom and democracy, perhaps many saw the Klan as the means to compensate for lost opportunities to serve.

Klansmen were both long-time residents and recent migrants to the city. Early joiners resided in Denver an average 13.5 years as compared to 9.5 years for the late joiners. One-third of the early joiners and one-fifth of the later members resided in Denver eighteen years or more. Fifty-three percent of the later joiners, as opposed to 37 percent of the early joiners, lived in Denver six years or less; 41 percent to 27 percent, three years or less. The visible impression that early joiners tended to reside in Denver for longer periods is supported by Pearson's coefficient of contingency (.53).

A striking contrast between early and late joiners appears in regard to membership in fraternities other than the Klan. Seventy-six percent of the late-joining Klansmen had no known fraternal ties. Forty-eight percent of the early joiners had no known fraternal affiliations, but 34 percent were members of two or more orders. These differences reflect changes in the methods of recruiting between the Klan's arrival and the stage of intensive organizing. Early in the Klan period the lodge was a prime site for contacting non-Klansmen. Later, as the saturation point was reached in the lodge room, other recruiting techniques were brought into play. A changing membership also indicated a transition in the Klan's appeal and meaning.

Occupational differences between the two Klan groups were considerable (Table 2.1.).[41] Early joiners engaged in high and middle nonmanual occupations comprised over 50 percent of their group, while just 21 percent of the late joiners shared an equal status. At the same time, 43 percent of the late joiners labored in occupations below low nonmanual as compared to a little over 16 percent of the early joiners. Only in the low nonmanual category do the groups contain similar proportions of men.

TABLE 2.1

Occupational Distribution of Denver Klansmen, 1921–25, Compared with the Occupational Distribution of Denver's Male Population in 1920.

Occupational Status Group	Early Joiners		Late Joiners		Male Population
	N	Percent	N	Percent	Percent
High nonmanual	58	15.5	15	3.0	4.7
Middle nonmanual	135	36.0	107	18.0	14.5
Low nonmanual	76	20.3	140	24.0	22.3
Skilled	32	8.5	110	19.0	18.0
Semiskilled and Service	28	7.5	102	17.0	21.0
Unskilled	2	0.5	40	7.0	13.5
Unknown	44	11.7	69	12.0	6.0
Total	375		583		

Source: *Denver City Directory;* U.S. Bureau of the Census, *Fourteenth Census of the United States, 1920: Occupations,* IV, 1095–98.

The late joiner's occupational distribution was a cross section of the wider Denver structure in all but the unskilled category. Conversely, high and middle nonmanual job holders among the early joiners are heavily overrepresented relative to the Denver population. When the two groups are united, the early joiners, skewed as a result of recruiting bias, disrupt the representative nature of the later joiners. In the combined Klan membership, the high and middle nonmanual categories are overrepresented, the low nonmanual bloc equivalent, and all blue-collar divisions underrepresented. Thus, a larger proportion of men in upper occupational groups appeared in the Klan than did in the outer environment. Semiskilled and unskilled workers were the least likely to share the secrets of the Invisible Empire. The numerical domination of clerical and blue-collar workers in the Ku Klux Klan is, therefore, misleading. The Klan attracted a greater number of men holding low nonmanual and manual jobs, not because of the alleged intolerance or status anxiety of these groups, but, rather, because of the character of Denver's economy. There were simply more Denverites in occupations below the middle nonmanual line than above it, and the Klan reflected this distribution. Hence, what at first glance seems to have been a movement of the lower middle and working classes was actually a wider-based organization, a somewhat distorted mirror image of the population encompassing all but the elite and unskilled.

Selective recruiting explains much of the socioeconomic variation between early and late joiners. Early joiners were contacted through restricted lodge, business, and professional channels, while the late joiners were conscripted in a mass membership drive. The early joiners were economically and fraternally one step below Denver's elite, while the later joiners closely approximated the larger society. Significant differences were observed in length of residence, number of fraternal ties, and occupational status; that is, early joiners tended to live in Denver for longer periods, belong to more lodges, and hold higher-status jobs than late joiners. Diversity within the two blocs helped to lessen intergroup differences. A sizable number of early joiners had lived in the city only a short time before entering the Invisible Empire. Also, men in high and middle nonmanual occupations comprised 21 percent of the late joiner sample. Similarly, common life and generational experiences united the heterogeneous membership. The knights were mature men with families. The majority had roots in the farms and small towns of Colorado and the Midwest. Almost all had remained on the home front during World War I. The men shared issue interests as well. Regardless of circumstances, they formed informal factions based on their specific needs and concerns.

The Denver case supports the conception of a highly diversified membership. The Klan's complex appeal, rooted in a shared Protestant identity and cache of symbols, was designed to attract men from every station on the socioeconomic spectrum. Excluding the elite and the unskilled, the Klan rank and file was a near occupational cross section of the local community. Modifications in recruiting methods and issue salience enabled any white Protestant, regardless of background, to find a home in the Invisible Empire. The young, the elite, and the proletariat were the only groups that could not be accommodated under the invisible panoply.

In preparation for the 1924 elections, John Galen Locke, now Colorado's Grand Dragon, outlined a plan of political organization designed to win the state's two U.S. Senate seats, the governorship, control of the state legislature, and scores of county offices. Every county was assigned a Klan major who appointed a captain to each bloc of six precincts. Captains designated a sergeant for each precinct, who in turn chose corporals if more than six Klansmen or women resided in his area of responsibility. To the sergeants and corporals was handed the primary mission of corralling voters, registering them, and inducing them to vote. The organization demanded strict discipline and a regular flow of information up the chain of command. Locke later boasted that Klan methods were modeled "on those of the United States army, . . . [with] the added advantage of secrecy maintained by the uniform worn by the members. In secrecy resides the element of mystery; mystery shrouds strength and members and fear as well."[42]

The Klan's political strategy eschewed violence and acceded to the accepted rules of acquiring power. Rather than forming a new political vehicle, Klansmen organized thoroughly at the grass-roots level and captured one of Colorado's major political parties. Absorbing new resources, continuing its intensive efforts, exerting strong discipline, and exploiting opportunities, the secret society triumphed where more conventional actors had failed. The minority had begun by outmaneuvering the majority and finished by commanding it.

When the state Democratic party fielded anti-Klan candidates for governor and Senate, the hooded order moved to infiltrate and capture the Republican party. The Klan selected as its candidate for governor District Judge Clarence Morley, a member of the Denver klavern and a loyal follower of John Galen Locke. Morley made no attempt to disguise his secret ties, hiring the leader of the Klan's foreign-born auxiliary as campaign manager and speaking at numerous Klan functions. With his two opponents splitting the anti-Klan vote, he told supporters: "Not for myself, mind you, do I wish to run, but for the benefit of the Klan. We must clean up the statehouse and place only Americans on guard."[43] For one of the U.S. Senate seats Locke chose Klansman Rice Means, Denver's city attorney. He, too, faced a divided opposition. The Klan endorsed Colorado's incumbent senator, who was unchallenged in his bid for renomination. Given little chance of reelection because of a lackluster voting record, the senator allegedly contributed a major share of the Klan's campaign funds to obtain the hooded endorsement.[44]

Flooding precinct meetings and county conventions, Klansmen and women placed their slates of candidates on the primary ballot for county offices and elected a sizable bloc of delegates to the Colorado Republican gathering. Klan candidates received their greatest support in the Denver area. Delegates pledged to Morley and Means swept a majority of the precinct selection contests and took control of the Republican county assembly. To increase its leverage, the Klan stationed Denver police officers at the entrance to the meeting with orders to deny admittance to "anyone who was not a member of the klan and, except delegates, no one but klansmen had tickets."[45] Under the guiding hand of Dr. Locke, who sat in the mayor's box in the rear of the auditorium, Klansmen committed 75 percent of their delegation to Morley and 55 percent to Means. The entire Klan ticket for county legislative and judicial offices was placed on the primary ballot. Although commanding only a minority of the votes at the Republican state convention, the Klan wielded sufficient strength to place its candidates' names on the primary ballot.[46]

During the campaign the Klan built momentum for its candidates with a continuous series of rallies, parades, and political meetings. Klan politicians, meanwhile, gathered support outside hooded ranks with promises of government efficiency, spending cuts, and stricter enforcement of the prohibition laws. In Denver, one hundred prominent Republicans led by District Attorney Philip Van Cise formed the Visible Government League to fight the Ku Klux Klan. The League organized a successful petition drive that collected enough signatures to field an anti-Klan county ticket in the Republican primary. The Klan stepped up its campaign activities to meet the challenge. Klan leaders decreed that failure to register to vote was sufficient grounds for suspension from the Invisible Empire. Regular Klan business was postponed and biweekly klavern meetings were devoted to political speeches, campaign pep talks, and the initiation of new voters.[47]

On election day, the Klan minority took advantage of Colorado's primary law, which permitted voters to choose ballots regardless of their party affiliation. Locke concentrated the order's strength in the Republican primary, reminding his men, "We are not Democrats or Republicans but Klansmen."[48] Klan bloc voting, combined with a split in non-Klan ranks, produced a sweep for the Invisible Empire. Klan candidates won nomination for every state office but one. Huge Klan majorities in Denver snowed under Van Cise's Visible Government ticket. Except for two district judgeships, Klansmen won every legislative and judicial contest in the Denver Republican primary.[49]

The Klan takeover of the Republican party fixed the course of the fall campaign. Although Colorado Democrats campaigned vigorously for farm relief and the rights of labor, they leveled their heaviest guns at the Ku Klux Klan. This assault on the Klan rallied their party and appealed to disaffected Republicans. Offsetting these defections were the new resources available for Klan use. Klan candidates, as the Republican party's official representatives, laid legitimate claim to the organization's vote-getting machinery and to its respectability. The Klansmen had also obtained the Republican birthright, the allegiance of dedicated party-line voters. This tie was so firm that many men and women voted for Klan Republicans against their personal principles.

Ignoring the invisible government issue, the Klan's candidates benefitted from a well-financed, grass-roots organization and rode to victory on the "Keep Cool With Coolidge" wave that engulfed Democrats throughout the United States in 1924. Klan supporters were elected to both Senate seats, and the offices of governor, lieutenant governor, and attorney general, among others. Only two Democratic candidates for state office survived the Republican onslaught; both had the endorsement of the Ku Klux Klan. Meanwhile, Klan-backed Republicans and Democrats won legislative and judicial offices in Boulder, Pueblo, Weld, and in many other Colorado counties. Returns were equally gratifying in Denver, where only three district judgeships and the juvenile court escaped Klan nets.[50]

A week after the election, Imperial Wizard Hiram Wesley Evans and the Grand Dragons of Georgia, Indiana, and Kansas arrived in Denver to bask in the Colorado Klan's victory. Dr. Locke, Governor-elect Morley, and Judge Albert Orahood, as well as a phalanx of newspaper reporters and photographers, greeted the Evans entourage at Union Station. After welcoming ceremonies were completed, a motorcade flanked by Denver police officers brought the Imperial Wizard to the Brown Palace Hotel for conferences with state Klan leaders. The climate had certainly changed since 1921 when the Klan's first Imperial Wizard, William Simmons, had found it necessary to enter Denver surreptitiously. The high point of Evans's visit came that night when he addressed a Klan meeting at the Cotton Mills stadium in South Denver. An estimated 35,000 persons, including 5,000 new recruits, heard the Imperial Wizard laud Locke, his knights, and the future leaders of the state of Colorado. In the winter of 1924–25, the Ku Klux Klan had reached the height of its influence. Mastering the means to power, however, would prove far simpler than exercising it.[51]

John Galen Locke and Denver Klan No. 1 confidently awaited the beginning of 1925. The Klan's phenomenal growth and electoral successes had shattered the opposition and left the Invisible Empire virtually unchallenged. One of the Denver klavern's own sat in the governor's chair while another represented Colorado in the United States Senate. Nineteen twenty-five was to be a year of consolidation, a time to rejoice in the organization's triumphs. In the new year, too, came evidence that the Klan was attempting to discard its image of notoriety and become a respected pillar of the community.

The Denver Klan began the year with a nine-day boxing and wrestling tournament given for the amusement of its members and all Denverites. A few months later the city was invited to the Cotton Mills stadium for an evening of musical entertainment by the 200-member Imperial Klan Band. Klan leaders became less reticent about their memberships, and their names and pictures appeared in the newspapers. Banquets honoring Klan notables were even broadcast over radio station KLZ for Denver's listening pleasure. The frenetic recruiting pace of 1924 gave way in the more relaxed atmosphere. Only 1,550 men were admitted into the Invisible Empire in the first six months of 1925, a sharp decline from the bumper harvests of the previous year.[52]

The Klan was not as invincible as it appeared; beneath the surface came rumblings of dissension. Dr. Locke's dictation of the Klan's course had alienated a group of its leading members, the most prominent of whom was Denver Mayor Ben Stapleton. In November 1924, he had recruited a powerful ally, United States Senator-elect Rice Means, angered by Locke's lukewarm support during the campaign. Hoping to solidify his position, Means sought to convert the Klan into his personal vote-getting machine. While Locke rode the crest, the opposition commanded little influence with the rank and file. Still, Stapleton's and Means's positions gave them power bases from which to mobilize resources. The dissidents now waited for events that would heighten dissatisfaction and fire their cause.[53]

They did not have to wait long. The Colorado Klan's and Locke's first defeat was suffered in state government during the early months of 1925. To make government more responsive to the Protestant majority, Governor Morley attempted to remove "disloyal" civil servants and minority group members by abolishing all government agencies. He then proposed to re-create the same bureaucratic boards under new names, this time with Klan staffs. In the state senate an opposition composed of Democrats and anti-Klan Republican holdovers elected before the emergence of the KKK coalesced to thwart administration intentions. Pursuing a strategy of delay and smothering Klan bills under the weight of procedure and debate, opponents stalemated the legislative process. Setbacks in state government drained the Klan of credibility, leading its members and nonmembers to reevaluate the movement's promise. So began a chain reaction that would reverse the factors that had been crucial to Klan growth.[54]

In April 1925, to reassert his authority over the Denver police force and to embarrass the Klan, Mayor Stapleton launched the Good Friday vice raids. Bypassing Klan Chief of Police, William Candlish, the mayor secretly deputized 125 American Legionnaires to execute the operation. The raiders were highly successful, arresting over two hundred bootleggers, gamblers, and prostitutes. A series of follow-up raids in May gathered almost one hundred more offenders, confirming Stapleton's commitment to his clean-up campaign. The arrests exposed a complex network of tipoffs, graft, and protection, at the center of which were the hand-picked men of the Klan vice squad. Fourteen police officers were suspended, all but two of whom were well-known Klansmen. Police hearings conducted after the raids substantiated the charges and forced the dismissal of two sergeants and ten patrolmen. Authorities would uncover other scandals implicating Klansmen in and out of government service. These revelations seriously damaged the Klan's prestige and image as the community's protector. Such instances of corruption, prominently displayed in the newspapers, heightened the anger and disgust of the faithful, who wore the now-sullied sheets of the Invisible Empire. The Klan foundation had begun to crack. When membership ties loosened, resources needed to exert influence were withdrawn. Imperceptible at first, the downward spiral had started and picked up speed with the rising number of Klan mistakes and failures.[55]

The Denver Klan, despite these setbacks, achieved two final victories. On May 5, Klan candidates emerged from a field of six to win places on the Denver school board. Their success was as much the product of apathy and surprise as the Klan's campaign organization. Two weeks later, Denverites went to the polls to elect a new nine-member city council. Remarkably, no organization was formed to mobilize anti-Klan voters. Election returns gave six of the council seats to Klan-endorsed candidates.[56]

The final act in the downfall of John Galen Locke began the day after the municipal elections. On May 20, Denver newspapers reported that federal officials were investigating the Grand Dragon's alleged failure to file income tax returns from 1913 to 1924. When Locke failed to cooperate with tax examiners he was imprisoned for ten days and fined. Jail buffered Locke from the dissension that was tearing his organization apart. Upon release, he moved quickly to rally his shaken followers. Locke held private conferences with leading Klansmen to convince them of his innocence. Klansmen were called to a special meeting to learn about the government's campaign to discredit their leader. Throughout the meeting Locke sat sullenly, his head in his hands, perhaps aware of the futility of his efforts. Many Klansmen, numbed by the spectacle of their leader behind bars, remained unconvinced. According to one member, Locke betrayed their trust and "took out a good part of the money."[57]

John Galen Locke had been the Klan's architect. His charismatic and dynamic personality gave the Klan much of its unity; he was the cement that bound together the organization's heterogeneous factions. In command from the beginning, he was the visible symbol not only of Denver but of Colorado Klandom. Thus his disgrace proved to be far more than a personal injury. Public opinion generalized the scandal to the movement and forced it upon the shoulders of every knight. Members reeled even more from the shock of their leader's alleged perfidy. The leadership variable, which had been so crucial to Klan growth, now stimulated community disapproval and turned members from the cause.

The income tax investigation, perhaps instigated at the suggestion of Senator Rice Means, was the decisive incident the insurgents had long awaited. Means met with Imperial Wizard Hiram Wesley Evans in Washington, D.C., and argued the case for Locke's removal. The debacle in the state legislature, the police department scandals, and now the imprisonment of the Grand Dragon had demoralized the knights and caused mass defections. Evans was receptive to these pleadings because he had for some time been suspicious of Locke's ambitions.

On June 30, 1925, the Imperial Wizard asked for Locke's resignation, later freezing all Colorado Klan assets. Seeing his opportunity, Mayor Stapleton declared his independence from secret influence by firing chief of police and Locke crony, William Candlish.[58]

Locke relinquished command but then moved to challenge the Klan for the allegiance of its members by setting in motion the Minute Men of America, a new secret society. Nearly 5,000 of Denver's 17,000 Klansmen followed Locke into the Minute Men organization. Less than 1,000 reaffirmed their loyalty to the Invisible Empire. For the majority of Kluxers, the revolt was a means to sever all ties to 100 Percent Americanism. Many who joined the cause to save Denver from lawlessness and to restore governmental responsiveness felt betrayed. The police scandals and the income tax investigation had corrupted the organization's law and order reputation. Further, as the crime issue gradually waned, men questioned their obligations to a now superfluous body. Similarly, the Catholic and Jewish conspiracies to seize Protestant rights never materialized. Blacks, after their initial challenges to the racial status quo, settled back into their prescribed positions. Thus the question of Klan governmental responsiveness could act in both a positive and negative manner upon the movement's fortunes. Those who perceived Klan authorities as responsible for the decline in minority challenges could leave the order assured that the crisis had passed. On the other hand, Klan governmental failures convinced many to withdraw their allegiance. Dramatic Klan growth had created other problems. Men entering the Invisible Empire in search of fellowship and fraternity instead found meetings to be random affairs attended by hundreds and sometimes thousands of anonymous men. Even the economic lure was dulled as Minute Men and Klansmen launched counterboycotts and Catholics shunned the merchants of both groups. The Minute Men revolt merely hastened the fall of the Ku Klux Klan. The Klan's fragile coalition could not survive the defeat of its program in city and state government, the humiliation of its leader, or the absence of a multitude of enemies. Lacking success and a reason for existence, the order could offer its members only worn platitudes about Americanism, Protestantism, and white supremacy. Interest and commitment vanished, and with them money, votes, skills, and the various resource tokens necessary to influence community decision making. The arsenal depleted quickly and the declension spiral spun out of control.[59]

By the end of 1926, the Minute Men had faded from the scene, never really expanding beyond its Denver base. Membership was, in effect, a highly emotional commitment to John Locke, a transitory state that quickly faded. Even the uniform proved debilitating; three-cornered hats and knee breeches could not replace the magic of the hood and robe. Dr. Locke lacked the patience and will to revive what had become moribund. Without issues or benefits, it could attract few men.[60]

Slipping from one failure to another, Denver Klan No. 1 never regained its balance after the July 1925 Minute Men secession. Meetings resumed on August 15 in the Woodmen of the World Hall, following a month-long reorganization. Slightly more than one hundred Klansmen attended the gathering, their beliefs made consistent by charges that the pope had bribed Locke to revolt. In October, Klansmen organized a drive to recall three Denver judges for their alleged Minute Men memberships, but gained little support. A December klorero of Colorado Klansmen elected Baptist minister Fred Arnold of Canon City as the new Grand Dragon. Arnold's selection ended Denver's hegemony and reflected the shift in the Klan balance of power toward Western Slope klaverns. The new year brought no relief. The second annual Ku Klux Klan boxing and wrestling tournament received scant notice and drew few paying spectators. In May Denver Klansmen hosted a Memorial Day klorero, with thirty to forty thousand people expected to attend. Unfortunately for the Denver Klan, far fewer appeared at the celebration, and a much touted parade of strength through the streets of Denver attracted only 468 masked Klansmen and Klanswomen.[61]

Infrequent press releases marked the final years of the Denver Klan. On the night of July 24, 1928, 200 Klansmen demonstrated and ignited a cross on the lawn of a woman convicted of child abuse. In March 1932, the Klan blamed the Depression for hindering its growth but predicted future expansion. A year later Klansmen announced that they had infiltrated the Denver Communist party and were aware of the red menace's every move. In December 1933, protests from Jewish and Catholic organizations barred the entry of two Klan floats in an NRA–Blue Eagle parade. Having influenced neither opinion nor events for years, the Denver Klan's demise shortly thereafter went unnoticed.[62]

Sheltering half of the state's hooded population, the Denver klavern was the center of Colorado Klandom. The Klan's initial objective had also been the first Colorado community to fall under the sway of invisible government. The Denver Klan's cafeteria of appeals, molded to time and local events, drew strength from government inaction and unresponsiveness. White Protestant men from almost all socioeconomic strata and backgrounds responded to the call to save their homes and communities from disruptive groups. The credit for the Klan's success rested with its able leaders, for they attracted and then held this heterogeneous membership together. They made it possible for the movement to be simultaneously an agency for law and order, a fraternal home, and, for the newly arrived, a way station bedecked with the symbols of the small town. Operating in an atmosphere of tolerance and unhindered by opposition sniping, the Denver Klan's rise to power was swift. Yet, the descent from the pinnacle was even more abrupt. In just seven months the Ku Klux Klan lost its standing in the Denver community. Once initiated, the demobilization cycle had gathered momentum as it proceeded. The initial wound was opened in the state legislature, where anti-Klansmen routed their inexperienced foes. Then, in rapid succession, revelations of corruption, dissension, and leadership errors appeared to weaken a movement suffering from a loss in relevance. The bonds that unified the unstable and diverse Denver Klan coalition had begun to unravel. Members withdrew their loyalty, time, money, and votes, and the coalition crumbled. Klan leaders who had seemed so perceptive during the order's organizing stage now were unable to prevent the exit from influence. Simultaneously, hostile community perceptions militated against an attempt to reverse the spiral through recruitment of former or new members. In this new environment, the Denver klavern of the Invisible Empire of the Knights of the Ku Klux Klan was rendered impotent.

NOTES

Portions of this essay appeared in Robert A. Goldberg, *Hooded Empire: The Ku Klux Klan in Colorado* (Urbana, 1981). Used by permission of the University of Illinois Press.

1. Edgar I. Fuller, *The Maelstrom: The Visible of the Invisible Empire* (Denver, 1925), 76; William G. Shepherd, "How I Put Over the Klan," *Collier's* 82 (July 14, 1928): 7. For a full discussion of the Colorado Klan, see Robert Alan Goldberg, *Hooded Empire: The Ku Klux Klan in Colorado* (Urbana, 1981).

---

2. Monsignor Matthew Smith, "Facts of How K.K.K. Got Colorado Start Are Given," *Denver Catholic Register,* February 26, 1948.

3. Colorado, Board of Immigration, *Year Book of the State of Colorado, 1919* (Denver, 1919), 5; Colorado, Board of Immigration, *Colorado: Eastern Colorado* (Denver, 1919), 8–38; U.S. Department of Commerce, Bureau of the Census, *Fourteenth Census of the United States, 1920: Population,* I, 82, 321, 323, 326.

4. Hiram Wesley Evans, "Where Do We Go From Here?" in *Papers Read at the Meeting of Grand Dragons, Knights of the Ku Klux Klan at Their First Annual Meeting* (Asheville, North Carolina, 1923), 7.

5. Personal interview, May 3, 1975.

6. William F. Christians, "Land Utilization in Denver" (Ph.D. dissertation, University of Chicago, 1938), 2–4; Homer B. Vanderblue, *Denver the Industrial City* (Denver, 1922?), 3–4; U.S. Bureau of the Census, *Fourteenth Census of the United States, 1920: Occupations,* IV, 1095–98; *1919: Manufactures,* IX, 162–65; *1920: Population,* II, 47, 49, 52; U.S. Bureau of the Census, *Fifteenth Census of the United States, 1930: Population,* I, 22, III, 307; U.S. Bureau of the Census, *Census of Religious Bodies: 1916,* I, 245–46; *Census of Religious Bodies: 1926,* I, 406–7.

7. *People of the State of Colorado v. W. R. Given,* 1922; *Denver Express,* September 17, 1921; *Denver Times,* June 17, 1921.

8. *Denver Post,* July 2, 8, 1921.

9. *Denver Express,* September 19, 21, 29, 1921.

10. Ibid., September 17, 28, 1921.

11. *Denver Catholic Register,* February 26, 1948; Lee Casey, "When the Ku Klux Klan Controlled Colorado," *Rocky Mountain News,* June 17, 1946; interview with Glenn Saunders by James Davis, Denver, September 1, 1963; and *Denver Post,* August 14, 1924.

12. *Denver Catholic Register,* February 26, 1948; interview with Monsignor Gregory Smith, Denver, February 21, 1975; personal interview, Denver, September 12, 1975; interview with Ray Humphreys by James Davis, Denver, February 27, 1963; Saunders interview by Davis.

13. *Denver Catholic Register,* January 26, 1922; *Denver Express,* March 1, 1922; *Denver Post,* February 25, March 13, 1922.

14. Letter to Ward Gash, 1922, Ku Klux Klan Collection, Western History Department, Denver Public Library.

15. *Denver Post,* February 25, March 11, 13, July 28, August 29, 1922; interview with Robert R. Maiden by James Davis, Denver, January 20, 1963; Don Zylstra, "When the Ku Klux Klan Ran Denver," *Denver Post Roundup* (January 5, 1958), 6.

16. *Denver Times,* June 6, 1922.

17. *Denver Express,* January 3, 1922.

18. Interview with Robert R. Maiden, Denver, January 25, 1975; *Denver Post,* February 7, April 2, June 2, 3, August 21, September 21, October 4, 8, 13, 1921; January 22, March 24, April 23, July 14, 16, December 5, 31, 1922; January 1, March 31, 1923; December 28, 1924; *Rocky Mountain News,* September 9, 1921; Philip Van Cise, *Fighting the Underworld* (Cambridge, Mass., 1936), 21, 143, 148, 149; *Denver Express,* April 27, June 3, 1922.

19. Telephone conversation, Denver, September 28, 1975.

20. *Denver Catholic Register,* April 7, July 21, September 1, 15, 1921; *Denver Post,* March 21, July 26, 1923; Maiden interview by author; Monsignor Smith interview.

21. Personal interview, Denver, May 17, 1975.

22. Ida L. Uchill, *Pioneers, Peddlers, and Tsadikim* (Denver, 1961), 208–30; interview with Glenn Saunders by author, Denver, July 8, 1975; *Denver Jewish News,* June 18, 1919; May 25, August 24, 1921; Van Cise, *Fighting the Underworld,* 39; Maiden interview by author; *Denver Post,* October 15, 1921.

23. *Denver Express,* February 7, 1924; Carleton H. Reed, "A Culture-Area Study of Crime and Delinquency in the Italian Colony of Denver, Colorado" (Master's thesis, University of Colorado, 1940), 15–18; *Denver Post,* August 21, October 15, 1921; October 1, 1922; January 10, 1924; Maiden interview by author; Saunders interview by author.

24. Interview with Dr. Clarence Holmes, Denver, March 21, 1975; *Denver Post,* May 19, 28, June 18, September 21, November 11, 1920; December 2, 1921; February 5, 6, 8, 9, 1923; *Denver Express,* February 13, 1923; March 19, 1924; September 30, 1925.

25. Saunders interview by author.

26. *Denver Post,* January 15, April 26, June 25, 1925; *Denver Express,* June 17, 29, 1925; *Rocky Mountain America,* July 3, 1925; Holmes interview; interview with Forbes Parkhill by James Davis, Denver, March 4, 1963; Zylstra, "When the Klan Ran Denver," 6; Philip Van Cise Spy Reports, April 28, May 5, 1924, Klan Collection, Denver Public Library.

27. Saunders interview by author; personal interview, Denver, March 1, 1975; personal interview, Denver, February 10, 1975.

28. *Denver Post,* April 30, May 3, 1923; *Denver Express,* March 30, May 1, 3, 8, 12, 14, 1923; interview with Charles Ginsberg by James Davis, May 5, 1963; *Rocky Mountain News,* April 23, 29, June 27, 1923; *Colorado Labor Advocate,* May 3, 1923; Denver Klan No. 1, Roster of Members, Ku Klux Klan Collection, State Historical Society of Colorado.

29. *Denver Post,* June 1, 2, 4, 6, 7, 16, 26, July 16, 26, August 2, 1923; March 12, 31, 1924; *Denver Express,* May 31, June 2, 6, 14, 16, 1923; March 31, April 4, 1924; *Rocky Mountain News,* February 2, March 29, April 1, 1924; Maiden interviews by Davis and author; Denver Klan No. 1, Roster of Members.

30. Monsignor Smith interview.

31. *Denver Post,* June 24, 27, October 29, November 13, 1923; January 12, 1924; *Denver Catholic Register,* April 3, June 19, 1924; July 2, 1925; *Denver Express,* October 29, November 3, 1923; January 12, 1924; *Rocky Mountain News,* November 11, 13, 1923; Van Cise Spy Reports, April 28, May 26, 1924.

32. *Denver Post,* August 9, 1924.

33. *Denver Post,* March 29, June 28, July 9, 13, 27, August 2, 3, 6, 1924.

34. *Denver Express,* February 25, 28, 1924; *Colorado Labor Advocate,* February 28, March 6, August 7, 1924; *Denver Times,* August 5, 11, 1924; *Denver Democrat,* August 16, 1924; *Rocky Mountain News,* June 27, July 15, August 7, 11, 1924.

35. *Denver Post,* August 3, 1924.

36. *Rocky Mountain News,* May 10, 1932; *Denver Express,* August 9, 1924; *Denver Post,* August 8, 11, 1924; Van Cise Spy Reports, July 14, 1924.

37. *Denver Post,* August 13, 1924.

38. Denver Election Commission Official Returns; *Denver Post,* August 12, 13, 1924; *Denver Express,* August 13, 1924; *Denver Catholic Register,* August 14, 1924.

39. *Denver Express,* April 1, 1924.

40. For a complete discussion of Klan membership in Denver, see Goldberg, *Hooded Empire,* 38–47.

41. Representative occupations for each category are:
High Nonmanual
banker, businessman (sufficient property), clergyman, lawyer, physician, teacher
Middle Nonmanual
accountant, businessman (small), farm owner (small), manager of a business
Low Nonmanual
bookkeeper, foreman, office clerk, salesman
Skilled
baker, brick mason, butcher, carpenter, furrier, machinist, painter, tailor
Semiskilled and Service
apprentice, barber, cook, driver, factory operative, janitor, policeman, waiter
Unskilled
laborer, porter

42. Philip Van Cise Scrapbook, private collection of Eleanor Drake, Denver; "Program of First Anniversary of the Realm of Colorado," May 13, 1924, Klan Collection, Denver Public Library; *Denver Post,* August 14, 1924.

43. *Denver Express,* August 8, 1924.

44. *Rocky Mountain News,* August 2, 1924; Ginsberg interview; interview with Morrison Shafroth, Denver, April 11, 1975; *Denver Post,* August 5, 1924.

45. *Denver Post,* August 5, 1924.

46. "The Rise and Fall of Dr. John Galen Locke," KOA radio broadcast, Denver, February 23, 1962; *Denver Post,* August 2, 3, 5, 6, 7, 1924; *Rocky Mountain News,* August 5, 7, 1924; *Denver Express,* August 4, 1924.

47. Van Cise Spy Reports, May 26, July 21, August 22, September 1, 8, 1924; *Denver Express,* August 19, 1924; interview with O. Otto Moore by James Davis, Denver, October 7, 1962; Parkhill interview.

48. Van Cise Spy Reports, May 26, 1924.

49. *Denver Post,* September 10, 11, 12, 1924.

50. *Denver Express,* November 5, 1924.

51. *Denver Post,* November 11, 12, 1924.

52. *Denver Post,* January 15, 16, 17, 1925; *Rocky Mountain News,* January 14, 1925; Roster of Klan Members.

53. Saunders interview by author; *Denver Post,* September 26, November 26, 1924; February 26, 1925.

54. Goldberg, *Hooded Empire,* 84–95.

55. *Denver Post,* April 11, 16, 30, May 1, 3, 22, 24, June 2, 4, September 22, November 22, 1925.

56. *Denver Express,* April 4, May 5, 13, 18, 20, 27, 1925.

57. *Denver Post,* May 20, 26, 27, 28, 30, June 2, 3, 8, 9, 12, 13, 15, 1925; *Denver Express,* June 13, 1925; *The United States of America v. John Galen Locke,* Case 7911, U.S. District Court for Colorado, 1925; Maiden interview by Davis; personal interview, Denver, March 1, 1975.

58. *Denver Post,* July 1, 23, 1925; Zylstra, "When the Klan Ran Denver," 7; *Denver Express,* May 28, July 2, 25, 1925; *Rocky Mountain American,* July 17, 31, 1925.

59. Personal interview, Denver, May 17, 1975; Ginsberg interview; *Denver Post,* May 10, 12, June 27, 1925.

60. John Galen Locke returned to his medical practice in 1927. In 1935, the U.S. Board of Tax Appeals ruled that Locke had earned no income from Klan sources and was even entitled to a refund on his 1925 assessment. On April 1, 1935, Locke died of a heart attack at the age of sixty-one. The night after his internment, a band of ex-Klansmen secretly entered the cemetery and burned a cross before his crypt.

61. *Denver Post,* August 15, October 6, 17, December 9, 1925; January 6, May 23, 28, 30, 1926; *Pueblo Chieftain,* March 14, 1926; *Protestant Herald,* May 28, 1926; *Denver Express,* May 31, 1926.

62. *Denver Post,* July 25, 1928; *Kourier Magazine,* March 1932; February, December 1933.

3

Imperial Outpost on the Border: El Paso's Frontier Klan No. 100

SHAWN LAY

The state of Texas served as one of the earliest and most fruitful recruiting grounds for the Ku Klux Klan in the 1920s. Imperial Wizard Simmons personally helped bring the organization to Houston in the latter part of 1920, and soon kleagles began visiting other cities and towns, making sales pitches that eventually brought tens of thousands of Texans into the ranks of the Invisible Empire. The precise appeal of the KKK in specific communities has yet to be explored adequately, but it has been persuasively argued that the order's spectacular rise primarily resulted from widespread anger and frustration over what was perceived to be a general breakdown of law, order, and social morality. Believing they were confronted with dangerously chaotic conditions, Texans hoped to use the KKK as a means of preserving traditional values and modes of behavior.[1]

Although they posed as the guardians of moral order, there can be little doubt that certain members of Lone Star State klaverns engaged in lawless violence. Especially notorious were the knights of Beaumont Klan No. 7, whose zealous vigilantism resulted in the suspension of the chapter's charter by Imperial officials. Klansmen elsewhere in Texas demonstrated a proclivity for extralegal action, as was indicated by numerous press accounts of whipping bees, tar-and-feather parties, and other violent incidents throughout the eastern and central parts of the state.[2] Nevertheless, the Realm of Texas also included a large number of respectable and peaceable members, some of whom were drawn from prominent social circles. Sam Houston Klan No. 1's initial recruits, for example, "represented literally a glossary of Houston's *who's who*," including "silk-stocking men from the banks, business houses, and professions."[3] Klan recruiting also made inroads among public officials and law enforcement officers, who often joined out of political expediency or because they viewed the order as a promising means of challenging lawlessness.[4]

Nineteen twenty-one was the year the Invisible Empire established itself as a major force in Texas, as recruiters under the direction of King Kleagle George M. Kimbro traveled across the state organizing new klaverns. The Klan's adaptable program of Americanism, Protestant fraternalism, better law enforcement, and a return to traditional morality proved very attractive: by year's end, more than one hundred local Klan chapters claimed some ninety thousand members. In May 1921, Dallas Klan No. 66 announced its existence with an eerie nighttime parade through the city's business district, and a few weeks later Austin Klan No. 81 received its charter in the state capital.[5] Eventually, the kleagles ranged westward, reaching the border city of El Paso sometime during the late spring or early summer. It was here, in Texas's most western and culturally unique city, that the state's hundreth klavern would be organized.

Acquired by the terms of the Treaty of Guadalupe Hidalgo after the Mexican War, El Paso remained an isolated desert outpost prior to the 1880s, a small supply and recreation center for the region's farmers, miners, and soldiers. The arrival of four railroad lines after 1881, however, transformed the community, linking it to the expanding mining enterprises of northern Mexico and the southwestern United States and to industrialized regions in the distant east and west. Once equipped with modern transportation facilities, El Paso became a major supplier of shipping and commercial services for a vast hinterland and also developed thriving industries in smelting, tourism, and health care.[6] Economic growth in turn produced a dramatic increase in population, as people from both sides of the border sought new opportunities. While there had been less than one thousand residents on the eve of the railroads' arrival, by 1920 the official census would place the local population at 77,580, certifying El Paso as the largest city for hundreds of miles in any direction.[7]

Although community leaders understandably took pride in El Paso's rapid development and expansion, certain difficulties accompanied growth. One major problem was that the local economy depended heavily upon extractive industries that extensively utilized low-paid, unskilled workers and thus provided many residents with very limited opportunities for economic and social advancement; even the few manufacturing establishments that existed by 1920–most notably cement plants and cigar factories–typically exploited cheap labor. Owing to the unusually heavy demand for unskilled workers, and because few working-class Anglos would accept the wages that prevailed along the border, a majority (probably at least 60 percent by 1920) of El Pasoans were of Mexican origin, most of whom resided in crowded ethnic neighborhoods where substandard living conditions predominated.[8]

Despite the presence of an economically deprived Spanish-speaking majority, race relations in El Paso remained remarkably stable as late as 1910. Although some degree of racial discrimination and prejudice influenced almost all forms of Mexican-Anglo interaction, local Anglos generally avoided the overt and vehement anti-Hispanic racism that characterized the southern and eastern parts of Texas.[9] Dependent on Mexican labor and trade, and relatively isolated from large American population centers, the Pass's Anglo community recognized the dangers of racial conflict. The Mexican Revolution of 1910, however, severely tested the limits of local tolerance. Shocked and frightened by eight years of violence and chaos along the border, many Anglos became increasingly convinced that Mexicans were a cruel mercurial people inherently prone toward social disorganization. Such sentiment particularly prevailed among El Paso's newer Anglo residents, many of whom were natives of east Texas and the Deep South and had never had the opportunity to be socialized into the Pass's tradition of cultural tolerance. Because they had arrived during a period of unusual tension and ill feeling, this important and growing segment of the city's population experienced few positive contacts with Hispanics and thereby failed to develop an appreciation for the social and economic realities that shaped life at the Pass.[10]

The unfortunate trend in ethnic relations established during the revolutionary period continued through the months of American participation in World War I. Encouraged by authorities to demonstrate "100 percent Americanism" in all aspects of civic life, Anglos strove to repress any features of local society that did not appear to be fully in tune with the war effort. Because Hispanics seemed to be a potential source of trouble, the Chamber of Commerce discussed disarming the city's Mexican population, and local officials registered all firearms and ammunition, noting each owner's nationality. At the same time, federal authorities ordered the censorship of all telephone and telegraph lines to Mexico and assigned a new cavalry unit to nearby duty patrolling the border.[11] A lack of wartime zeal on the part of El Paso's Mexicans appeared particularly evident when reformers sponsored a local option election on the prohibition of alcohol–a move intended to improve the city's vice situation and thereby persuade the federal government to locate a large military training base at the Pass. With the southside Mexican vote proving the deciding factor, El Paso narrowly rejected prohibition in 1918, proof in the eyes of "dry" advocates that Hispanics were preventing the community from fulfilling its patriotic and moral obligations.[12]

In large part because of El Paso's experiences during the Mexican Revolution and World War I, a sizeable Anglo bloc had developed by the early 1920s that distrusted the city's large and expanding Mexican majority. Although the intense feelings of the previous decade had abated somewhat, this group wanted to curb Mexican influence in local affairs and firmly assert Anglo dominance. When the Ku Klux Klan arrived in 1921, with its solemn vow to "strive for the eternal mainte- nance of white supremacy," the secret order found a ready audience. Moreover, because the Mexican majority was almost exclusively Roman Catholic and the bulk of Anglo newcomers were southern evangelical Protestants, the KKK had a splendid opportunity to pose as the local champion of imperiled "Protestant civilization."[13]

A number of serious social and political problems also contributed to the Klan's appeal, chief among which was an increase in crime. Throughout the first half of 1921, El Paso's location on the international boundary and the situation created by the recent advent of national prohibition resulted in numerous violent incidents. During the spring and summer, liquor smugglers killed or wounded at least five prohibi- tion agents, and a number of city policemen suffered physical assault, including the chief of police, who was assassinated by two Mexicans. An increase in the number of reported burglaries and car thefts supplemented these disturbing events. By the end of 1921, thieves had taken a record half million dollars worth of property, including 349 automobiles.[14] While it is difficult to assess whether the city was in the throes of an unusually severe crime wave or simply experiencing problems inevitably associated with rapid growth, there can be little doubt that residents of this period perceived a dangerous increase in the level of illegal activity. The police proclaimed an unprecedented midnight curfew, and civic groups such as the Rotarians and American Legion organized drives to combat "burglars and crime" and rid El Paso of "petty grafters, pickpockets, and other undesireables."[15] Yet, by the summer of 1921, these measures had not produced the desired result, providing the Invisible Empire with a powerful issue with which to attract a following. Furthermore, the fact that bootleggers and other criminals were often Hispanic (as was only natural along the border) added further inducement to join an order that simultaneously stood for strict enforcement of the law and Anglo-Saxon supremacy.[16]

The Klan's defense of traditional social morality also seemed of particular relevance at the Pass. Although the city had yet to shed the last traces of provincialism, El Paso found itself vulnerable to the same sort of ferment that characterized most of American society in the 1920s. Through local motion picture theaters, advertising in national magazines, and the daily newspapers, residents confronted sensational but disturbing innovations in dress, speech, and sexual behavior. As a result of these influences, increasing numbers of female El Pasoans began to "bob" their hair, smoke and drink in public, wear shorter skirts and "vampire" dresses, and make bold forays across the border to enjoy the nightlife in neighboring Ciudad Juárez.[17] Many men likewise abandoned Victorian social restraints, a trend greatly assisted by the privacy and mobility provided by the automobile. Indeed, in the view of a leading El Paso minister it appeared that "The automobile of today is replacing the red light district of yesterday."[18]

The proximity of Ciudad Juárez added to concerns over social morality in El Paso. With the general cessation of revolutionary activity in Mexico and the implementation of the Eighteenth Amendment north of the border, the Juárez economy had become almost exclusively dedicated to servicing the American tourist trade. Much of this trade involved essentially wholesome activities. As one El Pasoan recalled, "In the '20s, groups of us would go down there [to Juárez] on Saturday night to eat; and we had a drink or two, dance around.... I always got along very well in Juárez."[19] El Paso's sister city, however, also featured thriving trades in narcotics, prostitution, and open gambling, activities that might tempt a person (particularly a young person) to go on a spree. To those El Pasoans already unsettled by the rapid pace of social change and disturbing new moral codes, the Juárez vice industry represented a major threat. Moreover, as was the case with the law and order issue, concern over vice in Mexico reinforced racial prejudice against Hispanics. One can imagine the impression a new El Paso resident would form of Mexicans after a tour of the Juárez red-light district, with its "young teenage girls living in filthy hutches, a couple of babies on the floor and a cheap crucifix on the wall."[20]

Anti-Hispanic prejudice and alarm over vice and crime fueled the major source of frustration that the El Paso Klan would exploit: the perception that the community's established leaders were doing little to rectify, indeed were abetting, unsatisfactory local conditions. In recent years, many city politicians had openly opposed prohibition and did not seem adequately enthusiastic in supporting the war on liquor violators. The administration of Mayor Charles Davis, moreover, worked with dominant elements of the business community to promote El Paso as an ideal convention and tourist center in the early 1920s, stressing the convenient accessibility of the pleasures in "wet" Ciudad Juárez.[21] This open effort to profit from what were illegal activities in the United States seemed the height of hypocrisy and immorality in the eyes of many local residents who believed the spiritual welfare of the community should take precedence over economic opportunism. As a religious spokesman emphasized, moral reformers opposed making "the open conditions of booze, gambling, and licentiousness in Juarez an asset to El Paso in the sense of drawing people here."[22]

Earlier in El Paso's history, other groups had opposed the city's dominant politicians. In the decades prior to the final abolition of the community's officially sanctioned red-light district in 1917 and the beginning of prohibition, El Paso achieved national notoriety as a "wide-open" border town, and upright citizens had regularly formed civic reform and good government organizations to oppose both vice and those politicians and business leaders who allied themselves with the "sporting crowd."[23] Such reform efforts, however, had consistently run up against the tight control a series of powerful political bosses exerted over the local Mexican vote. These bosses–often Irish-Americans such as Joseph U. Sweeney and Charles E. Kelly–at times paid Mexicans for their votes and imported illegal voters from Mexico during close elections, creating great outrage among reformers who saw such unethical practices as a betrayal of the principles of honest and democratic government.[24] Yet, with the brief exception of a disappointing reform administration from 1915 to 1917, the political "Ring" of the bosses remained in power in El Paso throughout the Progressive era, combining the monolithic southside vote with enough Anglo votes from north of the railroad tracks to win elections year after year.[25]

Naturally, this state of affairs angered and frustrated those residents who felt they were being illegally denied a voice in local government. Racial and religious prejudice, moreover, enhanced such resentment. The unethical manipulation of the Mexican vote seemed to prove that Hispanics tended to be corrupt and had little genuine respect for American institutions. The fact that Roman Catholic bosses controlled the votes of Mexican Roman Catholics also appeared to indicate that Catholicism contributed to political corruption at the Pass. Therefore, the local desire for reform was almost inevitably related to racial and religious matters, a situation that would permit the Ku Klux Klan, with its particular ethnic and sectarian orientation, to proffer itself as the ideal agency for ending the reign of the Ring. The Klan's primary mission, a local Klansman proclaimed, was to forge "a combination of clean and decent American voters in such form and with such power as to bring the fear of the election laws into the hearts of the men who capitalize another's faith to their own political ends. . . . The real and vital reason for [the Klan's] existence lies in the political necessity for it."[26]

Exactly how and when the Ku Klux Klan first arrived at the Pass remains somewhat of a mystery. The local klavern received its charter in July 1921, but KKK recruiters had evidently been operating in the city for weeks, including a certain C. M. Kellogg, identified in the *New York World*'s exposé of the Klan as the "King Kleagle" for the Realm of New Mexico. Perhaps because he found few recruits in the sparsely populated and largely rural Land of Enchantment, Kellogg posted himself in El Paso's Sheldon Hotel, where he held a number of mysterious conferences with unnamed parties. Given that the local press later reported that an unknown outsider had founded the El Paso Klan, Kellogg may well have been the Invisible Empire's advance agent at the Pass.[27]

The KKK's recruiting in El Paso followed a pattern similar to that in other communities. One major method of soliciting new members was to exploit fraternal ties in men's social organizations such as the Masons, Shriners, and Odd Fellows; indeed, the Klan's local leadership would almost entirely be active members of these predominantly Protestant organizations. Even before the El Paso Klan secured its charter, visiting Masonic Grand Master Andrew L. Randell felt it necessary to warn the city's Masons against "standing sponsor for, or in any manner aiding and abetting, the Ku Klux Klan." A few weeks later, a leading Mason in nearby Las Cruces, New Mexico, also voiced concern over KKK recruiting among lodge members, claiming that "Definite evidence has come to my attention of solicitation among Masons and officers of Masonic lodges in this grand jurisdiction for memberships in the organization known as the Ku Klux Klan." El Paso's Al Maida Shrine would become a particular hotbed of Klan activity, with Klannish Shriners eventually attempting to purge the order's anti-KKK members. "The Shrine was rife with them [Klansmen]," recalled longtime city resident William J. Hooten, an active Shriner. "The Klan nearly wrecked the Shrine." The KKK also thoroughly infiltrated the local chapter of the Odd Fellows, whose meeting hall often served as the site of Klan gatherings."[28]

At the same time that it was recruiting within fraternal societies, the El Paso Klan made an early and concerted effort to bring prominent local officials into the ranks of the Invisible Empire. These overtures proved most successful among state and county officeholders, traditional adversaries of the Ring politicians who dominated city government. Those inducted into knighthood included State Representative John E. Quaid, State District Clerk Clarence Harper, County Treasurer Asa R. Webb, County Tax Assessor and Collector Frank Scotten, County Clerk J. E. Anderson, and County Attorney Will H. Pelphrey. The Klan also approached County Judge Ed B. McClintock, but the jurist declined to join because of the evasive manner in which the KKK representative made his sales pitch. McClintock later described the recruiter as a "soft-pedalling kind of man" who declined to state which organization he represented—only that it was a patriotic "American secret society for the assistance of law enforcement agencies." Officials in city government were also solicited, but with much less success. Although City Weights and Measurements Inspector Lucian T. Jones, City Tax Assessor and Collector William P. B. McSain, and City Alderman William T. Griffith joined the hooded order, city hall would eventually become a bastion of fervent anti-Klan sentiment.[29]

By mid-summer 1921 the local Klan had gathered enough members to be officially chartered as Frontier Klan No. 100, and within weeks there were more than three hundred Klansmen in the city. At this time, however—in contrast to the friendly, or at least tolerant, reception afforded the Invisible Empire in many other Texas cities—El Paso authorities made it clear that the Klan would not be allowed to engage in illegal or disruptive activities. County Sheriff Seth B. Orndorff and Captain of City Detectives Claud T. Smith issued forceful public denunciations of the KKK, and Police Chief Peyton J. Edwards pledged to "do all that is within my power to suppress the activities of the Ku Klux Klan or any other secret order that would attempt to mete out punishment to citizens of El Paso." This firm stance no doubt reflected a recognition that reckless vigilantism of the sort that was currently being practiced in east Texas could prove disastrous at the Pass, with its distinctive racial and religious mixture. Indeed, city officials committed themselves to dissuading the Klan from making any type of sensational demonstration within the city limits. Accordingly, when word reached authorities in September that the fledgling Klan planned a public procession, the city council speedily enacted an ordinance prohibiting "assemblages, parades and processions of masked people within the city of El Paso." Questions concerning the law's constitutionality later prompted the council to pass a substitute measure that imposed a permit requirement for parades.[30] Nevertheless, the city government had forcefully made its point: El Paso was not Dallas or Waco or Beaumont, and the Invisible Empire had best conduct itself with caution and restraint.

Because of the hostile attitude of city authorities, Frontier Klan No. 100 maintained a low profile during the first months of its existence, the secret order using this period to select its leadership, recruit additional members, and develop a program to address local problems. During this formative stage, the man who would dominate the El Paso Klan established firm control within the klavern. Samuel J. Isaacks, a former state district judge and prominent local attorney, represented an almost prototypical example of the type of disgruntled El Pasoan who was upset over local conditions. An east Texas native who had moved to the Pass in 1917, Isaacks was a devout member of the Christian Church, an ardent prohibitionist, and a dedicated family man who ran his home with an iron hand. He also was an ambitious politician who had previously served as the first mayor of Midland, Texas. After transferring to El Paso and setting up his new practice, the former judge had become a leading figure among local moral reformers, but found his political future limited by the Ring's hold on power.[31] The organization of Frontier Klan No. 100, however, gave Isaacks, and other ambitious men as well, new opportunities to play an influential role in El Paso's affairs. As a former newspaper reporter later observed, the local Klan "attracted a lot of people who liked to be joiners, and who thought they would get some political backing out of it. Certain individuals saw a chance to get a power group behind them out of the Klan."[32] Yet, this did not mean that men such as Isaacks utilized the Klan solely to advance their political fortunes. Most of them, as far as can be determined, sincerely desired to improve their community and felt that the application of Klannish principles was a positive and constructive way in which to proceed. "I personally knew most of them," remembered one longtime El Paso resident. "They were by and large good, sincere people—just average citizens."[33]

In November 1921, Frontier Klan No. 100 decided that the time had come for its first public announcements. In identical letters sent to the city's two major newspapers, the *El Paso Times* and the *El Paso Herald,* the Klan informed residents that the local klavern had been organized and chartered four months before and had recently been "quietly gathering information for future reference." Most of this investigative effort evidently concerned the local vice and crime situation, the KKK providing a list of the social "cancers" that required immediate attention:

1. The running openly of a large number of houses of prostitution.

2. Approximately 500 women of immoral character on the streets, and some of them residing in our best residential districts, openly plying their trade.

3. Approximately 1000 males here being supported by the above mentioned females.

4. Automobile thefts averaging nearly one each day. On account of such condition the automobile insurance companies have nearly doubled their rates; some of them have withdrawn from the city entirely and others have threatened to do so, leaving car owners without protection whatever.

5. Burglaries of private residences are of such frequent occurence and committed with such boldness as to put many good people in constant fear, and to the extent that insurance companies have nearly doubled rates covering these risks.

6. The United States government maintains, at great expense, the largest force of prohibition enforcement officers on the border, because smugglers, bootleggers, highjackers and confidence men without number have made El Paso their headquarters.

Despite the urgent need to address these problems, the Klan emphasized that it did not desire to serve as a "moral correction agency," that it was simply a civic group composed of "decent, respectable American citizens" who wanted "to make El Paso a better and cleaner city . . . a better place in which to live and rear our children." In fact, the KKK proudly asserted, many of the community's most respected and financially prominent residents had become knights of the Invisible Empire.[34]

Shortly after making this rather temperate announcement of its intentions, Frontier Klan No. 100 attempted to demonstrate its respectability and usefulness in a variety of other ways. Beginning with a donation to an El Paso Associated Charities fund drive in November, the KKK ostentatiously contributed to a number of charitable efforts over the next several months, bestowing monetary gifts upon the Young Men's Christian Association, the Salvation Army, the El Paso chapter of the United Confederate Veterans, and, in at least one instance, an ill and impoverished local resident.[35] The Klan also vigorously sought to forge an alliance with the city's leading Protestant clergymen, whose views concerning moral conditions at the Pass mirrored those of most Klansmen. In a circular that took special notice of the adverse influence of motion pictures in El Paso, Frontier Klan No. 100 urged local ministers to inaugurate a new moral cleanup campaign, promising the full support of the "worthy citizens" who composed the Klan's membership.

Not surprisingly, this appeal elicited a positive response from many Protestant men of the cloth, particularly those who had long denounced sin along the border. "It is refreshing, quite so, to find the Ku Klux Klan interested in a better El Paso," opined the Reverend Dr. Floyd Poe of the First Presbyterian Church, who later described the Invisible Empire as a "mighty engine" and openly declared his sympathy "with the purposes of the Ku Klux Klan as published in El Paso." Other churchmen were similarly impressed, and soon Protestant pulpits rang with a new series of sermons decrying decadence at the Pass. Moreover, the Klan's stand on behalf of morality and the organization's apparent potential for serving as an agent of reform convinced a significant portion of the local Protestant clergy to either join the order or serve as active fellow travelers. In the latter part of 1922, the *El Paso Herald* asked twenty-two prominent local ministers and church officers whether they supported the KKK. Revealingly, only two of those queried indicated their decided opposition to the Klan. "Of the remainder," reported the *Herald,* "ten expressed sympathy for the organization while the others gave answers so burdened with conditional phrases that they were practically evasive." At least nine of the Protestant leaders implied that they were currently members of the Ku Klux Klan.[36]

The cordial reception given the KKK by Protestant moral reformers contrasted sharply with the stance of El Paso's business and political establishments. The *El Paso Times,* spokespiece for major commercial interests and the administration of Mayor Charles Davis, utilized almost every conceivable opportunity to denounce Frontier Klan No. 100. *Times* editor James Black possessed an intense personal aversion to southern-style racism and religious bigotry, and viewed Klansmen as a dangerous element who threatened El Paso's "old spirit of tolerance and forbearance." Other longtime civic leaders likewise considered the Klan an alien intrusion incompatible with southwestern traditions. The venerable Walter D. Howe, an El Paso resident since the 1880s and justice of the 34th District Court, pointedly instructed grand juries that an individual had the right to use homicide in defending oneself from disguised parties, and State National Bank president George Flory—described by one former employee as a "tough old boy"—arbitrarily purged the banks' workforce of suspected Klansmen. Although he had long campaigned for reform in El Paso, *Herald* publisher Hughes D. Slater also found the Klan's secrecy and methods repugnant, and sided with the anti-Klan forces. "The old-time vigilantes of the west did not disguise themselves or attempt concealment," Slater argued. "They had ugly work to do but they performed it as men."

Many common citizens shared the elite's aversion to the Klan. To bookkeeper George C. Matlin the KKK appeared to be "just a bunch of do-gooders." "They told people how they should act," he later recalled. "In a little East Texas town that might go over.... [But] El Paso was not a town to ever take to something like that." El Pasoan W. L. Rider similarly felt that a majority of the community would not tolerate "any interference with the orderly processes of law and justice." "We are not," stressed Rider, "in the bigoted belt."[37]

The opposition of longtime southwesterners and the El Paso establishment did not surprise, and probably did not totally displease, Frontier Klan No. 100. The political opportunists in the order realized that in the context of local traditions and the local power structure the Klan was destined to be an insurgent movement, and they sought a major issue with which to challenge incumbent officeholders. At first, as the KKK's list of pressing community concerns indicated, the Invisible Empire probably intended to focus on the local vice and crime situation, but the *Times*'s and *Herald*'s refusal to print any more letters from the Klan prevented a public debate on those volatile topics. This caused Frontier Klan No. 100 to turn to another issue of intense local interest: the administration of the public schools.

Civic reformers directed considerable attention to El Paso's public school system in the early 1920s. Because of the inherently depressed nature of the Pass economy, the tax base for educational expenditures remained small, resulting in an inadequate number of classrooms and other essential facilities for the city's rapidly expanding school-age population. Although the predominantly Mexican southside schools were the most overcrowded, schools north of the tracks also suffered from a serious lack of space and equipment. "Pupils at Manhattan School," angrily asserted the members of the Manhattan Parent-Teacher Association in January 1922, "study on the stairs, many lower grade pupils are shifted about the building three times a day before finding a roosting place, and there is only one desk for each three students in the junior high school." It did not appear, however, that any type of relief was imminent. Although the El Paso School Board had energetically sought more money for the schools, the Davis administration controlled funding and proved very reluctant to raise taxes. The Ring's control over the educational system's budget angered many El Pasoans who believed that their children were being victimized by career politicians. Thus, the school issue promised to be an effective entering wedge for Klan insurgents.[38]

In early 1922, Frontier Klan No. 100 made its debut, albeit a secret one, in local politics. On January 28, Samuel J. Isaacks announced he would seek a seat on the school board at the coming election scheduled for April 1. Shortly afterward, Charles S. Ward, the foreman of the *Herald*'s composing room, and Dr. J. Hal Gambrell, a physician and prominent member of the Al Maida Shrine, joined Isaacks on a three-man ticket. Ward and Gambrell were school board incumbents and leading figures in the fight for increased school funding. The Ward-Isaacks-Gambrell (WIG) slate soon launched a spirited campaign that called for expanded school construction and an end to the hold that Mayor Davis's "rotten political machine" had on the educational system, claiming that city politicians were scheming to make unethical profits from school bond issues. Supporters of the WIG ticket stressed that their candidates were all respected family men with children currently

attending the public schools and thus would be sympathetic representatives of "the common people who . . . are most vitally interested in
the school system." It was not acknowledged, however, that all three
men were members of the local Klan and that Isaacks currently served
as Exalted Cyclops.[39]

The El Paso establishment responded to the Klan's challenge in a
belated fashion. Only three weeks before the election, political and
business insiders put forth their own school board slate. It consisted of
William H. Burges, one of the city's most distinguished lawyers and a
past president of the Texas Bar Association; Ulysses S. Stewart, president of the City National Bank and a prominent member of the Chamber of Commerce; and Dr. James A. Brady, a dentist and wealthy
businessman. All three candidates were longtime city residents, well-
known members of the local elite with close links to the Davis
administration. Predictably, WIG partisans wasted little time in exploiting
these connections, persuasively arguing that the Burges-Brady-Stewart
(BBS) ticket was the tool of the Ring, part of a ploy to consolidate the
city administration's hold on the schools. Opponents additionally noted
that none of the BBS candidates were currently patrons of the public
schools–their offspring were either grown or privately educated–and
therefore could not appreciate the crisis situation facing the El Paso
system.[40]

The appearance of an establishment-backed ticket did not catch the
Klan off guard. Even prior to the fielding of the BBS slate, Klansmen had
been the guiding force behind the recent formation of the El Paso Good
Government League, whose proclaimed purpose was to "keep aliens,
illiterates and others who have no right to vote, from entering the polls
at the coming school election and all future elections." George B.
Oliver, the owner of a local fuel yard and member of Frontier Klan No.
100, headed the league. Oliver deftly concealed the league's Klannish
connections and thus attracted the support of influential non-Klan
elements, such as the El Paso Central Labor Union and Hughes D.
Slater's *Herald.* An active and spirited group, the league waged an
all-out war on political corruption: it compiled a list of aliens who had
paid their poll tax, offered rewards for the arrest and conviction of
illegal voters, sent letters to suspected aliens and illiterates warning
them not to vote, succeeded in having the school board approve a list
of league-endorsed election officials, and posted poll watchers in suspect precincts on election day. Thus the league–in its role as a Klan

surrogate—represented a continuation of the reform efforts that had sporadically surfaced at the Pass during earlier decades.[41]

On April 1, the El Paso electorate endorsed the WIG ticket by a sizeable majority (fig. 3.1), each of the three Klansmen outpolling their nearest BBS opponent by more than eight hundred votes. A worried Mayor Davis described the primary reason for this victory after an election-day tour of the city: "They are certainly flocking to the polls in the districts north of the tracks. And in the southern part of town the voting is not as heavy as we expected." Mobilized by anger over the state of the public schools, Anglo voters, especially those residing in the expanding suburban additions in northeast El Paso, balloted in unprecedented numbers and provided Isaacks and his running mates with their margin of victory. Although a precise analysis of the WIG vote awaits the release of manuscript census data, most of these voters appear to have been relatively recent arrivals at the Pass, of southern or border state origin, and evangelical Protestants. In addition, a significant percentage of them were women. Whereas only 2,816 El Paso women had paid their poll tax in 1921, this figure rose to 6,098 the following year, the result of a new state law requiring that the 1922 tax be automatically assessed against all property owners. Most of these potential new voters were Anglo: out of 6,645 females paying the tax or being issued exemptions because of advanced age, only 830 had Spanish surnames. Because the bulk of these female Anglo voters resided in precincts carried by the WIG ticket, it can be reasonably surmised that women played a crucial role in the KKK's victory.[42]

The Klan's candidates benefited not only from a surge in the number of Anglo voters but also from the recent reduction of the potential Mexican vote. In the postwar atmosphere of nativism, Texas legislators decided that the time had come to fully Americanize the electorate, enacting a measure in 1921 that excluded all aliens from the franchise. This move had a profound, and confusing, impact along the border, where large numbers of Mexicans who had taken out first papers toward naturalization had previously voted legally. The school board election demonstrated that the Hispanic electorate no longer remained the exclusive key to political dominance in El Paso. Additionally, the vigilance of the Good Government League and league-approved election officials prevented any major influx of illegal Mexican votes on election day. At the 49th precinct in southeast El Paso, a judge at the polls turned back

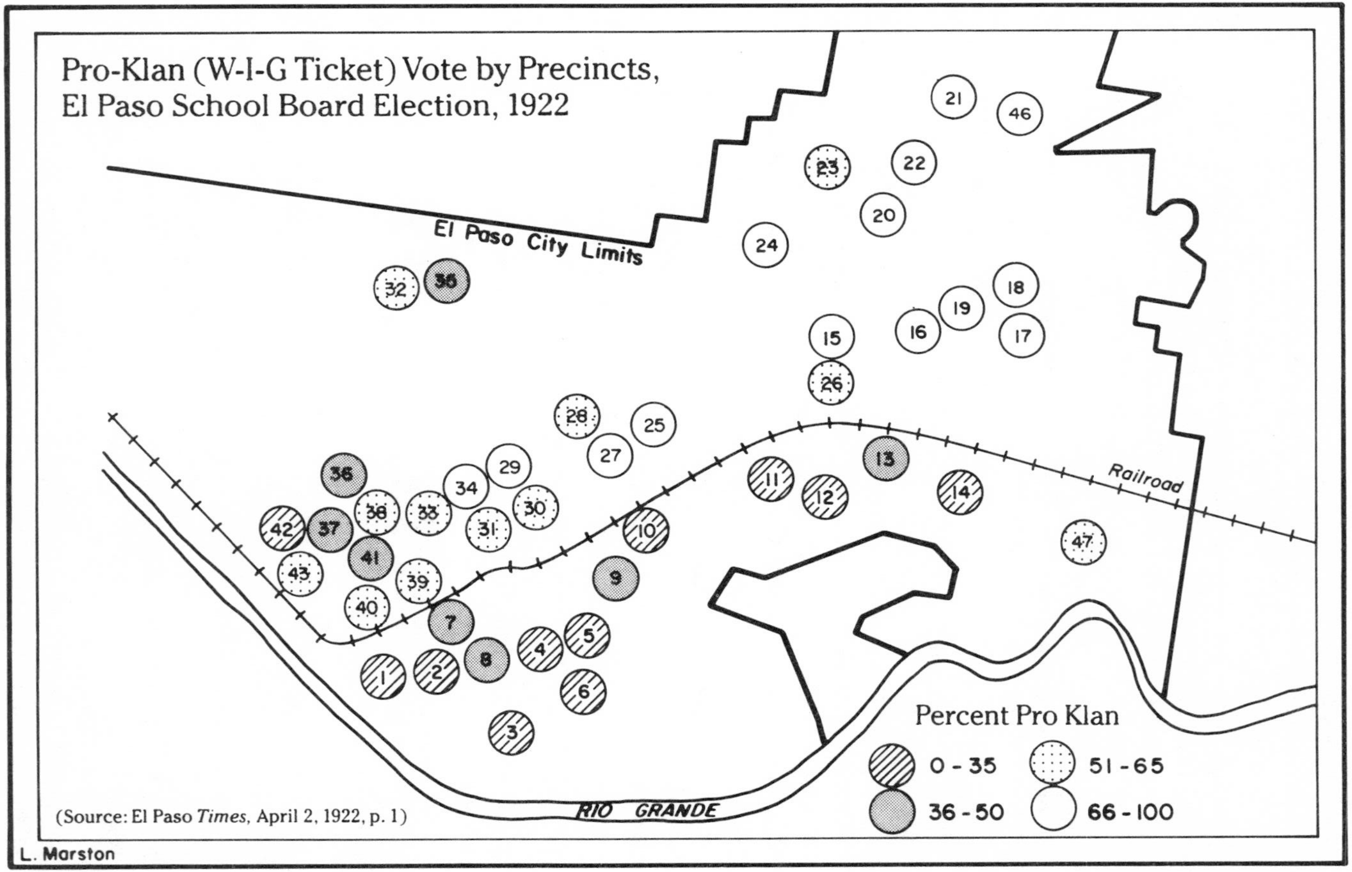

Pro-Klan (W-I-G Ticket) Vote by Precincts,
El Paso School Board Election, 1922

Percent Pro Klan

0 - 35   51 - 65

36 - 50   66 - 100

El Paso City Limits

Railroad

RIO GRANDE

(Source: El Paso *Times*, April 2, 1922, p. 1)

L. Marston

FIGURE 3.1.

forty suspect Mexicans who tried to vote, and George Oliver and other GGL members kept a close eye on proceedings in precincts where the Ring had previously voted Hispanics in large numbers. These efforts apparently paid off (or perhaps were unwarranted), the league only being able to identify ten valid instances of illegal voting.[43]

The outcome of the school board election provided a dramatic triumph for Frontier Klan No. 100, the result of the politically astute and disciplined manner in which the KKK had operated throughout the campaign. Realizing that they could not allow the Invisible Empire to become the focus of debate, Isaacks and his running mates succeeded in concealing their Klannish connections, utilized the Good Government League as an effective front organization, and directed the voters' attention toward the serious problems associated with the management of the schools. In doing so, they garnered the support of many citizens who were not affiliated with the Klan and scored an impressive win over the El Paso establishment. It still remained unclear, however, what the voters thought of the Ku Klux Klan itself. That judgment would not be rendered for several months yet.

Throughout 1922, Frontier Klan No. 100 became increasingly bold in asserting itself on the local scene. This confidence rested partly in the klavern's steady growth in membership, as hundreds of recruits were inducted into the order at elaborate ceremonies just beyond the city limits. According to one of the group's opponents, as many as thirty-five hundred El Pasoans may have belonged to the Klan at one time or another, but the organization's core strength was probably closer to fifteen hundred—still a very impressive percentage of the total number of adult white Protestant males at the Pass. The KKK's appeal was well demonstrated at a spectacular gathering—replete with cactus-fueled bonfires and burning crosses—in the western foothills in March. More than one thousand Klansmen in white hoods and robes stood in attendance while three hundred recruits awaited initiation. Automobiles of the participants were double-parked in a line extending nearly one hundred yards. At a subsequent Klan rally in the upper valley near the New Mexico border, 212 inductees took the KKK oath beneath a huge fiery cross, a ceremony witnessed by more than a thousand additional Klansmen. When the proceedings concluded, a reporter for the *Herald* managed to acquire a Klan costume that was misplaced during the confusion of departure. The number "2,706" was stamped on the back of the outfit, a possible indication of the minimum strength of Frontier Klan No. 100.[44]

While the total number of El Paso Klansmen can be roughly approximated, the unavailability of a comprehensive membership roster hinders any evaluation of the social and economic standing of the order's rank and file. The general features of local Anglo society, however, must have greatly influenced the types of recruits brought into the Invisible Empire. Because of the region's underdeveloped border economy and the presence of an ample supply of unskilled Mexican laborers, Anglos at the Pass usually filled middle-class roles in the marketplace. One study estimates that two-thirds of all non-Spanish-surnamed workers in El Paso in 1920 were white-collar employees; only slightly more than 3 percent of this group found employment as unskilled laborers or menial workers. Therefore, most El Paso Klansmen, because of the predominant features of the local pool of potential recruits, almost certainly came from the middle class. Such a middle-class membership would help to explain why Frontier Klan No. 100, in contrast to many other Texas klaverns, remained a law-abiding group and eschewed violent vigilantism. As a local Klansman noted, "We are constantly warning against [violence] in our meetings. . . . We are working here to assist in law enforcement. That's why we got into politics."[45]

Nevertheless, El Paso Klansmen pursued their moral and political agenda with insistence. In March 1922, "scores" of El Pasoans received mimeographed messages, affixed with the official seal of Frontier Klan No. 100, warning them against recreational trips to Ciudad Juárez. The missives ominously noted that "Dynamite has been handled by many men for many years, but it has been known to explode." Other perceived moral offenders also attracted the attention of the Klan: Frank H. Morris, a clerk at the Union Drug Store, was told to drop a pending divorce case; John E. McAllister received an unwelcome note concerning his "personal affairs"; and Charles Clark, an American residing in Juárez, was told by two men bearing KKK cards to return to the United States or face deportation. In addition, Frontier Klan No. 100 systematically monitored the activities of carousing juveniles, notifying parents when wayward teenagers made unauthorized visits across the border.[46]

Few actions taken by Klansmen created more public alarm than those of the KKK's victorious candidates on the school board. Soon after taking office, Ward, Isaacks, and Gambrell engineered the selection of fellow Klansman James A. Borders, president of the American

Trust and Savings Bank, to fill a vacancy on the board, giving the Invisible Empire a majority of four among seven trustees. Once their control of the board was secure, the Klansmen forged ahead with needed reforms—securing more funding for the schools and approving numerous construction projects—but also initiated a reevaluation of school employees on the basis of religion. At a secret "star chamber" session on May 26, the trustees decided they would not rehire three of the city's four Catholic principals for the coming academic year.

The firing of the Catholic principals created intense controversy. "The whole thing simmers down to the Ku Klux Klan and the anti-Ku Klux Klan," charged board member W. T. Power, a Klan adversary. "The majority of members of the school board are in sympathy with the Ku Klux Klan—I would not say they are members—and some of the principals they refused to re-elect are Catholic and are opposed to the Klan." Subsequently, school board meetings regularly degenerated into acrimonious confrontations between the pro- and anti-Klan factions. After engaging in a shouting match with Power on one occasion, Samuel Isaacks picked up a chair and appeared ready to use it on his opponent. As Isaacks later explained: "I guess I got a bit excited and I did jump up from my chair. Then Powers [sic] reached for his hip. I sat down."[47]

The disruptive impact of the Ku Klux Klan was not confined to the school board. By the latter part of 1922 the American Legion, the Al Maida Shrine, the El Paso Bar Association, and the League of Women Voters, among other groups, had divided into vociferous cliques that either supported or despised the KKK. "Almost *every* organization and club," recalled an El Paso resident of this period, "had its pro-Klan and anti-Klan factions." The tension and general unpleasantness resulting from this controversy disturbed El Pasoans and caused many of them, Klansmen included, to reassess the Klan's impact on the community. "If we do not put a stop to this discord and the fight between people of different creeds and get together in the old spirit that existed here," warned one resident, "we might just as well pull our freight and move to some other community where such conditions do not exist."[48] While the Klan had initially appeared a promising means of implementing reform, its adverse impact on community relations was, in the view of an increasing number of citizens, severely reducing the order's utility as an agency of progressive civic action.

At the same time that public sentiment began to shift against the

Klan, the enemies of the Invisible Empire took steps to undermine the tight secrecy that Frontier Klan No. 100 had thus far maintained. During the fall of 1922, William (Will) H. Fryer, a former county attorney and prominent member of the Knights of Columbus, filed a petition in 65th District Court requesting that the names of four Democratic nominees—John E. Quaid, Frank Scotten, Clarence W. Harper, and Asa R. Webb—be taken off the general election ballot in November. The petition asserted that these individuals had "forsworn allegiance to the constitution and laws of the state of Texas" through the taking of an oath of loyalty to a foreign power—the Invisible Empire. Fryer also provided a list of witnesses who could testify about the nominees' affiliation with the KKK, including Samuel J. Isaacks, J. Hal Gambrell, James A. Borders, George B. Oliver, and more than a dozen other Klansmen. Although Fryer's petition was based on unsound legal ground and he withdrew it before the court could deliver an unfavorable ruling, the publicity generated by the case dealt Frontier Klan No. 100 a severe blow. Many of the klavern's most influential members now found themselves exposed and KKK recruiting declined precipitously because the order could no longer guarantee secrecy.[49]

Others joined Fryer in his fight against the Invisible Empire. The *El Paso Times* posted "watchers" near the scene of Klan gatherings, who wrote down the names and automobile license numbers of those attending. Utilizing a series of paid informants, the *Times* managed to positively identify Samuel J. Isaacks as Exalted Cyclops and received detailed reports of KKK activities. In the latter part of 1922, the Davis administration also became more active in opposing the Invisible Empire, particularly after authorities learned that the personal automobiles of city policemen had been parked near Klan outings. Mayor Davis required that all members of the police department sign affidavits that they had "not been within six months next proceeding this date a member of the Ku Klux Klan, nor a citizen of the Invisible Empire," but he suspected that there were still active Klansmen on the force. Accordingly, on September 26, Clifford L. Sirmans, the recently identified kligrapp (Klan secretary) of Frontier Klan No. 100, was subpoened to appear before a justice of the peace to assist in an investigation concerning "making false affidavits." Under intensive questioning by Assistant District Attorney Charles L. Vowell, Sirmans revealed that at least four officers had been Klansmen in the past six months.

The policemen were shortly dismissed, and Davis ordered all other municipal employees to sign sworn statements that they had not recently been members of the Invisible Empire. To further ensure that city government had been purged of Klannish influences, police detectives stationed themselves near Odd Fellows Hall whenever it seemed a Klan meeting was in progress. This naturally angered Klansmen like George Oliver, who angrily shouted at the detectives on one occasion, "You'd better watch some of your officials instead of spying on decent citizens, peaceably attending a meeting!"[50]

The actions of Fryer, the *El Paso Times,* and the Davis administration took a heavy toll on Frontier Klan No. 100. Not surprisingly, many Klansmen began to doubt whether they wanted to belong to a group that was under surveillance by the police and newspaper reporters. Moreover, the El Paso klavern also suffered from internal disaffection. Although the mysterious ritual and romantic bonds of fraternalism had initially attracted many El Pasoans to the secret order, this allure quickly diminished. As one former Klansman explained, "I had misunderstood the real nature and purpose of the organization and very soon realized that I was not in sympathy with them." Another El Pasoan likewise noted that "Good men got into that organization but got out when they found out what they had joined." Some recruits sensed that the Klan was nothing but a "money-making scheme"; others were appalled by the open religious and racial bigotry that prevailed at meetings of the klavern and realized that ultimately such a group could not play a positive role in local affairs.

By late 1922, those who had joined the Klan out of political expediency also recognized the KKK's limitations. In contrast to the order's triumph in the school board election, the results of the 1922 state Democratic primary in July had been mixed. A number of Klan-affiliated candidates won local races, but almost all were incumbents and the Klan's opponents had held their own. The Invisible Empire's choice for United States senator, State Railroad Commissioner Earle B. Mayfield (who had spoken before Frontier Klan No. 100 during a campaign visit to El Paso), carried the city in a runoff with former Governor James E. Ferguson, yet the extremely low voter turnout indicated that local Klansmen apparently did not constitute a powerful and reliable voting bloc. Indeed, plagued by internal problems and beset by enemies, the El Paso Klan's core of active knights had dwindled to only 682 by January 1923.[51]

Despite their organization's difficulties, diehard Klansmen held firm. The Democratic primary for city offices was to take place in February

1923, and the Invisible Empire hoped it could again capitalize on anti-Ring sentiment and bring about the downfall of the Davis machine. "[One] victory is not enough," asserted a local Klansman. "We have to remake the political fabric of our city." During the closing weeks of 1922, the KKK assembled a full slate of municipal candidates, headed by mayoral hopeful Preston E. (P. E.) Gardner, an attorney and proprietor of the Gardner Hotel in downtown El Paso. In contrast to the school board election, however, the Klan ticket failed to conceal its connections to the Invisible Empire. Indeed, the local press revealed that the slate had been officially endorsed at a secret meeting of Frontier Klan No. 100.[52] Thus the pending primary increasingly appeared to be a referendum on whether the Klan would rule in El Paso.

No group of El Pasoans felt more concern about the possibility of a KKK-run local government than prominent members of the business community. With the Pass economy so dependent on Mexican labor and trade, the business elite feared the possible Hispanic reaction to such a city administration. Thus far, El Paso's Mexican majority had not actively involved itself in the controversy over the Klan, primarily because of a widespread lack of interest in American politics and because local Hispanics realized that Frontier Klan No. 100 was essentially law-abiding. "The Klan here wasn't like the Klan in other parts of Texas that attacked blacks and Mexicans, tarred and feathered them," observed Mauricio Cordero, a local Mexican immigrant. However, the accession of a Klan administration and police force might spur the Mexican community to belated action and disrupt the Pass's labor supply. A Klannish city hall, moreover, would certainly hurt the city's relations with Mexico. Delicate negotiations were currently underway for full United States recognition of the government of President Alvaro Obregon, and local interests looked forward to a great surge in business activity south of the border. The presence of municipal authorities who were members of a racist secret society would hardly be a favorable inducement for Mexican officials and businessmen to direct trade toward El Paso.[53]

Fearful that Frontier Klan No. 100 might again successfully exploit resentment against the Davis administration, El Paso business leaders searched for an alternate candidate. They chose State Senator Richard M. (Dick) Dudley, one of the city's most-respected businessmen and officeholders, then serving as president pro tem of the Texas state senate. A "business progressive" free of links to the Ring, Dudley had actively supported prohibition, woman suffrage, and the movement to bar alien voters; he was also a staunch Baptist. Nevertheless, he had no use for the Klan and called for a reunited El Paso that would "not be governed or controlled by any one class or sect, but rather by broad-minded businessmen who represent its full citizenship."[54]

Dudley's candidacy received a great boost in December 1922 when Charles Davis announced that he would not seek a fourth term as mayor. Although he would have liked to remain in office, Davis realized another mayoral bid would divide the anti-Klan forces and provide the Invisible Empire with considerable political ammunition. His withdrawal meant that the enemies of the KKK could unite behind Dudley's progressive record and attract the support of non-Klan voters who had balloted for the WIG ticket in the school board contest.[55]

Dick Dudley and the El Paso establishment conducted an impressive and effective campaign during the early weeks of 1923. While the senator made lofty speeches praising the nation's traditions of religious and racial tolerance, his supporters unleashed a furious attack on the Invisible Empire, stressing the organization's incompatibility with southwestern culture, "In this great southwest," asserted District Attorney Charles Vowell at one Dudley rally, "we are used to meeting each other man to man and fighting it out. That's the way of the great southwest—we don't want to look at each other through the holes of a pillow slip." All three daily newspapers (including the new *El Paso Post*) joined in the anti-Klan crusade, denouncing the Invisible Empire's impact on community relations and helping to focus the voters' attention on the exclusive question of whether the Klan would run local affairs. By election day, one city resident noted, "The only issue in this campaign is whether El Paso is a Ku Klux town or not."[56]

P. E. Gardner and the other officeseekers on the Klan ticket proved to be no match for the establishment. Needing to obscure the KKK issue, the Gardner forces attempted to direct the public's attention to a variety of other matters—civic improvements, vice, drug smuggling, bootlegging—but to no avail. In desperation, Gardner's campaign manager charged that Dick Dudley had sought Klan aid in his recent senate bid and that the senator's friends had once characterized him as "as good a Klansman as ever wore shoe leather." These false assertions demonstrated that even the KKK realized that membership in the Invisible Empire had become a distinct political liability.[57]

On February 23, Dudley and his running mates rode the rising tide of anti-Klan sentiment to a decisive victory in the city primary (see fig. 3.2). The senator outpolled P. E. Gardner 7,572 to 5,452. Although Gardner did well in the northeastern suburbs, Dudley managed to make sizeable inroads among Anglo voters in the western and central precincts in older parts of the city, the same areas that had supported the WIG ticket in 1922. Combined with the senator's solid southside backing, these Anglo votes produced an impressive win.[58] In the process, an important decision had been reached: El Paso's city government would not be handed over to the Ku Klux Klan.

The results of the city Democratic primary spelled the imminent demise of Frontier Klan No. 100 as a significant political and social force. Most Klansmen who anticipated political rewards left the organization, and by early 1924 only a little more than two hundred members regularly attended meetings of the order. The group attempted a few more forays into local politics, but these efforts proved decidedly unsuccessful. Indeed, the Klan's electoral clout was so diminished that Charles Ward, Samuel J. Isaacks, and J. Hal Gambrell decided not to seek reelection to the school board at the end of their two-year terms. Nevertheless, the enemies of the Klan remained on guard. The Dudley administration carefully monitored Klan activities, and Will Fryer hired a private detective to infiltrate the El Paso klavern. This unyielding vigilance further reduced the organization's membership. By the end of 1924, the year that Texans as a whole were rejecting the Invisible Empire, Frontier Klan No. 100 had become a negligible community influence.[59]

El Pasoans joined Frontier Klan No. 100 for a variety of reasons, but the primary explanation for the rise of the Invisible Empire at the Pass is that the order appeared to many citizens to be a promising means of changing local society. El Paso's rapid growth had brought a large Anglo group who had little affinity or tolerance for traditional border culture, and who wished to establish a new political and social order. Members of this group were drawn from a broad cross section of Anglo middle-class society and tended to be new arrivals, evangelical Protestants, and natives of the South. These residents used the Klan for a period to address local problems and to contest the dominance of established business and political interests, but eventually the organization proved to be an ineffective agency of progressive civic action. For a tension-filled year and a half, however, the Ku Klux Klan had

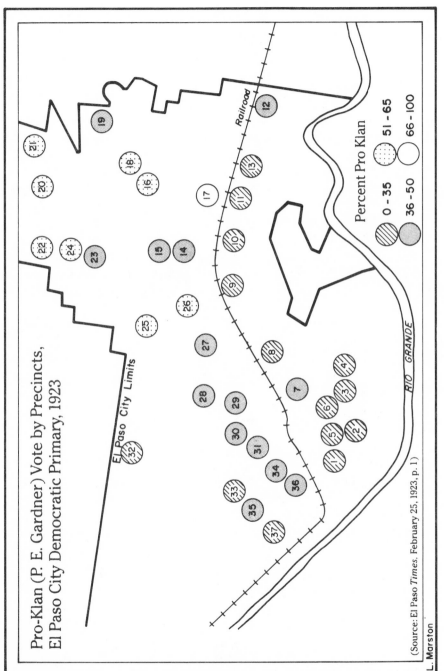

Pro-Klan (P. E. Gardner) Vote by Precincts,
El Paso City Democratic Primary, 1923

Percent Pro Klan

0 – 35   51 – 65
36 – 50   66 – 100

El Paso City Limits

Railroad

RIO GRANDE

(Source: El Paso *Times*, February 25, 1923, p. 1)

L. Marston

FIGURE 3.2.

served as a formidable weapon in the hands of local insurgents, a means of challenging El Paso's unusual cultural traditions and economic arrangements.

NOTES

The author would like to thank Texas Western Press for permission to use material from his book *War, Revolution, and the Ku Klux Klan: A Study of Intolerance in a Border City* (El Paso, 1985). He would also like to thank Claude M. Mathis, Nella Cunningham, and Joe Cunningham for their able services as research assistants.

1. Charles C. Alexander, *Crusade for Conformity: The Ku Klux Klan in Texas, 1920–1930* (Houston, 1962) and *The Ku Klux Klan in the Southwest* (Lexington, Kentucky, 1965). An excellent survey of the Texas Klan experience is included in Norman D. Brown, *Hood, Bonnet, and Little Brown Jug: Texas Politics, 1921–1928* (College Station, Texas, 1984), 49–87. There is a great need for local case studies of Lone Star klaverns in the eastern, central, and southern parts of the state. The one such study to date, Lois E. Torrence, "The Ku Klux Klan in Dallas, 1915–1928: An American Paradox" (M.A. thesis, Southern Methodist University, 1948), is of minimal usefulness.

2. For a summary of the violence, see "The Reign of the Tar-Bucket," *Literary Digest* 12 (August 27, 1921): 12, and Albert De Silver, "The Ku Klux Klan— 'The Soul of Chivalry'," *The Nation* 63 (September 14, 1921): 285–86.

3. Brown, *Hood, Bonnet, and Little Brown Jug,* 51.

4. Ibid., 58–59; Alexander, *Crusade for Conformity,* 11.

5. Brown, *Hood, Bonnet, and Little Brown Jug,* 52; *El Paso Times,* May 23, 1921.

6. For the best general history of the El Paso area, see C. L. Sonnichsen, *Pass of the North: Four Centuries on the Rio Grande* (El Paso, 1968). Economic developments at the Pass are ably surveyed throughout Mario T. García, *Desert Immigrants: The Mexicans of El Paso, 1880–1920* (New Haven, 1981).

7. U.S. Bureau of the Census, *Fourteenth Census of the United States, 1920: Population,* III, 81, 710, 1015, 1016, 1024. The actual population of the city was probably significantly higher than the official total because of the difficulties in accurately determining the number of local Hispanic residents. When the populations of neighboring Fort Bliss and Ciudad Juárez are taken into consideration, there can be little doubt that more than a hundred thousand people resided in the El Paso metropolitan area by 1921. See *El Paso City Directory, 1921,* 186, and Oscar J. Martínez, *Border Boom Town: Ciudad Juárez Since 1848* (Austin, 1978), 161.

---

8. García, *Desert Immigrants,* passim.

9. Such racism is well detailed in Arnoldo De León, *They Called Them Greasers: Anglo Attitudes Toward Mexicans in Texas, 1821-1900* (Austin, 1983).

10. Shawn Lay, *War, Revolution, and the Ku Klux Klan: A Study in Intolerance in a Border City* (El Paso, 1985), 16-32.

11. *El Paso Times,* April 10, 26, May 12, 1917; El Paso Chamber of Commerce, "Minutes of a Specially Called Meeting of the Board of Directors of the El Paso Chamber of Commerce, April 20, 1917."

12. Lay, *War, Revolution, and the Ku Klux Klan,* 40-45.

13. U.S., Congress, House, Committee on Rules, *Hearings on the Ku Klux Klan,* 67th Cong., 1st sess., 1921, pp. 96, 127. For a survey of the city's church memberships, see *El Paso Times,* June 29, 1921.

14. *El Paso Times,* January 4, 11, 25, 26, March 3, 5, 21, May 1, 7, July 11, 25, August 17, 28, 1921; January 1, 1922; *El Paso Herald,* March 22, May 2, June 14, 1921.

15. *El Paso Times,* January 7, March 1, 1921.

16. The ethnically biased manner in which the El Paso press regularly reported crimes committed by Hispanics also enhanced the impression of a direct correlation between race and crime. Although I have not attempted a systematic survey, it seems from a reading of the local papers that the great majority of reported criminal offenses in the early 1920s were attributed to Mexicans.

17. *El Paso Times,* January 23, 27, March 20, August 16, 23, November 27, 1921; *El Paso Herald,* July 23-24, August 3, November 4, 1921.

18. *El Paso Times,* August 30, 1920.

19. Institute of Oral History, University of Texas at El Paso, Chris P. Fox transcript, ACC 214, p. 18.

20. Edward Lonnie Langston, "The Impact of Prohibition on the Mexican-United States Border: The El Paso-Ciudad Juárez Case" (Ph.D. dissertation, Texas Tech University, 1974); Interview with William J. Hooten, El Paso, December 1, 1983.

21. See *El Paso Times,* January 1, 19, 1921; January 1, 1922.

22. Ibid., January 3, 24, February 21, 1921.

23. Sonnichsen, *Pass of the North,* 348, 353.

24. García, *Desert Immigrants,* 158, 162-64; Jack C. Vowell, Jr., "Politics at El Paso: 1850-1920" (M.A. thesis, Texas Western College, 1952).

25. García, *Desert Immigrants,* 169-70; Hooten interview.

26. *El Paso Post,* January 12, 1923.

27. *El Paso Times,* September 15, October 4, 1921.

28. *Las Cruces Citizen,* October 22, 1921; John W. Denny, "One Hundred Years of Freemasonry in El Paso, 1854-1954" (M.A. thesis, Texas Western College, 1954), 150-51; Hooten interview.

---

29. *El Paso Times,* September 27, 1921; October 29, 1922; May 15, 1924; *El Paso Herald,* February 24, 1923; telephone conversation with Mr. and Mrs. William E. Griffith, February 18, 1985.

30. *El Paso Times,* September 10, 16, 23, 25, 29, 30, 1921; *El Paso Herald,* July 26, September 15, 1921; "Minutes of a Regular Meeting of the El Paso City Council, September 15, 1921," Book M-2, p. 65; "Minutes of a Regular Meeting of the El Paso City Council, September 29, 1921," Book M-2, pp. 88–89.

31. Interview with Mr. and Mrs. Bill Isaacks, El Paso, November 28, 1983. For more on Isaacks and his family, see the Isaacks family file in the Barker Center, University of Texas at Austin.

32. Institute of Oral History, University of Texas at El Paso, S. L. A. Marshall transcript, ACC 181, p. 73.

33. Hooten interview.

34. *El Paso Times,* November 4, 1921; *El Paso Herald,* November 3, 5–6, 1921.

35. *El Paso Times,* November 11, 17, 20, 1921; May 17, 1922; *El Paso Herald,* November 16, 1921; April 8, May 12, 17, June 12, 1922.

36. *El Paso Times,* November 17, 1921; *El Paso Herald,* November 17, 1921; October 11, 1922.

37. *El Paso Times,* June 20, August 7, November 8, 1921; October 1, 1922; March 18, 1984; *El Paso Herald,* July 20, November 7, 9, 1921.

38. *El Paso Herald,* July 5, 13, 1921; February 9, 1922.

39. *El Paso Times,* January 29, 1922; February 17, 1923; *El Paso Herald,* January 28–29, March 25–26, 29, 1922; May 14, 1924; *El Paso Labor Advocate,* February 3, 1922; Institute of Oral History, University of Texas at El Paso, Msgr. Henry D. Buchanan tape, ACC 3.

40. *El Paso Times,* March 10, 12, 14, 26, 1922; *El Paso Herald,* March 10, 23, 1922; J. F. Hulse, *Texas Lawyer: The Life of William H. Burges* (El Paso, 1982).

41. *El Paso Herald,* March 6, 7, 8, 14, 27, 28, April 1–2, 1922; *El Paso Times,* March 7, 14, April 2, 1922.

42. *El Paso Herald,* April 1–2, 1922; *El Paso Times,* February 10, 1921; February 1, March 30, April 2, November 5, 1922.

43. Texas, *General Laws of the State of Texas Passed by the 37th Legislature of the Regular Session, 1921,* 275–276; *El Paso Herald,* March 29, April 1–2, 1922; *El Paso Times,* April 2, 1922.

44. *El Paso Herald,* March 11–12, May 31, 1922; Edward F. Sherman, "The Ku Klux Klan and El Paso Politics Following World War I" (History seminar paper, Texas Western College, 1958), 21.

45. García, *Desert Immigrants,* 89; *El Paso Post,* December 29, 1922.

46. *El Paso Times,* April 23, August 7, 1922; *El Paso Herald,* April 12, July 19, 1922.

47. El Paso School Board Records, vol. 11, "Minutes of a Special Meeting of the El Paso School Board, April 4, 1922," "Minutes of a Special Meeting of the

El Paso School Board, May 8, 1922," and "List of Superintendant's Comments on Principals, with Recommendations"; *El Paso Times,* April 7, May 17, 27, September 20, 1922; *El Paso Herald,* April 7, May 27–28, September 20, 1922; *El Paso Post,* September 20, 1922; Sherman, "Klan and El Paso Politics," 14.

48. Marshall transcript, 69–71; Hooten interview; *El Paso Times,* May 19, June 2, 1922; *El Paso Herald,* June 2, July 6, 1922; April 30, 1923; May 14, 1924.

49. *El Paso Times,* October 29, 31, 1922; *El Paso Herald,* October 30, 31, 1922.

50. *El Paso Times,* September 9, 16, 27, 28, October 1, 3, 1922; February 14, 16, 1923; *El Paso Herald,* September 16–17, 27, 30, October 1, 2, 5, 1922.

51. Hooten interview; *El Paso Times,* March 29, August 27, September 28, 1922; *El Paso Herald,* July 24, September 27, 28, 1922; January 11, 1923.

52. *El Paso Times,* April 12, 1922; February 2, 14, 1923; *El Paso Herald,* December 16–15, 1922; January 11, 1923; *El Paso Post,* December 16, 1922; January 15, 1923.

53. Institute of Oral History, University of Texas at El Paso, Mauricio Cordero transcript, ACC 142, p. 43; Hooten interview; Lay, *War, Revolution, and the Ku Klux Klan,* 137–38; *El Paso Times,* September 22, 1922.

54. *El Paso Times,* November 12, December 19, 31, 1922; January 7, 1923; *El Paso Herald,* November 11–12, 1922; *El Paso Post,* December 19, 1922.

55. *El Paso Times,* December 10, 1922.

56. Ibid., January 7, February 2, 10, 13, 22, 1923; *El Paso Post,* December 19, 1922.

57. *El Paso Times,* February 9, 13, 18, 1923; *El Paso Herald,* February 9, 12, 1923.

58. *El Paso Times,* February 25, 1923.

59. Ibid., April 5, 6, May 15, 1924; *El Paso Herald,* May 14, 1924; Brown, *Hood, Bonnet, and Little Brown Jug,* 211–52.

4

The Invisible Empire and the Search for the Orderly Community: The Ku Klux Klan in Anaheim, California

CHRISTOPHER N. COCOLTCHOS

As a result of an extensive recruiting effort, a number of klaverns were operating in southern California by the spring of 1922. California Klansmen shared many of the beliefs and concerns of their brethren elsewhere, but the origin, development, and decline of the region's local chapters were intimately bound up with specific community conditions. In the case of Anaheim and surrounding Orange County, the overall Klan experience can best be viewed as a contest between an entrenched commercial-civic elite and a rising group of politically oriented citizens who strongly disagreed with the elite's notion of how communities should be ordered.

Located twenty-five miles southeast of Los Angeles, Anaheim originated as a vineyard colony established by a group of German merchants and tradespeople from San Francisco in 1857. The vineyards did not survive the phylleroxa epidemic of the 1870s, but the community retained its Germanic leadership for decades. German remained the official language of municipal transactions until the 1880s, and a Germanic majority dominated the city council well into the twentieth century. The town's ethnic heritage resulted in, among other things, a toleration of alcoholic beverages. On the eve of World War I, Anaheim was one of the few "wet" communities in Orange County and served as a recreation center for the oil company employees who worked the fields in nearby Brea and La Habra.[1]

By 1917, prominent German-Americans represented an important element within a closely knit elite that dominated Anaheim's economic, civic, and social arenas. This elite's influence extended throughout northern Orange County, a region delimited by La Habra and Brea on the north, Buena Park on the west, and the Santa Ana River and Garden Grove on the south. The first families of this area had definite views about what constituted the best interests of their community and how civic priorities should be accordingly ordered. They also possessed a stranglehold on the successful development of civic leadership. Throughout Orange County, local politicians were elected in nonpartisan, at-large elections. The politics of acquaintance and local reputation were key factors in achieving and maintaining political office. In the informal millieu of a small city like Anaheim, occupational success, as measured by wealth, was not the only determinant of political leadership. The endorsement, or at least the tacit approval, of key groups such as the Elks, Masons, Kiwanis, Chamber of Commerce, and the local newspapers was extremely important for electoral success. Membership and active participation in these groups could help secure their endorsement. Although Anaheim had no organized political machines, informal word of mouth, or the lack of it, by one of the prominent civic or social clubs could spell the difference between defeat and success. A network of quasi-interest groups underlay the town's informal and apparently open civic culture.[2]

Anaheim's leaders had their critics, residents who were highly active in local affairs and possessed their own distinct vision of the commonweal. These citizens wanted to be part of a community that was fully cognizant of all its constituents (at least all its white constituents) and accorded them a certain minimum of respect and dignity regardless of their socioeconomic and political prominence. Increasingly, from 1917 to 1923, this dissident faction became convinced that Anaheim was being run in a patently arbitrary, undemocratic, and corrupt fashion.

The manner in which the elite alienated certain townspeople was well demonstrated by a dispute involving R. W. Earnest, the editor of the *Orange County Plain Dealer* (which would later evolve into the publicity organ of the Anaheim Klan). Shortly after he had arrived from Ohio in 1916 and assumed his editorial duties, Earnest discovered, as did other future Klansmen and Klan allies, that the town's dominant civic elements had set ideas concerning what should be said about Anaheim. In late December 1916, Earnest wrote a seemingly innocuous article about smudge pots "working overtime" to save the citrus crop during recent cold weather, poking a little fun at the town's official slogan, "Anaheim, The Frostless Belt." These remarks infuriated prominent Anaheimers, including Henry Kuchel, the owner, publisher, and editor of the weekly *Anaheim Gazette*.

A descendent of one of the first families to settle in Anaheim, Kuchel served as an influential and respected spokesman for the town's traditional leaders, whose booster-oriented views he shared. He took Earnest's remarks as a major affront to Anaheim's leadership: "Our slogan, 'Anaheim, The Frostless Belt,' was adopted by the board of trade, a body of honorable men, who would never dream of using a false motto, or sending forth misleading literature to induce investors to come here." Kuchel noted that Earnest was a "newcomer here" and perhaps did not appreciate that "We are endeavoring to induce good people in the north and east to locate here and the fact that Anaheim is the frostless belt is one of our greatest inducements." The leading merchants of the Anaheim Board of Trade, forerunner of the Chamber of Commerce, held similar views and passed a resolution condemning the article, demanding that Earnest withdraw his comments. The wrath of community leaders, among whom were many of the *Plain Dealer*'s advertisers, forced Earnest into a quick about-face. He avowed that Anaheim was, indeed, at the heart of the Frostless Belt.[3]

The outspoken editor did not long remain quiescent, and by July 1917, he had again clashed with the local establishment, this time over a flood protection district. The previous year, Anaheim had been partially inundated when the Santa Ana River had broken through the levees protecting the eastern part of the city. The city council subsequently demarcated a flood protection district that excluded westside neighborhoods. This angered many of that area's residents, who felt arbitrarily shut off from the protection that such a district would provide and who resented the prospect of paying for a large construction project that would not benefit them. With Earnest and several future Klansmen leading the fight, the westsiders succeeded in defeating a bond issue for the project in October 1917, despite the elite's insistance that the district would boost overall property values.[4]

Perhaps the controversy that most underlined the divisions between the elite and its critics (including many who would join the Klan) was a protracted battle over the construction of a new city hall. Dominant civic elements sought such a structure in order "to keep pace with the spirit of progress manifested by the enterprising citizens of the town." These leaders described the present municipal building as "a disgrace to the town and an eyesore" that would repel new residents and visitors. Many Anaheimers, however, did not think matters were so urgent, especially at a time when the country needed to concentrate its resources on the war effort. R. W. Earnest's *Plain Dealer* threatened a recall of municipal trustees should they press ahead with construction without consulting the voters, asserting that the city council's enthusiasm for the project had been enhanced by quid pro quo kickbacks. Many rank-and-file citizens supported the paper's stand, believing that civic improvements should not come at the price of popular sovereignty.

The vehement protests of the anti-city hall forces convinced the city council to schedule a bond election to determine if $100,000 could be raised for the construction of a new municipal building and a surrounding park. Despite the elite's intense electioneering, the measure failed at the polls in the fall of 1917.[5] Refusing to concede defeat, the council proceeded to approve plans for a new structure that would be funded through Anaheim's general fund. This prompted their adversaries to renew the threat of a recall, the *Plain Dealer* characterizing the incumbents and their allies as a "booze and boodle gang." In response, the city administration accused their opponents of being small-minded people with "personal axes to grind."[6]

The controversy over a new city hall persisted throughout early 1918, with critics of the edifice presenting petitions asking for another referendum on the issue. After the petitions were declared invalid on a technicality, the Anaheim council arbitrarily ordered the city engineer to tear down the old city hall. Before demolition began, however, a prominent local banker (and future Klansman), August Nagel, filed a legal protest that led to a superior court injunction prohibiting construction of the new municipal center. Like others who would join the KKK, Nagel resented the elite's ruthless exercise of power and the decision to spend tax revenues on a project over which the community was deeply divided. Meanwhile, the trustees appealed the injunction and fumed that for the present the "old decrepit city hall" would stand.[7]

At the same time that the city hall controversy was being handed over to the courts in 1918, the *Plain Dealer* and other antielite elements inaugurated an effort to "dry up" Anaheim. Largely owing to its Germanic traditions and leadership, the town remained the site of a considerable liquor trade. Numerous prominent citizens owned saloons or package stores, including Mayor William Stark. In the view of the elite's political opponents, prohibition and the issue of arbitrary community control were overlapping concerns, and both matters were regularly injected into Anaheim's municipal and school board elections.

As a result of the burgeoning outcry for tougher liquor law legislation in 1918, the Anaheim city council considered a "bone-dry" ordinance that even Mayor Stark had been persuaded to vote for. A number of leading merchants responded with angry protests that the law would ruin their businesses, since much of their trade came from oil field workers "who are attracted here on account of the liberal manner in which the city is governed." Executing a sudden reversal, the council voted down the prohibition measure.[8]

Not content to let matters rest, dry advocates headed by R. W. Earnest circulated a petition calling for a special election on the bone dry law. This greatly distressed established leaders, who felt their critics were simply motivated by personal vendettas and political opportunism. The elite felt that character defects rather than a sincere alternative view of the commonweal lay behind the protests of prohibition supporters. Instead of stirring up a senseless factional fight, Anaheim's leaders argued, residents such as Earnest should realize that "the business interests are the backbone of the city" and "cooperate with the merchants and boost for trade." Nevertheless, the prohibition forces pressed ahead and presented a special election petition with 475 signatures in July 1918. Accepting the inevitable, the council approved a bone-dry law that took effect in early 1919.[9] The elite, however, neither forgave nor forgot Earnest's efforts.

The uniform implementation of prohibition in Orange County by 1919 presented the problem of effective enforcement. Almost immediately, rumors circulated of large-scale liquor law violations, rumors that seemed to be confirmed by the public statements of local prohibition agents. By 1921, officially sanctioned "vigilance committees" had been set up in several communities, including Anaheim, to assist in cracking down on bootleggers. In June 1921, a group of Protestant church representatives met with the city council and urged even stronger methods, including a tougher liquor law. The representatives received a cold reception from the council and Mayor Stark, who resented the implication that Anaheim officials were not fully enforcing prohibition; they also tended to be skeptical about the extent of bootlegging operations.[10]

An analysis of arrest records for Orange County for the period 1917 to 1930 lends strength to the city administration's view that the local "crime wave" was more myth than reality. Even when the Klan assumed power in 1924, the arrest rate for liquor violations, as well as for most crimes, did not significantly increase; motor vehicle citations was the only category in which there was a significantly higher arrest rate during the period of Klan ascendency.[11] However, the sensationalistic media coverage of the crimes that did occur in the early 1920s and the official endorsement of vigilante activities to suppress the alleged crime spree created the perception of a criminal bootlegging element that eluded ordinary means of control. Thus, to many citizens, the Klan would appear as a promising means of fighting fire with fire.

At the same time that concerns over prohibition enforcement were growing, the city hall issue resurfaced. Throughout the period 1920 to 1923, the *Plain Dealer* and other critics of Anaheim's leadership battled the city council over the proposed facility's cost, location, and source of funding. Two future Klan leaders led the opposition to the elite and even ran for council positions in 1920. Despite their defeat and the eventual funding approval for the city hall that occurred after two bond elections, these dissident elements had succeeded in focusing and consolidating the growing opposition to the commercial-civic elite's tight hold over city policy.[12] By the time of the new municipal building's completion in 1923, the elite's opposition had become fully aroused, emphasizing the issues of autocratic leadership and indifferent prohibition enforcement.

It should be realized that the series of intense civic controversies that took place in Anaheim between 1917 and 1923 occurred at a time of dramatic community expansion. A small city of approximately five thousand inhabitants on the eve of American participation in World War I, Anaheim would more than double in population (as would all of Orange County) during the next seven years, primarily owing to the booming fortunes of the oil and citrus industries. Most of the new arrivals were native-born white Protestants, many from the Midwest, who possessed a strong interest in moral issues such as prohibition.[13] Thus, critics of the elite had a splendid opportunity to develop a constituency that could challenge Anaheim's traditional power structure.

The next step in the generalization of the growing split over the direction of community affairs was the formation of the American Civic League of Anaheim, which stressed the issue of better law enforcement. The league, which included a number of future Klansmen, claimed that local officials were neglecting their duties and challenged city council incumbents during the April 1922 municipal elections. The Civic League lost the election but served notice that the level of dissatisfaction in Anaheim had reached serious, sustainable proportions.[14] It was at this time that the Ku Klux Klan made its first appearance in Orange County.

Two separate klaverns developed a following in Anaheim during the 1920s. The first organized during March 1922 and lasted only two months. It was a small group of only 200 people, mostly non-Anaheimers, whose use of vigilante tactics evoked little lasting sympathy from most citizens and led to its speedy demise under pressure from Orange County authorities. The second klavern experienced much greater success, garnering over 410 members in Anaheim (and nearly 1,300 countywide) and winning political control of the city for a period.

The first klavern announced its existence in April 1922 via a threatening letter to J. H. Clark, an Anaheim hotelowner. The missive allegedly warned Clark to leave Anaheim within ten days or suffer the consequences. One newspaper, the *Anaheim Daily Herald,* heartily approved of this warning, claiming that Clark was "operating as a bootlegger with a large clientele among patrons of three large business houses here." The paper later reported rumors of additional messages sent by this klavern to other suspected bootleggers. The *Anaheim Gazette,* spokespiece for the local elite, disapproved of these tactics and strongly censured the order for acting as the "self-constituted guardians of the morals of the city."[15] Considering the *Gazette*'s opposition to prohibition, its condemnation surprised no one.

On April 22, the fledgling klavern announced its virtues in a public letter. The notice said that the KKK stood for law and order and that "good law-abiding people have nothing to fear." Asserting that the police were "not in a position to cope with the [crime] situation," the Klan declared it intention to deal with "whiskey runners," "scalawags," and "grafters."[16]

The next day, important events occurred in Los Angeles that quickly threw the klavern into disarray. Elements of the Los Angeles klavern led a raid on a suspected winery in Inglewood that met armed resistance from a local marshal, resulting in the death of a Klansman (an Inglewood constable). Los Angeles District Attorney Thomas Lee Woolwine then raided the Klan's headquarters and seized membership rolls for the entire state. On April 30, Orange County District Attorney Alex P.

Nelson announced that Woolwine had given him a list of all Klansmen in the county. The list included the names of 203 Klan members, 178 of whom lived in the Santa Ana area and 10 in Anaheim. These Santa Ana-based Klansmen must have perceived Anaheim as a center of particular moral terpitude and corruption, because they had sent letters of warning only to Anaheimers.[17]

Orange County officials took prompt action against the klavern. The Board of Supervisors ordered all county employees to withdraw from the KKK or tender their resignation, and District Attorney Nelson revealed the names of Klan leaders in the local press. Exposed and under assault by the authorities, the klavern expired by the end of May 1922.[18]

The Santa Ana-based klavern's inept publicity efforts and apparent emotional gratification in scaring people under the guise of preserving law and order were poor methods of insuring its growth and power, and did not address the deeper concerns of most Orange County residents. Perhaps as a result of this experience, the founding and development of the Anaheim Klan in the fall of 1922 proceeded under a shroud of absolute secrecy and demonstrated a much greater degree of political astuteness. It was during this formative period that the Reverend Leon Myers, the pastor of the First Christian Church of Anaheim, assumed control of the klavern through his role as Exalted Cyclops. Myers had recently arrived from Redlands, California, with a reputation as a bold community activist. Like many moralistic reformers of this period, he ardently embraced the prohibition cause, viewed Roman Catholicism with great distrust, and believed that evangelical Protestantism had a historic mission to fulfill throughout the world. Myers evoked either strongly positive or negative responses from those who knew him, being variously characterized as a power hungry opportunist or a strict moral Christian with an abiding sense of mission.[19]

The first public indication of the Anaheim Klan's existence came in an article in the *Plain Dealer* on February 13, 1923, that stated the KKK might "favor with a visit this evening" a visiting evangelist preaching at Myers's church. True to prediction, a group of silent, hooded Klansmen appeared at the gathering and presented the minister with a donation and a letter of gratitude for his efforts to have the Bible read in the public schools. The letter also set forth the ideals and purposes of the Klan: "Wrong rules the land and waiting justice sleeps. God give us men! Men who serve not for selfish booty, but real men, courageous, who flinch not at duty. . . . Wrongs will be redressed, and right will rule the earth."[20] Having deposited their gifts, the shrouded Klansmen vanished into the night.

Over the course of the next few months, the Klan also made its presence known by cross-burnings in Anaheim, Fullerton, and Yorba Linda. These fiery displays and a few more church visitations were, however, exceptions to the klavern's generally low-key method of recruitment and organization. Faced with the organized strength of the Anaheim elite, the Klan believed that quiet appeals through an informal network of friends and acquaintances would gain the most headway.

The hooded order utilized a variety of sales pitches. One longtime Anaheimer recalled being asked, "Wouldn't you like to join a Protestant organization that's trying to keep the Catholics from trying to take over the public school system?" Another common type of solicitation was the assurance that "the Klan people would do business with you" if you entered the fold. One businessman who refused the Klan's overtures and later became an opponent was offered the contract to install the heating system in the Odd Fellows lodge. Klan recruiters also stressed the important role their order could play in maintaining personal and social morality. Typically, these different appeals were intertwined with varying emphases in an effort to find the most effective ways of inducing a particular individual to join.[21]

For years, historians have debated about what type of men joined the Ku Klux Klan of the 1920s. Fortunately, in the case of Orange County, a comprehensive Klan membership list dated August 25, 1924, is extant. The roster contains the names of 1,280 individuals. Through a variety of random sampling, record linkage, variable construction, and error detection techniques, the list and other local records have been used to construct detailed group portraits of the Klan and non-Klan populations of Anaheim. An additional list of 299 prominent Klan opponents also allowed an analysis of the city's most outspoken anti-Klansmen.[22] As is indicated in Table 4.1, Anaheim Klansmen were very similar to the community's non-Klan male population in a number of important regards. Contrary to any notion that the typical Klansman was left behind in the race for economic success, he possessed almost the same exact amount of real and personal property as the average non-Klansman in Anaheim. The high proportion of property-owning Klansmen also reflects their relative prosperity and substantial stake in the community. Their jobs were a bit more prestigious than those of their non-Klan counterparts. With the exception of the difference in the proportion of property owners, Klansmen and non-Klansmen possessed remarkably similar demographic, occupational, and wealth characteristics. When non-whites are excluded from the non-Klan population, the preceding assessments remain essentially unchanged. Anaheim Klansmen appeared to be neither economically nor socially insecure.

TABLE 4.1

A Comparison of the Klan, Non-Klan, and Anti-Klan
Adult Male Populations of Anaheim, California, Circa 1924

	Median Age	Median Years Residence in Orange County	Median Wealth	Professional, Trade, Clerical, Administrative Employment	Property Owner	Voter Reg. 1922	Voter Reg. 1924	Civic Club Member
Anaheim Klan	37.64	7.98	$432	43.36%	70.98%	54.15%	92.44%	9.51%
Non-Klan of Anaheim	37.06	7.9	$433	31.51%	61.45%	27.71%	54.64%	3.01%
Anti-Klan of Anaheim	41.8	10.7	$3984	61.21%	76.25%	67.22%	93.21%	33.11%

It can be argued that insecurities and anxieties are internal, psychological affairs that quantitative data cannot measure. This may be true; however, no historian to date has unearthed direct evidence of such insecurity from a representative cross section of the KKK's membership. If such direct evidence is lacking, any claim to have fathomed Klansmen's psyches is suggestive at best. An analysis of the group's ideology is not a proper substitute for this evidence, since its ideas can be tied to varying personality types, especially in an era when racism was the rule and not the exception among white Protestant Americans. The preceding criticism also applies to any psychologically based interpretation of Klansmen as a group of moral authoritarians. A belief in strict morality and law enforcement during the 1920s did not necessarily constitute the outward manifestation of a maladjusted authoritarian personality.[23]

Surprisingly, as was the case with economic factors, ethnicity and religious affiliation did not serve as strong determinants of whether an individual would join the Invisible Empire. The non-Klan population was predominantly composed of white native-born Protestants. Even Anaheim's anti-Klan elite, which included a sizeable contingent of German-American Catholics, was largely Protestant. Of far more importance in differentiating Klansmen from non-Klansmen was an individual's degree of civic involvement. As is indicated in Table 4.1, Klansmen registered to vote in significantly higher percentages in both 1922 and 1924 than non-Klansmen. Being registered to vote is the most general way a person, especially if time and money dictate a limited ability to be active in civic groups, can show interest in local affairs. This was especially so in 1922, when there were few major national elections. The higher percentage of registered Klansmen in 1922 also demonstrates that the Invisible Empire did not stimulate political involvement, but that civic involvement provoked interest in the KKK. Thus, being registered to vote in both elections is a crude, but effective, sign of an on-going concern with community affairs. The problem with such measures of involvement is the extremely high rate of in-migration to the city in the 1920s. Many Klansmen simply did not live in Anaheim in 1922. Nevertheless, the discrepencies between the Klan and non-Klan populations are striking. The anti-Klan group was even more highly registered to vote, but this is precisely what would be expected of a faction that was largely composed of members of the local elite.

The Anaheim Klan's civic involvement had a second component. Klansmen joined civic groups such as the Chamber of Commerce, Kiwanis, and Rotary in higher proportions than non-Klansmen. For those with the time and extra energy, joining such organizations represents an extensive level of community involvement. The difference between the Klan and non-Klan groups along this dimension is even greater than that between voter registrations. This difference indicates the solid core of civic leadership that guided the Klan and clearly represents a strong interest in local affairs. Once again, the anti-Klan group showed a higher level of civic group membership than the KKK–which is the expected pattern for an elite. Thus, in placing Klansmen somewhere between the elite and the ordinary non-Klan population, we can more clearly see why KKK members resented Anaheim's traditional leadership.

By November 1923, the Anaheim Klan had recruited nearly nine hundred members (including many from smaller outlying communities) and felt confident enough to involve itself in local political affairs. As the first step toward improving municipal government, Exalted Cyclops Leon Myers and the members of his Bible-study class (many of whom were Klansmen) sent an open letter to the newspapers accusing Judge G. B. Brown, who held positions as both city recorder and justice of the peace, of inefficiency, drunken behavior on the job, and a failure to enforce the law. They additionally charged the city government with complicity in these matters and indicated that the records on which the charges against Brown were based had been "mysteriously stolen" from police department files. Although it was not announced at the time, this information had been supplied to Myers by three Klansmen on the Anaheim police force.[24]

The KKK's charges against Judge Brown inaugurated a bitter two-month confrontation between the city administration of Mayor Stark and local dissidents. Recognizing that the local klavern was behind the assault on Brown, the *Anaheim Bulletin* charged that "the cogs of an organization within an organization are grinding to tear down . . . the entire city administration and our local court of justice." An official investigation revealed, however, that most of Myers's accusations were valid. After admitting to several indiscretions, Brown relinquished his city recorder post, and thereby gave the Klan its first important victory.[25] At the same time, two incumbent city councilmen, perhaps unnerved by recent developments, announced that they would not stand for reelection. This meant that four of the council's five seats would have to be filled at the upcoming city elections in April.[26] The Invisible Empire now had a golden opportunity to seize political power.

Emboldened by its recent success, the Klan launched an ambitious plan to exert its influence throughout northern Orange County in the spring of 1924. The KKK worked hard to secure the election of favored candidates in Fullerton, but the main effort was reserved for Anaheim. One tactic was the initiation of an economic boycott of "un-American" businesses. As a former Klansman recalled:

> I attended the meeting and they talked about their plan of all sticking together. A Klansman was supposed to trade with nobody but someone who was in the Klan, and you could tell who was a member of the Klan because they had the American flag hung way back in a certain place. And if you didn't see that flag in the store, you weren't supposed to trade there. They said, the first time you're caught trading in a store that's not a Klansman's store, you'd be warned. The second time you'd be fined, and

the third time, God help you! ... They said, "You don't need to be afraid. We'll know where you'll be shopping."

Leon Myers allegedly directed an extensive spy network whose task it was to monitor the membership's shopping habits.[27] Since 27 percent of Anaheim Klansmen earned their livelihood from retail or wholesale trade, the klavern's effort to develop an economic fellowship is not too surprising.

The Invisible Empire also decided to field a four-man slate of candidates at the approaching city election. The ticket included Elmer H. Metcalf, a prominent local rancher and Anaheim school board trustee; Dean Hassom, a member of a leading Orange County family and an active Mason; Arthur Slaback, the owner of a small grocery; and Emons Knipe, like Metcalf a rancher with a solid civic reputation.[28] The fielding of this ticket had been anticipated by the hooded order's enemies, the *Anaheim Bulletin* warning on March 21 that "It is time that the people of Anaheim were fully acquainted with the invisible menace that threatens to dislodge the very rocks of the municipal foundation and has as its cat's paw the *Orange County Plain Dealer.*"[29]

The *Plain Dealer*'s subsequent endorsement of Metcalf, Hasson, Slaback, and Knipe should have alerted residents to their Klan affiliation, but apparently it did not. Three important factors worked against exposing the KKK's candidates. First, no one outside of the klavern could present absolute evidence that they were Klansmen, or that they had even been endorsed by the KKK. Second, the nonpartisan politics of a small California city in the early twentieth century militated against exposure. Newspapers were supposed to boost the town, not dissect the connections and motivations of candidates for civic office, unless these leaders clearly threatened the community's peace, economic prosperity, or the elite's influence. During the spring of 1924 no one could establish that any of the Klan's candidates had this potential, especially since they were well-known citizens. The candidates' personalities and the appearance of probity and efficiency were ultimately more important to the newspapers and voters than any possible Klan connections. Finally, the election would be fought over matters that deeply concerned the entire community. The intense debates raised by the issues, which the Klan candidates were able to effectively wield, offered their opponents no opportunity to broach the KKK's role in the election.

During the course of the campaign, Metcalf, Hasson, Slaback, and Knipe, in close association with R. W. Earnest's *Plain Dealer,* commenced a full-scale assault upon Anaheim's civic leadership, harping upon the alleged sins of the Stark administration over the last seven years. The insurgents cited the reckless fashion in which Stark had proceeded with municipal improvements, especially the new city hall, and decried "sky-rocketing taxes." The *Plain Dealer* charged that the mayor ran Anaheim like a "dictatorship" and predicted that Metcalf and his running mates would receive a heavy vote from "the many new subdivisions where scores of lot owners and home builders have been delayed for months in obtaining water and sewer services while the Stark administration was spending $200,000 for an uncompleted city park." The Klan ticket and its supporters stressed that they were not opposed to civic expenditures promoting the town's growth. They only wished to balance expenditures with efforts to achieve what they believed was a more open, democratic, and moral government.[30]

Realizing that their opposition was making considerable headway with their out-group political rhetoric, the Anaheim elite intensified its efforts on behalf of William Stark and two other favored candidates. A week before the election, a group of prominent businessmen formed a "Good Government League," which advocated keeping Anaheim on its "present path of progress." Efforts were also made to discredit Elmer Metcalf's term as school board trustee, it being charged that he had mismanaged school construction funds. On the day before the election, Mayor Stark desperately tried to influence the electorate by restating his vision of the community's future. Castigating his opponents for their narrow-minded approach to civic welfare, Stark declared that, but for his personal efforts, "this group and their discontented friends would not have the fine streets and sidewalks, nor the City Park, nor the City Hall, nor the Outfall Sewer on all of which I have spent years of endeavor to bring to pass." The mayor boasted that "civic improvements in Anaheim and the fair condition of our community have placed us in an enviable position before the eyes of the rest of California and the United States." He remained convinced that the essence of the good community consisted of things such as "fine streets and sidewalks" and ignored the moral elements that the Klan believed should share equal footing with economic growth.[31]

On April 14, 2,689 out of Anaheim's 3,487 registered voters cast their ballots in the city council election. The results revealed that Metcalf,

Hasson, Knipe, and Slaback had easily secured the vacant seats on the city council. All four of the Klan's candidates garnered more votes in each of Anaheim's six precincts than any of their opponents, but the northeastern and southeastern sectors of the city, where the newer subdivisions were located, balloted particularly heavily for the Invisible Empire's slate.[32] Since only 410 Klansmen lived within the city limits, many other residents probably agreed with the Klan's assessment of the previous administration's approach to civic problems.

A week later, on April 21, the new Klan-dominated council assumed its duties. The councilmen appointed Elmer Metcalf as mayor, who promised that efficiency and clean government would be his administration's watchwords. Metcalf revealed that the Stark administration had spent over $221,000 on an uncompleted city park and over $135,000 on the new city hall—figures far above the original estimates. The mayor vowed that his administration would not be so careless in the expenditure of the public's money. Surprisingly, both the anti-Klan *Bulletin* and *Gazette* called on the city to unite behind the Metcalf administration. The Anaheim elite, including former Mayor Stark, pledged to cooperate fully with the council to continue local economic growth. Perhaps the elite felt that once in power these councilmen could be won over to its vision of the community welfare.[33]

Such hopes were soon dispelled. Less than three days after assuming power, the council received a letter from the kleagle of the Anaheim Klan that noted that "It is now no secret that the Knights of the Ku Klux Klan were a considerable factor in your election to the positions you now occupy." The letter falsely stated that the new trustees were not members of the KKK, "yet nevertheless are men, real men." Apparently, Exalted Cyclops Myers and the klavern's leadership did not want opponents to know the true extent of Klan influence in city affairs. The missive also indicated the Invisible Empire's willingness "to assist you in the enforcement of the law. . . . Nearly a thousand men are ready at a moment's notice to serve and sacrifice for the right. All that we expect or seek is that your lives be clean . . . and that in the fear of God you administer the laws of our city to the best of your ability."[34]

From late April to July 1924, Anaheim's city council pursued a policy of dismissing non-Klan city employees and replacing them, in most cases, with Klansmen. On May 8, the council added eleven officers to the Anaheim police force, raising the total from four to fifteen. Ten of the eleven appointees were knights of the Invisible Empire. As a reward for its efforts in the election campaign, the council granted the *Plain Dealer* the contract "for all advertising to be done by said city government required to be published in a daily newspaper within said city." The councilmen appointed Klansman Walter A. Ground, a local carpenter, as city building inspector, while three other members of the klavern received jobs as city health officer, city garbage collector, and assistant rate collector. During June and July, four Klansmen were appointed as deputy city marshals, and a Klan majority was installed on the Anaheim board of health.[35]

Beyond looking at its hiring procedures, evaluating the Klan's policies is difficult because the group did not hold unopposed power long enough to develop its own coherent framework for guiding civic life. The Anaheim Klan operated freely from late April to the early part of August 1924. Thereafter, the rise of a powerful opposition group shaped most of the KKK's public actions. The brief period of unchallenged Klan dominance, however, demonstrated the order's desire for a more moral, law-abiding, and formally bound community.

The first ordinance passed by the Klan council was a strict new prohibition law that provided harsh punishment for liquor offenders. The measure was very detailed and revealed a scrupulous concern with having the existing laws strictly obeyed and enforced. The Klan wanted more than a pro forma observance of prohibition and more than a token commitment to the community's welfare. In many ways, the Invisible Empire harkened back to the seventeenth-century New England Puritan ideal of the regulated community. Specifically, the Klan hoped to abolish civil disorders such as bootlegging and to establish a responsive leadership sincerely interested in the community's social morality.[36]

The council's other actions reflected the KKK's specific and general objectives. A long unenforced ordinance requiring property owners to help maintain the streets and sidewalks fronting their property was reactivated, the Klan council outlawed slot machines, traffic laws were more strictly enforced, and an additional prohibition measure came on the books. The most controversial move at this time was the policing of the city by on-duty officers dressed in full Klan regalia. According to one former Klansman, only a few officers worked in their robes, but those who did "generally made themselves offensive." Apparently, Leon Myers and Councilman Slaback had suggested this practice.[37]

The Invisible Empire's increasingly overt involvement in the community was dramatically demonstrated at a mammoth open air rally and initiation ceremony at Anaheim City Park on July 29, 1924. The Klan apparently hoped to overawe the city with a display of its power and show the elite that Anaheim would be run along different lines than had been the case in the past. The rally attracted the largest crowd in Anaheim history up to that date. Ten thousand Klansmen from all over southern California attended and paraded down Center Street in an impressive show of strength. A Klan band from Santa Monica provided marching music while a plane decorated with glowing crosses flew overhead. At the city park between ten and fifteen hundred "aliens" were led into the center of a "human square" formed around a thirty-foot-high electric cross. The recruits listened to a recitation of the KKK's induction ritual and swore to obey the order's rules and officers. A fireworks display completed the festivities.[38]

This monster initiation frightened many Anaheimers and helped give rise to an organized crusade to destroy the Klan, as the city's traditional leaders belatedly realized that the KKK upstarts would not forget the issues and concerns that had put them into office. During August, the founders of what would soon be known as the U.S.A. (Unity, Service, and Americanism) Club committed themselves to procuring a membership list of the Anaheim Klan. Eventually the roster was acquired through a payment of several hundred dollars to a prominent California Klan officer.[39]

The anti-Klan forces soon put the list to effective use. In the summer of 1924, the Invisible Empire was making a strong effort to secure the nomination of Klan-affiliated candidates for state and county offices in a primary election scheduled for August 26. The U.S.A. Club provided a copy of the Klan roster to the staunchly anti-KKK county district attorney, Alex Nelson, who revealed to the press which officeseekers were Klansmen or fellow travelers. The Invisible Empire's elite opponents now posed, ironically, as the defenders of small-town America's tradition of open government against the alleged secret, corrupt, dictatorial rule of the Klan. This shift in tactics paid off handsomely, as most of the Klan's favorites went down to defeat in the primary.[40]

Buoyed by the primary results, the U.S.A. Club and allied elements marshalled their resources to rid Anaheim of Klannish influences. They wrote newspaper articles denouncing the hooded order, circulated petitions calling for a recall of the Klan city council, and began holding meetings at which speakers attempted to educate the electorate about the merits of open versus invisible government. Sometimes patently trivial matters were used to discredit the KKK councilmen. One anti-KKK petition asked the trustees to restore a flagpole at the center of the intersection of Los Angeles and Center streets, which had been removed as a traffic hazard. The petition sharply questioned the reason for removing the flagpole: "What cause was there for that action? We believe that no authority should have taken it down without having given reasons for its removal." Over nine hundred people signed the flagpole petition, submitted to the council on September 4. The anti-Klan forces clearly wished to use this minor episode to impugn the Klan's patriotism and to reveal to local citizens the Invisible Empire's undemocratic methods.[41]

Throughout the latter months of 1924, the anti-Klan campaign began to take effect. The local Kiwanis, Lions, Rotary, and Elks clubs all officially denounced the KKK, as did the Anaheim Masonic Lodge. The Klan responded with full-page advertisements in the *Plain Dealer* detailing its virtues and decrying the "propaganda being spread in Anaheim by some highly misinformed people." Nevertheless, by early November the U.S.A. Club had gathered enough signatures to force a city recall election, scheduled for February 3, 1925.[42]

Faced with the possibility of being removed from power, the Klan countered by initiating its own recall effort against the only non-Klansman on the council, Godfrey Stock, whom the *Plain Dealer* characterized as the "last remnant of the old Anaheim wet machine." The Klan attempted to depict the recall struggle as a wet versus dry fight. At the same time, Leon Myers forcefully defended the Klan's reputation, arguing at public gatherings that the Klan championed free speech, free public schools, just laws, and the pursuit of happiness "against encroachment by any hostile force." The U.S.A. Club responded with charges that the Invisible Empire was failing to address the only major issue that truly mattered: whether Anaheim should be ruled by a secret government.[43]

Hoping to revive its sagging political fortunes, the Klan, in association with local law enforcement officers and the Anti-Saloon League, launched a massive dry raid throughout Orange County on the night of November 19—an effort intended to prove the existence of large-scale bootlegging operations. Although the raid netted fifty-two purported violators, this scheme backfired on the Invisible Empire when the city councils of several northern Orange County communities refused to pay the dry raiders' expenses. During subsequent legal proceedings, it was publicaly revealed that the KKK had planned, organized, and financed the antiliquor assault, thus allowing Klan opponents to cite the raid as an example of the clandestine and allegedly sinister way in which the Klan operated. Moreover, Klansmen never recovered the $9,500 that they had subscribed for the raid, a setback that threw the klavern into considerable financial disarray.[44]

During January and February 1925, the opposing forces began slinging political mud with great frequency. A week before the recall election, the Klan council held spirited rallies denouncing their "wet" opponents and promoting the councilmen's "fine record of civic leadership." The pro-Klan *Plain Dealer* printed a barrage of articles in the hope of scoring some last-minute political points. One story emanating from the police department urged citizens to retain the current council because "we don't have our hands tied now." In response, the U.S.A. Club accused the council of altering the recall ballot to confuse the voters and claimed a leading anti-KKK spokesman had received a death threat from the Anaheim klavern.[45]

Election day saw a heavy turnout at the polls. With passions running high, Orange County Sheriff Samuel Jernigan and District Attorney Nelson provided armed guards to protect the polling booths. One longtime resident recalled that "there were men with sawed-off shotguns at the various booths. There were men from the sheriff's office, and the other side had their men. There were quite a few challenges to votes, but no violence occurred." Nearly 4,200 out of a possible 5,399 registered voters (77.37 percent) cast ballots. The results were a decisive victory for the anti-Klan candidates: all the Klan councilmen were recalled by substantial, although not overwhelming, margins, and Godfrey Stock easily won his recall race. An analysis of the polling reveals that the KKK managed to hold onto precincts where the percentage of Klansmen was relatively high, but the organization had lost much of its following among non-Klansmen.[46] Once the elite and the U.S.A. Club had managed to turn the issue of secret and undemocratic government on the hooded order, the Invisible Empire's fate was sealed.

The unfavorable verdict rendered in the recall election was a setback from which the Anaheim Klan never fully recovered, but the klavern carried on. The boycott of non-Klan businesses continued, and a series of articles in the *Plain Dealer* dramatized a crime wave that had allegedly blossomed in the wake of the recall election and the subsequent firing of KKK-affiliated police officers. Klansmen assailed the record of the newly appointed chief of police (who eventually had to resign) and gave indication that they might soon launch a recall campaign of their own.[47]

The Invisible Empire's continued activism convinced the order's enemies that additional action had to be taken. The first step was to deny the organization access to the media. The *Bulletin* and *Gazette* stopped reporting any KKK-related activities after February 1925. A few weeks later, a prominent Klan opponent filed a libel suit against the *Plain Dealer,* after which R. W. Earnest's paper also fell silent on Klan issues. The suit was settled when the *Plain Dealer* printed a front-page retraction and agreed to be acquired by the *Bulletin.* On May 8, 1925, the *Plain Dealer* ceased publication. The new city council then passed two laws expressly designed to keep the Invisible Empire from ever again achieving political power in Anaheim. The first law forbade the distribution and posting of handbills and flyers in public places. The second required that any group seeking to solicit members within the city limits first obtain a permit from the city council, which would decide if "said applicant will not be detrimental to the public." The local press also published a warning that "every employee of a business house or industrial plant who belongs to the order [KKK] ... or is a sympathizer, will find himself out of a job if Cyclops Myers attempts to stage a recall election."[48] The combined effect of these measures was to force the Klan underground by June 1925.

Beset by his enemies, Leon Myers decided to cede leadership of the Anaheim klavern. On October 29, he delivered a welcome surprise to his opponents by announcing his resignation from the pastorate of the First Christian Church. By December, the former Exalted Cyclops had left to accept a call from a Dodge City, Kansas, congregation. This left the Klan without its most talented organizer and dynamic publicist.[49]

The Klan, however, refused to die. Indeed, from 1926 through 1930, the feud between stalwart Klansmen and the anti-Klan elite remained as bitter as ever. The Invisible Empire dominated city governments in neighboring Brea, La Habra, and Fullerton for the remainder of the decade and fielded city council candidates in Anaheim in 1926, 1928, and 1930. In 1928, the order secured the election of a Klansman to the council by resurrecting the issue of extravagant government spending. This prompted the Klan's enemies to utilize a co-optation strategy by placing a recently reformed Klansman on a Citizens Harmony Ticket in 1930. This strategy worked well. The ticket won all the seats on the council by sizeable majorities and dominated local government throughout the 1930s.[50] At the same time, the Klan faded into insignificance.

Anaheimers joined and supported the Ku Klux Klan in the 1920s primarily because they hoped to create a more moral, law-abiding, better ordered, more balanced, and formally bound community. In a very basic sense the Klan was attempting to transform the traditional informal social controls of small-town American civic culture by intensely scrutinizing and regulating the behavior of the community's residents. The KKK in Anaheim was not defending a culture under attack by outside forces; instead, it was responding to the consequences of certain indigenous developments within Protestant culture. In particular, the order opposed the group-interest concept of the commonweal exposed by the town's elite, a concept that allowed Anaheim's traditional leaders to bend or break the rules to their advantage. Thus, the Klan, in its essence, represented an effort to find a middle ground between the disorder engendered by the informal social and political controls of traditional small-town America, and what were perceived to be the undemocratic, arbitrary, self-serving policies of the dominant commercial-civic elite.

NOTES

1. Thomas B. Talbert, ed., *Orange County Historical Volume* (Whittier, California, 1963), 128–30; Samuel Armor, *History of Orange County, California* (Los Angeles, 1921).

2. For an extended discussion of the Anaheim elite, see Christopher N. Cocoltchos, "The Invisible Government and the Viable Community: The Ku Klux Klan in Orange County, California, During the 1920s" (Ph.D. dissertation, University of California, Los Angeles, 1979), 176–94.

3. *Anaheim Gazette,* January 4, 11, 17, 1917. Unfortunately, the earliest surviving issues of the *Orange County Plain Dealer* date from January 1919. Thus much of what I know about Earnest and his paper's policies during 1917 and 1918 comes from rather hostile and biased sources—opposing newspapers. However, a good deal of reliance can be placed on the basic informational context of these sources.

4. *Anaheim Gazette,* July 26, August 16, 20, September 13, 27, October 4, December 27, 1917; Files of the City Clerk of Anaheim, miscellaneous peti-

tions dated July 1917; Charles H. Rinehart, "A Study of the Anaheim Community with Special Reference to its Development" (M.A. thesis, University of Southern California, 1932), 1-9.

5. *Anaheim Gazette,* March 1, 15, May 17, 31, July 5, 19, September 27, 1917.

6. Ibid., October 4, 18, 1917; January 10, 24, 1918.

7. Ibid., February 14, 21, 28, May 21, July 18, 1918.

8. Ibid., May 16, June 13, 20, 27, July 4, 1918; *Anaheim Daily Herald,* June 28, 1918.

9. *Anaheim Gazette,* July 25, August 1, 15, 22, 29, 1918.

10. *Orange County Plain Dealer,* June 16, 1921; City of Anaheim, "Minutes of the Board of Trustees for the City of Anaheim," vol. 10, p. 150; *Anaheim Daily Herald,* June 10, 1921.

11. Crime statistics for these years were compiled from City of Anaheim, "Criminal Docket of the City of Anaheim," 12 volumes. For more information on the local crime situation, see Cocoltchos, "Invisible Government and the Viable Community," 95-98.

12. *Orange County Plain Dealer,* April 7, 1920; August 24, September 14, 1922; *Anaheim Gazette,* April 15, 1920; September 27, October 19, November 30, 1922; City of Anaheim, "Minutes of the Board of Trustees of the City of Anaheim," vol. 11, pp. 132-35.

13. California, Office of the State Controller, *Annual Report of the Financial Transactions of Municipalities and Counties of California* (Sacramento, 1917-1927). See Cocoltchos, "Invisible Government and the Viable Community," 76-78, for a detailed ethnic and religious profile of Anaheim. In 1924 the community's population was overwhelmingly (nearly 90 percent) white and Protestant. The only sizeable minority were Hispanics, a group the local Klan totally ignored.

14. *Anaheim Gazette,* March 9, April 6, 13, 1922; *Orange County Plain Dealer,* April 7, 8, 11, 13, 1922; *Anaheim Daily Herald,* April 8, 1922; "Minutes of the Board of Trustees of the City of Anaheim," vol. 10, pp. 388-391.

15. *Anaheim Daily Herald,* April 11, 1922; *Orange Daily News,* April 21, 1922; *Anaheim Gazette,* April 20, 1922.

16. *Anaheim Daily Herald,* April 22, 1922.

17. Ibid., April 25, 27, May 1, 1922; *Los Angeles Times,* April 23, 24, 25, 1922; *Los Angeles Herald,* April 23, 24, 25, 1922; *Orange Daily News,* April 26, 27, 28, 29, May 1, 2, 1922.

18. Orange County, "Minutes of the Board of Supervisors of Orange County," vol. 16, p. 231; *Orange Daily News,* May 13, 14, 16, 1922.

19. First Christian Church of Anaheim, "Records of Meetings of Church Officers," entries for March 31, April 8, 9, 1922; interview with Warren Ashleigh, Anaheim, April 16, 1973; interview with Warren Hodges, Anaheim, May 6, 1970; interview with Fred Whitman by Duff Griffith, Anaheim, October 2, 1970,

Community History Project, Oral History Program, California State University, Fullerton.

20. *Orange County Plain Dealer,* February 13, 14, 1923.

21. Interview with Harry Horn, Anaheim, April 17, 1973; interview with Victor LaMont, Jr., Anaheim, May 6, 1973; Ashleigh interview; Hodges interview.

22. Professor Stanley Coben of the Department of History at UCLA obtained a copy of the list while researching at the Library of Congress. Based on personal interviews that I and others have conducted and on local newspaper accounts of that time, the list is indeed a valid and complete catalog of Klansmen in Orange County to the middle of August 1924. Considering the strength of the Klan's opposition that developed in Anaheim and the consequences of joining the KKK, and based upon my research in other sources, few, if any, people joined the Klan after August 1924.

23. The overall portrait of Anaheim's Klansmen particularly differs from the depiction of the typical KKK member presented in the work of Kenneth T. Jackson, Richard Hofstadter, and Charles C. Alexander.

24. Ashleigh interview; *Orange County Plain Dealer,* November 22, December 14, 1923; City of Anaheim, personnel file of G. B. Brown.

25. *Anaheim Bulletin,* January 4, 6, 1924; *Anaheim Gazette,* January 24, 1924; *Orange County Plain Dealer,* January 25, 1924; City of Anaheim, personnel file of G. B. Brown.

26. *Orange County Plain Dealer,* February 1, 1924.

27. Ashleigh interview.

28. Interview with Arnold EnEarl, Anaheim, July 20, 1976; Horn interview; Ashleigh interview; and Hodges interview.

29. *Anaheim Bulletin,* March 21, 1924.

30. In particular see, *Orange County Plain Dealer,* April 9, 10, 1924. The campaign is extensively analyzed in Cocoltchos, "Invisible Government and the Viable Community," 337–353.

31. *Anaheim Bulletin,* April 13, 1924.

32. *Orange County Plain Dealer,* April 15, 1924; *Anaheim Bulletin,* April 15, 1924.

33. *Orange County Plain Dealer,* April 22, 1924; *Anaheim Bulletin,* April 15, 22, 1924; *Anaheim Gazette,* April 24, 1924.

34. "Minutes of the Board of Trustees of the City of Anaheim," vol. 12, p. 183; A copy of the letter can be found in the file of Ku Klux Klan materials located in the vault of the City Clerk's office, Anaheim city hall.

35. *Orange County Plain Dealer,* April 25, 1924; *Anaheim Bulletin,* April 25, 1924; *Anaheim Gazette,* May 1, 1924; "Minutes of the Board of Trustees of the City of Anaheim," vol. 12, pp. 189, 195, 232, 242–43.

36. "Minutes of the Board of Trustees of the City of Anaheim," vol. 12, pp. 208–9; *Orange County Plain Dealer,* May 30, July 31, 1924; *Anaheim Gazette,* June 19, 1924.

37. "Minutes of the Board of Trustees of the City of Anaheim," vol. 12, pp. 198, 220; Hodges interview.

38. Interview with Joseph Peterson, Anaheim, May 9, 1973; Horn interview; LaMont interview; Hodges interview; *Orange County Plain Dealer,* July 30, 1924; *Anaheim Gazette,* July 31, 1924; *Anaheim Bulletin,* July 30, 1924.

39. Lafayette A. Lewis tapes, located in the Mother Colony History Room, Anaheim Public Library.

40. *Anaheim Bulletin,* August 20, 21, 23, 1924; "Statement of Vote for August 26, 1924 Primary" in "Minutes of the Orange County Board of Supervisors," vol. 18.

41. *Anaheim Bulletin,* August 28, 1924; *Anaheim Gazette,* September 4, 1924; "Flagpole Petition" dated September 4, 1924, in Ku Klux Klan file of Anaheim City Clerk's records.

42. *La Habra Star,* September 26, 1924; *Anaheim Gazette,* September 18, 25, October 2, November 6, 13, 1924; *Anaheim Bulletin,* September 16, 17, 19, 21, November 5, 8, 10, 14, 1924; *Orange Daily News,* September 24, 1924; *Orange County Plain Dealer,* September 22, November 4, 5, 6, 8, 1924; "Minutes of the Board of Trustees of the City of Anaheim," vol. 12, p. 328.

43. *Anaheim Bulletin,* November 14, 15, 18, 1924; *Anaheim Gazette,* November 20, 1924; *Orange County Plain Dealer,* November 11, 13, 14, 17, 18, 19, 1924.

44. *La Habra Star,* November 21, 1924; *Anaheim Gazette,* November 27, 1924; *Orange Daily News,* November 20, December 5, 1924; *Fullerton Daily News Tribune,* December 3, 4, 5, 1924; January 4, 14, 1925; City of Fullerton, Civil Case Docket, Case #17890, *C.S. Chapman v. The City of Fullerton,* December 4, 1924.

45. *Orange County Plain Dealer,* January 27, 28, 29, 30, February 2, 1925; *Ananeim Bulletin,* January 30, 31, February 2, 1925; *Orange County News,* January 26, 1925.

46. Lewis tapes; *Fullerton Daily News Tribune,* February 3, 1925; *Orange County Plain Dealer,* February 3, 1925; *Anaheim Bulletin,* February 3, 4, 1925.

47. *Orange County Plain Dealer,* February 14, 16, 17, 18, 1925; *Anaheim Bulletin,* May 29, 1925; *Anaheim Gazette,* April 16, May 14, June 4, 1925; *Orange Daily News,* May 11, 1925.

48. *Orange County Plain Dealer,* March 26, May 8, 1925; *Anaheim Gazette,* April 2, 16, May 7, 1925; "Minutes of the Board of Trustees of the City of Anaheim," vol. 12, pp. 457–458.

49. *Anaheim Gazette,* October 29, December 3, 10, 1925.

50. See Cocoltchos, "Invisible Government and the Viable Community," 588–606.

5

A Battle of Empires:
The Klan in Salt Lake City

LARRY R. GERLACH

When kleagles directed by Ku Klux Klan headquarters in Atlanta, Georgia, spread across the country in the early 1920s to transform the Invisible Empire from a regional to a national organization, they recognized the key to success of Klankraft in the Intermountain West was Salt Lake City–capital and largest city in Utah, seat of the most populous county in the state, and commercial, communication, and transportation hub of the region. However, the community proved to be a major challenge for the Klan because it also served as the headquarters of the Church of Latter-day Saints, a denomination that strongly opposed the Klan. Thus, any analysis of Salt Lake City's experience with the KKK must consider not only local municipal circumstances but the unique historical and religious context of the Beehive State.[1]

At first glance Utah did not appear to afford an environment conducive to the growth of Klankraft. Geographically extensive and demographically restricted, the state contained only 449,396 residents in 1920, dispersed across 84,990 square miles of valleys, deserts, canyonlands, and mountains. Salt Lake City constituted the lone metropolitan center, with 118,100 residents; the next largest town was Ogden (32,804). The state's racial and religious homogeneity seemed to provide little basis for ethnic or sectarian conflict. The vast majority of the inhabitants were classified as white (441,901); the 1920 census detected only 1,446 blacks, 2,711 American Indians, and 3,338 persons of "other" (mostly Asian) stock. The three largest religious groups in 1926 were LDS, 337,200; Roman Catholic, 13,595; and Greek Orthodox, 6,000. Jews numbered only 1,290 and the combined memberships of the five largest Protestant denominations totaled only 10,468.[2]

Additionally, although far removed from the Deep South, Utah had been affected by the Reconstruction Klan in ways that created an enduring hostility toward the Invisible Empire among the Morman majority. LDS church leaders had denounced the original KKK partly because of its record of violence, but primarily because of the numerous scriptural proscriptions in the Book of Mormon against "secret combinations" and the numerous acts of coercion, physical abuse, and even murder suffered by Mormon missionaries in the post–Civil War South by persons acting under the name of the Klan.[3] In short, Utah in the 1920s was a markedly homogeneous state, one that was largely rural, overwhelmingly Anglo-Saxon and Mormon, and attitudinally anti-Klan.

Mormonism has been a crucial influence in Utah's development ever since the first white settlers entered the valley of the Great Salt Lake in July 1847. The original pioneers intended to create an LDS Zion, therein zealously to promote and defend the Kingdom of God. Scattered in village communities amid the forbidding mountains and deserts, the faithful existed largely as a people apart, united in a common mental and spiritual effort to "build walls around Zion" and thus live in, but not be of, the world. The process of "Mormonization"–the forging of group identity and solidarity–virtually eliminated ethnic differences within the LDS community, thereby producing an extraordinarily homogenous culture. Because the Saints have never constituted less than two-thirds of the population, Mormonism–an easily discernible, but essentially undefinable, array of attitudes and assumptions, personality traits, and behavior patterns–has always been the most conspicuous and distinctive feature of life in Utah. As one scholar has observed, without the LDS influence "Utah would just be another Wyoming or Nevada."[4]

Cultural distinctiveness, however, did not immunize Utahans from the prejudices that prevailed elsewhere. Racial minorities routinely experienced overt discrimination in housing, public accommodations, employment, and social intercourse.[5] While animosity toward Asians was subtle and paternalistic due to their admired work ethic and social insularity, Native Americans–"redskins" in the popular white vernacular of the day–found themselves relegated to remote reservations. Blacks, most of whom lived in Ogden or Salt Lake City, were openly despised. Some manifestations of racism (such as an antimiscegenation law passed in 1898) mirrored practices in other states, but Utah's racism was bolstered by religious orthodoxy as the LDS church officially placed its black members in a position of moral inferiority by denying priesthood status to black males. In Utah, white supremacy was a doctrinal and social reality as well as a state of mind.[6]

Religious bigotry also permeated Utah society. Despite the financial success and civic contributions of the state's small but influential Jewry, anti-Semitism flourished in the form of covert hostility and private derision. While often highly respected as individuals—as evidenced by the election in 1916 of Simon Bamberger as the second Jewish governor in the United States—Jews as a group were distrusted and commonly banned from social organizations. Similarly, although anti-Catholicism was blunted by the prominence of Irish Catholics such as Thomas Kearns, mining magnate and publisher of the *Salt Lake Tribune,* the religious orientation of the "new immigration" produced alarm. Utahans believed the state's Italian and Hispanic immigrants owed primary allegiance to a foreign potentate, the pope. The Eastern Orthodoxy of Greeks, like the mystical spiritualism of Asians, also appeared decidedly alien. As members of a homegrown American faith believed to be the "true" church based on the "restored" Christian gospel and thus fervently committed to international missionary activities, the LDS looked especially askance at what were perceived to be foreign religions. A more general source of religious disputation, however, was the long-standing antipathy between Mormons and the various groups of non-Mormons. Less a sectarian squabble than a secular struggle, latent tension, if not open animosity, between Saints and "gentiles" (i.e., non-Mormons) had, since the early 1850s, affected almost every major public issue. Thus, while some Utahans would embrace the Klan's militant Protestantism with its corresponding condemnation of parasitical "Christ-killers" and idolatrous followers of "the Dago on the Tiber," many non-Mormons would endorse the Klan because of its demand for "an absolute separation of church and state."[7]

Unsettled economic conditions and labor unrest also concerned Utahans in the 1920s. Although increasingly integrated into the national economy after statehood in 1896 through the commercialization of agriculture and the development of corporate mining and manufacturing, Utah in 1920 ranked only seventh among the eight Intermountain states in per capita income. The advent of a commercial-industrial economy, moreover, brought social disorder, as unionization activities by such organizations as the Western Federation of Miners and the Industrial Workers of the World resulted in tense confrontations and periodic strikes. In large part because the LDS church took a clear, if unofficial, anti-union stand, the labor movement in general seemed to many residents to be a conspiracy perpetrated by outside agitators and foreign radicals. No single episode more clearly demonstrated the suspicion surrounding the labor movement in the Beehive State than the controversial trial and execution of IWW martyr Joe Hill in 1915 in Salt Lake City. Consequently, the Klan's call for "a closer relationship of capital and labor" and "the prevention of unwarranted strikes by foreign labor agitators" found a receptive audience in Utah.[8]

To many of the state's residents, especially those in the cities and towns, cultural modernity and attendant unrest posed the most dangerous threat to postwar America. Virtually every sizeable Utah community had its flivvers and flappers, speakeasy saloons, whorehouses, gambling dens, and dope dealers.[9] Symbolic of the perceived breakdown in both the moral code and the legal system were bootleggers, who plied their trade in illicit liquor with apparent impunity, the state attorney general conceding in 1921 that prohibition in Utah "is a farce and is developing a citizenry of sneaks and lawbreakers."[10] The answer to these problems, in the view of Utah traditionalists, lay in stronger efforts at social regulation, such as the banning of cigarettes in 1921.[11] Among this group, the Klan's call for a return to "law and order" made considerable sense.

The "One Hundred Percent Americanism" trumpeted by the Invisible Empire also possessed considerable appeal. At the advent of the twentieth century, Anglo-Saxons made up over 90 percent of the state's population. The next two decades, however, witnessed a significant influx of southern European immigrants that immediately produced tensions.[12] The Catholicism of the Italians and Slovenes and the Eastern Orthodoxy of the Greeks and Serbs clashed with Mormon and Protestant theology, while the cultures of the Mediterranean and Balkan peoples violated the staid social mores of the majority of the native white population. The conspicuous role of immigrants in violent labor disputes and bootlegging operations, moreover, branded them in the public mind as radicals and criminals. Although relatively small in numbers, the concentration of the foreign-born in the mining camps and towns of Carbon and Salt Lake counties hindered assimilation, as did the attitudinal legacy of the early Mormon attempt to "build walls around Zion." The LDS concept of a unified corporate community fostered a "we-they" perception of a world divided between acceptable

124

insiders and encroaching outsiders, and reenforced a general postwar xenophobia concerning "unassimilable" aliens. As evidence of this trend, in 1919 the Utah state legislature passed a law requiring all non-English-speaking residents between the ages of sixteen and forty-five to attend Americanization classes.[13]

The bloody Carbon County coal strike of April–September 1922 gave Utah nativists an occasion to vent pent-up social and cultural frustrations.[14] In ordering units of the National Guard to occupy the coalfields in June, Governor Charles R. Mabey declared that martial law was necessary to "teach a proper respect" for law and order as well as to preserve the peace. In his opinion, primary blame for the violence could be placed on "the many people of foreign birth and traditions who had not yet learned proper reverence for American laws and American ideals."[15] A suburban Salt Lake weekly likewise snarled: "Apparently these foreigners can only understand drastic action and they should have plenty of it." Another newspaper editor blasted the "alien population" of Carbon County for "its utter disregard and contempt for the laws of the state and nation" and declared that "the right to dominate and direct this country is inherent in our native born and selected citizenry."[16] The implication was clear: concerned citizens should act forcefully to impose order and maintain traditional values. Perhaps not coincidentally, a group expousing these goals had already been organized in the state.[17]

On June 21, 1921, the *Deseret News* announced with bold, front-page headlines: "Ku Klux Klan Will Organize Branch Here." Surprised, Utahans were both uninformed about the modern Klan and unprepared for its appearance in the state. Those who read the scant newspaper coverage about the new Invisible Empire probably thought it an exclusively southern organization dedicated to the maintenance of white supremacy through the intimidation of blacks. That view conformed with the popular sense of the Reconstruction Klan obtained when D. W. Griffith's *The Birth of a Nation* played to overflow audiences in Salt Lake City for six weeks from March to June. The precise impact of the film remains a matter of speculation, but reviews of the "wonderful American History play" indicate that it enhanced the general appeal of the hooded order.

Faced with the prospect of the Klan becoming a local reality instead of legendary romance, the *Deseret News* launched a devastating attack upon the secret order. That the *News* would lead the initial opposition to the Klan was both predictable and significant. The secular oracle of the LDS, the paper disseminated the political opinions of the Mormon hierarchy to the approximately 70 percent of Utahans who belonged to the church. Given the denomination's longstanding antipathy toward the KKK, it was not surprising that the *News* viewed the arrival of the Klan with "disapprobation and contempt" and detailed editorially why there was "No Room Here For This Outfit":

So far as [the Klan's] operations are known—its secrecy, its mummery, its terrorism, its lawlessness—it is condemned as inimical to the peace, order, and dignity of the commonwealth. These mountain communities of ours have no place whatever for it in their social scheme of things. It should be spurned and scorned, and any individual presenting himself as authorized or qualified to establish branches, "domains," camps or Klans should be made emphatically to understand that his local endeavors will be worse than wasted, and his objects are detested, and that his room is preferred to his company. The people of Utah have no taste or patience for such criminal nonsense, and there should be all plainness in making that fact known. Meanwhile they are to be warned against smooth-tongued advocates or promoters who are doubtless drilled in unfolding a plausible, attractive, and loyal tale, acceptance of which by those inveigled into the order is bound to bring mistrust, servitude to evil, suspicion, base subservience to passion and everlasting regret.

While perhaps correct in its assessment of the KKK, the *News* incorrectly went on to assert that no Utahans were "favorably interested in the Ku Klux Klan or its method or its purposes."[18]

The Klan's initial organizing effort naturally focused on Salt Lake City. The community's size not only afforded the greatest potential for recruiting, but its political and economic primacy meant that a successful klavern could possibly serve as the linchpin for a unified Klandom in the Great Basin region. The largest city between Denver and the Pacific coast, Salt Lake in the twenties enjoyed general prosperity and rapid growth, the population exceeding 140,000 by the close of the decade. Notwithstanding its role and image as the LDS capital, Salt Lake was the least Mormon place in Mormondom. Its population, approximately 56 percent non-LDS in 1923, featured a diverse admixture of religions, races, and nationalities, including Chinese, Greek, Hispanic, Japanese, and Italian commercial enclaves scattered throughout the central business district. Six Masonic lodges with almost twenty-three hundred members likewise attested to the strength of non-Mormon influences. Salt Lake boasted a wide range of cultural opportunities as well as a progressive-minded city commission form of government that had instituted numerous social reforms and urban improvements since its adoption in 1911.[19]

Salt Lakers shared many of the concerns, and were beset with the same prejudices, that preoccupied residents in other major urban areas. As commonly occured elsewhere, blacks in Salt Lake found themselves barred from public accommodations and ridiculed in the local press by antiblack cartoons, "Rastus" stories, and racial epithets. When a suburban Salt Lake social club advertises its minstrel show at the local LDS ward as "Nigger Night" and a *Salt Lake City Tribune* article about legislative log-rolling carries the headline "Senate Concerned Over Nigger in the Woodpile," racism is deep-seated.[20] Ethnic and racial animosity was kept in check, however, because of the "bottom line" realities of business intercourse, the urbane atmosphere that pervaded the seat of state government and home of the University of Utah, and the fact that most of the county's ethnic minorities lived not in the city but near the Bingham Canyon copper mines, the Magna mills, or the Garfield-Murray-Midvale smelters. Native-born whites composed the great majority (82.4 percent) of capital city residents, while northern Europeans accounted for 73 percent of the non-native-born; only 718 blacks and 611 other "non-whites" lived in the city. Nonetheless, Salt Lake daily newspapers invariably identified the race and nationality of alleged offenders in reports of crimes by blacks, Hispanics, and southern Europeans, thereby fueling the racial fears of whites.[21]

Probably of greater concern in Salt Lake than race and ethnicity was the new urban culture, a multifaceted social issue that divided the community between the defenders of traditional social codes and the proponents of modernist manners and mores. Signs of the new morality could be discovered everywhere, as young men raced around in fast cars and swayed sensuously to the sounds of jazz music with female counterparts who wore cosmetics, bobbed hair, and short skirts. Compounding moralistic concerns was the bootlegging, prostitution, and gambling that existed beneath the sober social mantle of Salt Lake Mormonism. Yet, crime and other urban problems were probably not as extensive in Salt Lake as in other metropolitan centers, owing to the exceptionally powerful influence of the Mormon civic and religious elite.[22]

What set Salt Lake City conspicuously apart from other American cities and ultimately tied together disparate local issues was deep-seated, endemic conflict between Mormon and gentile residents. This situation was less the result of a perception of the LDS as a parochial religious cult built upon bizarre practices such as secret temple rituals and polygamy than resentment over the church's political domination and competition between Mormon and non-Mormon merchants. Despite the pragmatic cooperation required to insure community stability and prosperity, distrust and suspicion pervaded both factions as gentiles actively opposed the LDS establishment while Mormons zealously defended their ideal of a theocratic corporate culture.[23] Thus the Klan entered a profoundly divided community in the early 1920s.

In the fall of 1921, E. T. Cain, a national Klan organizer, arrived in "the different world of Utah" to establish a KKK chapter in Salt Lake City. His efforts met with considerable success and by early 1922 the local chapter had secured an official charter from Imperial headquarters. Alexander W. Christensen, the recently appointed King Kleagle of Utah, now assumed direction of the klavern's recruiting. A native Utahan born in 1879 to Danish converts to Mormonism, Christensen at an early age ceased being active in the church. Occupationally a white-collar drifter, he held twelve different jobs from 1905 to 1918, usually as an insurance agent or manager of a small business. In 1919, Christensen's career took a turn toward stability when he became the managing partner of a printing supply house. Two years later he utilized his accumulated sales and managerial skills in an effort to establish the Invisible Empire as a permanent force in Utah.[24]

Christensen encountered no more success as a Kluxer than he had as a businessman. Despite the fortuitous (and probably Klan arranged) return of *The Birth of a Nation* to Salt Lake's Gem Theater in early 1922, recruiting entered an extended slump. The King Kleagle reported on February 22 that while receiving as many as fifteen applications in a single day, he had so far only "secured nine [new] members."[25]

To help attract recruits, the Klan launched a spring publicity campaign emphasizing the civic-mindedness and charitable nature of the order. The first public announcement of the existence of the KKK in Utah came on March 6 in the form of advertisements in the *Salt Lake Tribune* and the *Salt Lake Telegram*. Asserting that "the best citizens" in the community had "associated themselves with us" to further "the sublime principles of pure Americanism," the notices emphasized the Klan's commitment to charity, chivalry, humanity, justice, and patriotism.

Of special interest to Salt Lakers were the following objectives: "THE SEPARATION OF CHURCH AND STATE. Freedom of speech and press. Closer relation between Capital and American Labor. Preventing strikes by foreign agitators. THE MUCH-NEEDED LOCAL REFORMS. Law and Order."

The initial public appearance of the KKK occurred dramatically on April 19 in suburban Sandy at internment services for Gordon Stuart, a young Salt Lake County deputy sheriff killed in the line of duty. To the shock of the nearly five hundred mourners in attendance, a group of eight or nine Klansmen in full regalia suddenly appeared at the graveside services, placed a cross of lillies bedecked with a banner inscribed "Knights of the Ku Klux Klan, Salt Lake Chapter No. 1" on the casket, and then sped off in two cars with curtained windows and covered license plates. The Klan later contributed $150 to the *Telegram*'s campaign to raise funds for Stuart's widow and two-month-old son. In announcing that the Klan's donation was the largest single contribution to the fund, the paper noted that "it is one of the principles of this order to commend honest service by public officers." In September, the Salt Lake Klan also sent a $200 check to the Voiture 230 La Société des 40 Hommes et 8 Chevaux, a patriotic order associated with the American Legion, to help send the local rifle team to the Legionnaires convention in New Orleans in October.[26]

These publicity efforts could not compensate for the klavern's faulty recruiting strategy. Unwilling to risk incurring personal censure or opposition from the LDS church, Klan leaders conducted an essentially clandestine word-of-mouth membership campaign. Instead of utilizing extensive newspaper advertisements and such traditional attention-getting devices as parades, public lectures, and outdoor ceremonies featuring cross-burnings, Christensen and his cohorts talked up the Klan without revealing that they were members of the Invisible Empire, except when approaching close friends and associates. This meek approach garnered few recruits and, combined with ineffective local leadership and infighting among the members, led to the virtual disintegration of the nascent Salt Lake klavern by October 1922.[27] The subsequent inability to attract new recruits or to reestablish organizational unity finally forced leaders to admit that "our plan of campaign was impracticable." In fact, by the summer of 1923 the entire Utah Klan found itself in such disarray that the state charter was surrendered to Imperial headquarters, ex-King Kleagle Christensen publicly admitting that "the Ku Klux Klan is no longer active."[28] The spirit of Klankraft remained alive in the capital city, however, as a group of disaffected Klansmen founded the Minute Men of Utah in November 1923 as a "social, benevolent, charitable, and patriotic" organization.[29]

The unavailability of membership lists, klavern minutes, and other records hinders any precise determination of the reasons for the failure of the Klan in Salt Lake City from 1921 to 1923. However, the journal and correspondence of a charter member and officer of the klavern provide insight not only into the motivations of an individual Klansman but also into the early history of the Salt Lake Klan.

Charles Kelly was born on February 3, 1889, in Cedar Springs, Michigan, the son of an itinerant Baptist preacher. As a youngster, Kelly learned the printing trade, and he later wandered about the Midwest and Far West as a tramp printer. Following a brief stint in the Army, he arrived in Salt Lake City in 1919, married, and in 1921 established his own printing business. At the time he joined the Ku Klux Klan in early 1922, Kelly's establishment had fallen on hard times, so he took in Clarence E. Huber as a partner. An avowed atheist, Kelly openly criticized the LDS church's dominance in secular affairs. Possessed of a maverick "barbed-wire personality," guided primarily by individualism and pragmatism, Charles Kelly seemed a most unlikely candidate for the hood and robe.[30]

Yet Kelly became one of the Klan's first recruits in Utah and an officer in the Salt Lake klavern. On January 8, 1922, he noted optimistically in his journal: "I have joined the KKK, and it seems to be a good thing. Looks like I will get some business out of it eventually. They are a good bunch, but I don't know if they are all going to stick or not. If they do, they can do a lot of good sooner or later." On February 3 he remained enthusiastic: "I recommended Huber for the KKK and he was taken in, not knowing what it was until he had been through. He is crazy about it now. We are in the new quarters and have the charter, and everything seems to be going fine. I believe we will do big this year if they live up to the obligations." By May 21 he had become less optimistic: "Things are going slow with them, and I don't know if they are going to make it or not, but I will keep on hoping anyway." By September 23, disenchantment had set in: "I am wondering if I should resign from my job with the klan. Things are getting rotten. Nobody comes anymore except a few who have a motive for coming. . . . I don't know if it is worth while [sic] after all. I don't want to be any officer there any more [sic], because I hate to sit through a session and see the new members humiliated by having klansmen call each other liars so I guess I will resign the job and await developments." By October he was through with the order: "The kkk have disbanded here, so I am out of that."[31]

Economic considerations had first brought Kelly into the fold. In dire financial straits at the time he joined the Klan, he frankly admitted that he hoped to "get some business out of it eventually." When expectations failed to materialize, he began to wonder whether membership was "worth while," and by September he had determined to quit the organization because "we are getting very little work on the strength of it anyway."[32]

Like Kelly, many of the first Salt Lake Klansmen were tradespeople. Indeed, a group of non-Mormon businessmen apparently constituted the main force behind the establishment of the KKK, viewing the secret society as a promising means of challenging Mormon mercantile power.[33] Ever since the LDS church in 1868 created Zion's Cooperative Mercantile Institution, a wholesale-retail conglomerate designed to monopolize Mormon trade in the territory and thus undermine gentile businesses, commercial interaction between Mormon and non-Mormon merchants had been laced with a rivalry that transcended routine economic competition. That the Salt Lake Klan conceived of itself as an economic force is indicated by plans to print a "business directory of the KKK" that would guide members and supporters of the order to firms owned by Klansmen. Such entrepreneurial expectations, however, did not materialize. The directory remained unpublished, and many Klansmen failed to practice economic exclusivity, probably for the reason assigned by Kelly: "The fools are so scared of the Mormons they won't go into it for fear of losing a dime."[34]

The downfall of the first Salt Lake City klavern can be attributed to more than economic considerations. The chapter suffered from a lack of inspiring and effective leadership and never developed a wide-ranging following. Most importantly, the klavern failed to offer itself as an effective means of addressing community problems. The Klan simply seemed to have little reason to exist. The order, moreover, faced a number of major external challenges and problems.

Negative publicity that arose during the spring 1922 recruiting campaign hurt the Klan. Several residents known to operate speakeasies gambling parlors, and other illicit enterprises received letters signed "Leading Knight, K.K.K." threatening them with a coat of tar and feathers unless they left town.[35] Jim Bing, the lone black in suburban

Murray, was terrorized, "severely beaten," and run out of town by men who "rigged themselves up in ghostly attire."[36] A band of teenagers dressed in white hoods and robes with the initials "K.K.K." at the belt frightened residents as they roamed the streets at night "to put down lawlessness among the younger element" in the neighborhood. And a number of citizens received threatening telephone calls made in the name of the KKK.[37] Klan leaders correctly denied responsibility for such incidents, but the tendency of miscreants and pranksters to imitate the violent national reputation of the Invisible Empire surely hampered any effort to portray the KKK as an agency of constructive civic action.

Klan growth also suffered from the hostility of influential shapers of community opinion. In addition to its unfavorable news reports, the *Deseret News* repeatedly took dead editorial aim at the "cowardly" and "sinister" band of "night riders garbed in pillow slips and sheets," claiming the group "enraged race prejudice" and "fed upon religious intolerance." The *Telegram* likewise stepped up its reportage of incidents involving the Klan in other states that cast the hooded order in an unfavorable light. Taking a different tack, the Catholic-owned *Tribune* virtually ignored the Klan, no doubt in order to avoid publicizing the group.[38] The most sensational anti-Klan exposé came on September 20, 1923, when the local press printed two letters written in February 1922 by King Kleagle Christensen to Imperial Wizard Simmons wherein he remarked of the Utah membership drive: "We will not stop until we control this state and these great United States, because our cause is just and we cannot fail." To counter the negative publicity produced by this revelation, Klan spokesmen stressed that the hooded order stood four-square for law and order and pointed proudly to the *Telegram*'s admission that the Salt Lake chapter "has never been accused of acts of violence nor of having taken the law into its own hands on any occasion." Nevertheless, many residents suspected the pacificity of the local klavern was more a reflection of its weakness than of its intentions. In any event, the weight of adverse reports of Klan violence elsewhere and the opposition of the local press combined to persuade most respectable citizens to steer clear of the Invisible Empire.[39]

Another major factor inhibiting Klan expansion was the unrelenting opposition of the LDS church. In addition to editorials and articles in the *Deseret News,* Mormon leaders voiced their opposition to the KKK through exhortations at church conferences and in the monthly magazine *Improvement Era.* For many Mormons the final word on the subject came during the church's semiannual conference in October 1922. Following President Heber J. Grant's firm admonition to "sustain and live the law," Presiding Bishop Charles W. Nibley of Salt Lake specifically named the Ku Klux Klan in condemning "secret societies" formed in time of "contentions":

> Some of these organizations like the Ku Klux Klan have undertaken to administer what they call justice, independent of Constitutional law, and the rights of men, and they have taken the law into their own hands and have dealt with certain people in a way which can only result in disorder, turmoil, strife, and the breaking down of Constitutional law. For these secret organizations undertake to administer punishment upon men and women, irrespective of the laws of the land.

The message to Mormons was unmistakable: avoid the Klan and render strict obedience to duly constituted authorities.[40]

The Klan's attitude toward Mormonism helped fuel this antagonism. Although Mormons appeared in many ways to be ideal candidates for the order—overwhelmingly Anglo-Saxon, intensely patriotic, culturally puritanical, and oriented toward social regulation—they were technically non-Protestant and thus failed to meet the KKK's membership standards. Moreover, certain western Klan leaders deliberately placed the KKK on an anti-LDS footing. At the 1923 Imperial Klonvocation, the Grand Dragon of Wyoming warned the delegates that "in the Realm of Utah and scattered over the west in general, we have another enemy, which is more subtle and far more cunning in carrying out his efforts against this organization than Roman Catholics." He then condemned Mormons for using the public schools for religious purposes by "teaching the Latter-day Saints religion constantly in the classroom"; for "seeking rather than avoiding the inter-marriage of their women with Protestant men, thereby hoping for conversions and the concentration of capital into their stronghold"; and for setting "at naught the laws of the land when the same conflict with their teaching, even going so far as to practice polygamy and other things that are equally distasteful to the majority of American citizens." He also decried Mormon "ecclesiastical influence" in politics, claiming church members utilized bloc voting to wrest concessions favorable to the LDS church from government officials.[41]

To what extent Mormons were aware of such sentiments is not

known. Nevertheless, although the kleagles never openly attacked the LDS church in Utah, their emphasis on the principle of "the absolute separation of church and state" was not misunderstood. In other states the call for such separation permeated anti-Catholic rhetoric, but in Utah this principle clearly referred to the involvement of the Mormon church in secular affairs—an involvement that was particularly pronounced in the city and county of Salt Lake.

Interestingly, opposition from an organization nationally considered to be a prime source of recruits—the Masons—also served initially to retard Klan expansion. During the Salt Lake membership drive in early 1922, King Kleagle Christensen advised officials in Atlanta that "most of the opposition here at present comes from a few of the leading Masons of this state, who evidently have been circulating propoganda detrimental to the organization and have prevented a large number of them from joining our order." A short while later, Christensen, himself a Masonic official, reported that "while the opposition is not entirely overcome here (masonically) they are not getting very far now; many of the boys are getting very apt in soliciting members, yet not admitting that they are associated with the Klan." "It seems a pity," he lamented, "that a few narrow minded people who should be eligible to this organization will go as far as they have in this matter, when they should as American citizens get behind the movement and do all in their power to assist in building it up."[42] Eventually, however, the Salt Lake Klan managed to recruit extensively among local Masons; indeed, by the summer of 1922, almost all of the known or suspected members of the klavern belonged to some type of Masonic society.[43]

Finally, local partisan politics, specifically the reappearance of the anti-Mormon American party, handicapped Klan growth. Initially organized by non-Mormons in 1904 to counter the overt political influence of the LDS church, the American party had disbanded by 1912 because of its lack of success in state and local elections. However, the spirit behind the third party, which had controlled Salt Lake City government from 1906 to 1911, remained strong in the capital into the 1920s.[44] Already angry over the role of the LDS church in securing the enactment of an anticigarette law in March 1921 that made it illegal to sell tobacco products or smoke them in public places, anti-Mormon forces coalesced over two issues in the fall of 1922.[45] The first was the creation by county Republican boss George Wilson and United States senatorial candidate Ernest Bamberger of a secret anti-Mormon political clique known as the Order of the Sevens.[46] The second was the blatant interference in county politics by the First President of the LDS church, Heber J. Grant, who not only personally encouraged and endorsed an independent candidate, Benjamin R. Harries, to run for county sheriff but also publicly urged Mormons to support his choice for office. Harries eventually scored a smashing victory, but the election results produced a prolonged court battle, which lasted until 1926, keeping religious tensions high.[47]

Although Harries had received support from non-Mormons and non-partisan groups concerned with lax law enforcement, Heber Grant's impolitic interference raised old fears of LDS involvement in secular affairs. With church-state antagonisms once again the talk of the town, gentile activists reorganized the American party at a mass meeting of "at least 1,200" on August 30, 1923, at the Orpheum Theatre. The gathering endorsed the candidacies of non-Mormons Joseph E. Galigher for mayor and George N. Lawrence and Parley L. Williams for city commissioners in the upcoming city election, stressing a platform of lower taxes, more efficient government, and the "complete and absolute separation of church and state."[48] The latter plank, the party's *raison d'etre,* plainly represented an attack on LDS influence and guaranteed a heated campaign. In one of the bitterest municipal contests in Salt Lake City history, incumbents Mayor C. Clarence Nelsen, a Mormon bishop; Commissioner Theodore T. Burton, an LDS church official; and Commissioner Herman H. Green soundly defeated the American party's non-Mormon slate in November 1923.[49] This decisive outcome spelled the end of the American party, as its Democratic and Republican followers soon returned to their respective parties or the Order of the Sevens.

The Ku Klux Klan had become an issue, albeit a subsidiary one, in the election. For weeks rumors had circulated that the American party's candidates and campaign manager Henry C. Allen belonged to the hooded order. Allen, a week before the election, denounced the "whispering campaign" and vehemently denied that he been an officer in the local Klan and that the remnants of the Salt Lake klavern used the American party's headquarters as a meeting place. The bulk of the evidence indicates, however, that Allen and candidates Galligher and Wilson were or had been Klansmen. Nevertheless, it would be erroneous to label the American party as a front for the Klan, which had already collapsed as a force on the local scene. Rather than being

KKK-sponsored, the political activism of gentile insurgents in 1923 can best be viewed as yet another round in the longstanding political battle between Mormons and non-Mormons.[50]

Notwithstanding the flurry of Klan activity in Salt Lake City in 1921–22, the Invisible Empire gave scant attention to Utah during the first phase of westward expansion. Skipping from Colorado over the sparsely populated states of the Great Basin to the more fertile recruiting grounds along the Pacific coast, the order realized marked success in California, Oregon, and Washington. Therefore, Klan recruiters in mid-1924 again turned their attention to Utah as part of a larger campaign to establish Klankraft in the Intermountain West. That the Kluxing of the Beehive State was part of an orchestrated membership campaign is evident in the systematic progression of Klan activity from the northernmost counties of Cache and Box Elder southward through Weber, Davis, Salt Lake, Utah, and Carbon counties.[51]

When the field representatives arrived in Salt Lake City in late summer 1924, they found the Klan on the verge of extinction. The few diehard Klansmen were part of a truly invisible empire, having relinquished their charter and ceased to operate as an organized unit. Still, the kleagles found the recruiting climate much improved from two years before. In particular, the recent activism of the American party and the Order of the Sevens, both of which had drawn support from the first Salt Lake klavern, had heightened political consciousness in ways that made Klankraft more appealing. Recruits were quickly enrolled in towns throughout Salt Lake County, but the primary target remained the capital city. With the Empire Insurance Company serving as a front for Klan operations, William M. Cortner, an Imperial representative from Ohio, directed the new recruiting campaign in Salt Lake City, assisted by "stenographer" Myrtle Galvin, field organizer for the Women of the Ku Klux Klan, who spearheaded the formation of a woman's auxiliary. To Dr. John C. Polly, national Klan lecturer from Washington, D.C., went the task of publicizing the virtues of the Klan's program.[52]

With an advertisement in the *Telegram* on September 15 inviting the "entire public" to "come and hear the truth about this great American movement" the next evening, the Ku Klux Klan formally announced the beginning of an aggressive and open membership drive in Salt Lake City. The response proved extraordinary. A throng estimated at four thousand persons, including nearly one hundred uniformed Klansmen, gathered at Heath's Auto Tourist Camp at 1017 South State Street at 8:30 P.M. to hear Dr. Polly outline "the ideals for which the Klan stands" and the problems confronting "red-blooded Americans." Appealing to the traditional religious, social, and ethnic prejudices of Protestant Caucasians, Polly identified the enemies of the Klan: the bootlegger, the "men and women of the underworld," the "grafting politician," and the "uneducated immigrants" who "take the jobs of Americans." After the speech, according to one newspaper report, so many men came forward to get membership applications that Klan officials exhausted their supply of 250 and accepted names on slips of paper. In marked contrast to their earlier recruiting effort, Klansmen made no effort to hide their identity, as "most of them" mingled with the crowd without their hoods. Polly lectured to another large crowd on October 20, and it soon became apparent that the Klan's recruiting strategy of holding public rallies had been successful. Membership increased dramatically, with chapters of both the Knights and the Women of the Ku Klux Klan holding large and spirited meetings in Odd Fellows Hall on Post Office Place.[53]

In contrast to its success in Salt Lake City, the Klan did not fare well in other parts of the state or county where Kluxing featured highly visible and provocative recruiting methods—parades, cross-burnings, and outdoor ceremonials—and occasional acts of violence. While such tactics produced an initial rush of new recruits, they also generated determined community opposition from municipal officials, newspaper publishers, and immigrant residents. By the end of 1924, the Klan had been destroyed in Logan and driven underground in Ogden by antimask ordinances; elsewhere, as in Bingham, Brigham City, and Magna, Klansmen had been forced to disband because of intense community pressures.[54]

The fall membership drive in the Beehive State also provoked strong condemnation from the LDS church. President Heber J. Grant refused a visitation request from Klan organizers, and Mormon leaders reaffirmed their disapproval of the secret society during the general church conference in October 1924. In censuring the Klan, Elder George Albert Smith pointedly declared: "There are those who are misguided in the belief that they may organize groups and take into their own hands the punishment of those who have differed from them in their ideas of religion or government.... We may know that no man is a faithful member of this Church, in good standing, who refuses to sustain the law of the land, and who lends himself in any way to break down that organized system of laws that has been prepared for the good of the community."[55] For many Utahans, the official admonition against Mormon membership in the Klan sealed the fate of the organization in Zion.

Unbeknownst to both rank-and-file Klansmen and their critics, Klan leaders at this time made an audacious move to establish a permanent statewide administrative structure by successfully filing a petition with the Salt Lake County clerk for the incorporation of the "Knights of the Ku Klux Klan" as a "Patriotic, Secret, Social, Benevolent Order." The incorporation of the Klan was fraudulent as none of the petitioners—William Cortner; Harry Sawyer, the new King Kleagle of Utah; and L. W. Tavenner, the King Kleagle of Idaho—lived in the county, and two were not even residents of the state. Moreover, by avoiding reference to the Georgia Klan, its administrative structure, and traditional Klan terminology in identifying offices and officers, Cortner and his cronies had in effect incorporated an unauthorized and independent Utah Klan. A desire for personal power and profit primarily motivated this course of action, but there was also a larger political purpose: under the terms of its charter, the new Utah Klan was open to all "white male persons of sound health, good morals, and high character"; the conspicuous absence of "Protestant" and "native-born" qualifications therefore opened the door of Utah Klandom to Mormons and theoretically even to Catholics, Jews, and unnaturalized immigrants. Realizing this brash innovation would lead to defections and jurisdictional warfare if discovered by Imperial officials, Cortner kept the incorporation of an autonomous Klan a secret from most other members of the order.[56]

Presuming the Klan to be in hibernation for the winter, Salt Lakers were caught off guard when the Invisible Empire provided a spectacular conclusion to Washington's Birthday celebrations the evening of February 23, 1925, with an unannounced parade through the heart of the city's business district. A blazing red cross appeared just before 9:00 P.M. on Ensign Peak north of the city, near the spot where Brigham Young and a small band of LDS leaders had "set up an ensign for the nation" nearly eighty years before. A few minutes later, a hooded and robed contingent estimated at "several hundred" left the klavern meeting hall on Post Office Place. A color guard bearing the American flag headed the Klan's first parade in the city. Next came the "three leaders of the klan in Utah"—probably Cortner, Sawyer, and Tavenner—who lifted their hoods during part of the parade. Following close behind the trio was John Held's "city band," which played lively patriotic airs along the entire parade route.[57] Then came four hooded horsemen leading a long line of Klansmen in full regalia. Some of the masked marchers carried banners with inscriptions such as "We Stand for the Church," "America for Americans," and "We Stand for the Sanctity of the Home." Interspersed among the marchers were three automobiles, each bearing an electrical "flaming" cross. In one of the vehicles rode the Great Titan, whose name was "carefully guarded," bedecked in the distinctive purple robes of his office. A mounted posse brought up the rear of the parade. The provocative procession passed without incident, there being no reports of heckling by the spectators who "densely lined" the eight-block parade route.[58]

As surprising as the unannounced parade was the apparent strength of the order. Although the marchers included Klansmen from throughout the county (who normally participated in the rites of the Salt Lake klavern), KKK recruiting in the city had clearly been more successful than enemies of the order had suspected. Indicative of the enhanced popularity of Klankraft were the pro-Klan sentiments expressed by the *Citizen,* an influential Republican weekly aimed at the Salt Lake business community. Whereas the paper had merely commented favorably on the Klan in September 1924, it openly endorsed the order just one week prior to the February 1925 parade. In railing against the leniency shown by the courts in a recent murder trial, the paper editorialized that "many openly state" their desire "to see the Ku Klux Klan or some other organization [insure] that our laws are more strictly enforced."[59]

The rapid growth of the Salt Lake Klan culminated with the first interstate Konklave ever held in the Beehive State. Scheduled to coincide with the spring conference of the LDS church, several hundred knights from Utah and Nevada met in Salt Lake City on Sunday, April 5, 1925, to discuss "affairs pertaining to the Invisible Empire." The next evening, Ensign Peak was again aglow, this time from several immense fiery crosses, which burned so brightly they could be seen in almost every part of the valley. On a mesa just below the peak, hooded and robed Klansmen formed a circular guardline nearly a mile in diameter around the ceremonial site. Inside the circle a joint demonstration of men and women of the Klan took place, as two large "classes" were inducted into the male and female orders. The exact number of Klansmen who participated in the Konklave is not known, but one press estimate placed it "into the thousands." In addition, thousands of spectators reportedly witnessed the gathering, which, with its pagentry, mysterious garb, mystical ritual, fiery crosses, billowing flag displays, and martial music, presented a spectacular sight.[60]

A Klan spokesman claimed that Salt Lake's first Konklave was the "greatest affair held by the Klan of Utah" and "in every way a great success." It was, however, wishful thinking to report to Atlanta that "from all indications Utah will soon be classed as one of the great Klan states." This excessive enthusiasm perhaps stemmed from the recent diminution of two major barriers to Klan expansion in Utah. First, the Masons had experienced an almost complete change of heart and now served as a major source of Klan recruits. Second, despite the admonitions of their spiritual leaders, an appreciable number of Mormons, including some bishops, had joined the Invisible Empire. Although Mormons were a distinct minority in every klavern and although Robert F. Howard, klabee of the Salt Lake chapter, was the only Mormon known to be a Klan officer, LDS officials were so deeply concerned about the secret society that President Grant felt it necessary to reiterate the church's vehement opposition to the Klan in April 1925.[61]

With Klan activity outside of the capital either nonexistent or operating behind closed doors, Klankraft in Utah had come full circle and was again primarily a Salt Lake phenomenon.[62] Concerned about setbacks elsewhere in the state, Cortner and his kleagles hit the hustings in late May. At a dinner meeting in June attended by more than six hundred Salt Lake knights, the Klan leader announced that seven new chapters had recently been established "in various places."[63]

This flurry of recruiting activity in the eastern, western, and southern areas of the state proved ultimately unsuccessful and even counterproductive as the Salt Lake City Commission, alarmed by renewed Klan activity, now challenged local Kluxers. Unlike the situation elsewhere in the state and nation, the Salt Lake Klan did not incur opposition from the city government because of any tangible transgressions of the law or breaches of the peace. Cross-burnings and parades were indirectly frightening and threatening, but no instances of direct physical abuse of persons or property by capital city Klansmen have come to light. Instead of lawlessness, it was the increased boldness and strength exhibited by the Klan that alarmed municipal officials.

To prevent any disorders that might result from increased Klan activity, the city commission attempted to legislate the secret society out of existence, as had been done in Logan and Ogden. Acting upon a motion of Theodore T. Burton on June 15, the commission three days later unanimously enacted an ordinance making it unlawful for anyone "to appear or participate in any parade, assemblage or demonstration in or upon any of the streets, parks, or other public places of Salt Lake City while wearing any mask, disguise, or device whatsoever which shall be intended to or shall have the effect of preventing the entire face . . . from being at all times plainly visible to the public." Deemed "necessary to the health, peace and safety" of the citizens of Salt Lake, the law carried a maximum penalty of $299 in fines and six months in jail.[64]

The antimask ordinance hurt, but did not bring an end to, the Klan's publicity efforts. After arranging for a showing of *The Birth of a Nation* on August 30–31, Klan leaders scheduled the first public rallies to be held in almost a year: lectures on September 1 and 2 at Heath's Auto Campgrounds by John A. Jeffrey, Imperial Lecturer from Atlanta, and a gathering at the Richards Street auditorium on September 3.[65] But these functions were for the public, not exclusively for Klansmen, and the attempt to follow up the rallies with a parade ran afoul of the recent antimask ordinance. William Cortner, using an alias and presenting himself as a Klan representative from Georgia, appeared before the city commission on September 22 and sought permission for a masked march on October 5, arguing that Klansmen had been singled out for unfair treatment.[66] The commissioners took the matter under advisement but the following morning denied the Klan's request.[67]

In keeping with Cortner's pledge to obey the law, the Klan marched robed and hooded but unmasked as scheduled shortly after 9:00 P.M. on Monday, October 5. Preceded by several weeks of advertising and timed to coincide with the state fair, the procession of "several hundred" Klansmen and Klanswomen was by far the biggest and most elaborate Klan parade ever held in the Intermountain West. An honor guard of army and marine veterans resplendent in their military uniforms and bearing the Stars and Stripes led the marchers. A Klan band blaring patriotic music, twenty-five to thirty Klansmen astride prancing horses, and a pair of automobiles carrying red fiery crosses gave an air of martial excitement to the four-block-long cavalcade. The Klan conveyed its message by numerous banners stressing "law and order" and "the preservation of the rights of liberty" and by several floats depicting symbols such as the Goddess of Liberty, the Little Red School House, and Uncle Sam. The band, the flags, and the floats reportedly received "many ovations" along the route.

After the parade, the marchers reassembled at Walker's Field for a public initiation. Klansmen and a throng of curious spectators witnessed naturalization ceremonies for both men and women and then heard Cortner lecture on the principles and purposes of the Klan. Paying his respects to the city commission, he claimed that the antimask law, "instigated by groups of persons not eligible to the American order and opposed to the belief in Americanism," had actually served to "whet the enthusiasm" of Klan members and heighten public interest in the organization. Klansmen, he declared, were "patriots who see the need of rising to the defense of their country today just as much as did the patriots of the Boston tea party when they donned the mask in order to deliver their country from the hands of the oppressor." He detailed special problems in the city and county of Salt Lake relating to graft, corruption, and excessive taxation and spoke of the need to elect to government office "men who would not pledge themselves to groups or cliques to enrich themselves."[68]

Cortner's pointed reference to local politics indicated that the KKK would again become a factor in municipal elections. For some time, rumors had circulated that the local Klan supported non-Mormons Berkley Olson and Patrick J. Moran, the principal challengers to incumbent city commissioners Arthur F. Barnes and Harry L. Finch in the upcoming November general election. Ostensibly, the Klan was out to defeat Barnes and Finch because they were part of the "Mormon machine" of Mayor Nelsen that dominated city government and because of their role in passing the antimask ordinance. The Klan denied support for either Olson or Moran, but remained a definite, if largely unacknowledged, issue. Because the Invisible Empire constituted an unknown political quantity, none of the candidates mentioned the hooded order during the campaign, opting instead to stress the relatively benign themes of law and order, and honest, efficient government. Olson's slogan that he "Stands for the Homes, the Schools, and a Clean, Orderly Community" was indistinguishable from the campaign themes of his rivals, as well as the stated goals of the Klan.[69]

The KKK finally became an open issue on the eve of the election. During the night of November 2–3, downtown Salt Lake City was "covered" with thousands of posters urging the election of the rather improbable combination of Harry Finch and Patrick Moran, claiming they were "Backed by the Klans." The next morning both candidates vigorously disavowed any association with the KKK and denounced what they termed "a dirty last-hour" trick to convince voters they were affiliated with the Invisible Empire. Klan officials initially refused to comment on the circulars, remarking: "The Klan has a perfect political machine in this election, but it is not prepared to divulge whether it fostered the move to campaign for Finch and Moran." Later in the day, however, Klan headquarters announced that the secret order "knew nothing of the printing or distribution of the dodger." This was probably a truthful statement: the posters, unlike all other KKK literature, used the terms "Klans" instead of the official "Knights of the Ku Klux Klan." Whatever the effect, or purpose, of the posters, voters turned out in unusually large numbers despite the first snowfall of the year and elected Finch and Moran by commanding margins.[70]

A few weeks later, the Klan suffered a public relations setback when the group was blamed for the farcical banishment of Santa Claus at Christmas. At the December 23 meeting of the city commission, Harry Finch reported that Ku Klux Klan officials had called his attention to the fact that the Santas who wore false beards on the streets of Salt Lake City soliciting funds for the poor were violating the municipal antimask ordinance. Another commissioner, Herman H. Green, concurred and pointed out that it would be class legislation to apply the ordinance to some but not to others. Mayor Nelsen had no choice but to order the police department to enforce the law against bewhiskered St. Nicks.[71] Because city commission minutes are silent on the incident, it is not possible to determine with certainty whether the Klan actually instigated this ludicrous protest or whether Finch raised the issue to embarass either local Klansmen or anti-Klan commissioners. In any event, the local klavern suffered popular ridicule by being blamed for driving Santa Claus from the streets of Salt Lake City.

As 1925 drew to an end, it increasingly appeared that the denouement of the Salt Lake chapter of the KKK was near. William Cortner realized, the October parade notwithstanding, that many rank-and-file members of the secret order, which included a number of "prominent business and government leaders," were unwilling to brave the possibility of further public exposure. Consequently, he attempted to ally Beehive Klansmen with Dr. John Galen Locke's Denver-based Minute Men of America, an organization that had abandoned the more controversial features (secrecy, overt anti-Catholicism and anti-Semitism) of the Invisible Empire while retaining the Klan's concern with law, order, morality, the separation of church and state, and immigration restriction.[72]

Following preliminary inquiries in the late fall of 1925, Cortner journeyed to Denver in early January 1926 to confer with Locke. Upon returning to Salt Lake he presented a merger proposal to the officers of the Salt Lake Klan and then to the membership at a klavern meeting on January 25. The next day Cortner formally announced that Salt Lake Klan No. 1 had seceded from the Knights of the Ku Klux Klan (Inc.) and affiliated with the Minute Men of America because the national Klan had "given no support" to the local chapter and was an "undemocratic and Un-American" organization. He hastened to point out, however, that the principles and purposes of the Minute Men were "essentially the same as the Klan with the exception . . . that the new body is purely democratic and pro-American." Noting that the local chapter's women's auxiliary had "unanimously voted" to join the Minute Women of America, Cortner expressed confidence that "every klan unit in Utah, Nevada, and Idaho will also secede."[73]

Cortner's schismatic maneuver backfired. Although a majority of the Klansmen present at the klavern meeting on January 25 had presumably voted for secession, the move met strong opposition from the many members who had not attended. Whether based on institutional loyalty or a struggle for power within the chapter, the resulting dispute proved so disruptive that "it broke the Klan wide open." When it became clear that the secessionists composed a clear minority, Cortner departed for greener organizational pastures.[74]

Torn by internal dissension, buffeted by negative publicity, and handicapped by the antimask ordinance, Salt Lake Kluxers met only behind close doors in 1926. That the principal chapter in Utah Klandom held no public parades, lectures, initiations, or Konklaves during the year indicated the moribund state of Klankraft. Out of sight for the first nine months of the year, the Klan suddenly became a major issue during the fall election campaign.

The 1926 general election in Salt Lake County produced one of the most vicious campaigns in Utah history as Democrats charged that the Republican candidate for sheriff, Clifford W. Patten, was both a member of the "secret, oath bound, un-American" Order of Sevens and an "ex-member of the Ku Klux Klan." While the campaign turned largely on charges and countercharges concerning Patten's purported affilia-tion with the Invisible Empire, the actual Democratic target was the powerful Sevens, a "secret political gang of self-seeking slickers and manipulators" that "has secured a throathold on the Republican County organization." The attempt to undermine Republican hegemony by exposing the "UN-AMERICAN ALLIANCE of the SEVENS and the KU KLUX KLAN" proved counterproductive. Whatever the merit of the Demo-cratic charges—Patten probably had once been a Klansman, and there certainly was Klan influence in the Order of the Sevens—the electorate reacted to the negative campaign tactics by making Patten the leading vote-getter in a GOP sweep of offices.[75]

Patten's victory did not signal a revival of the Klan's fortunes. Despite the assurance of Klabee Robert F. Howard in November 1926 that the Salt Lake Klan was "still functioning with great vigor and holding meetings every Monday evening," interest in the order was drastically on the wane.[76] With William Cortner gone, leadership of the klavern had devolved to lesser hands. The new exalted cyclops by late 1926 was David Patten (no relation to Clifford Patten), an itinerant laborer who soon departed.[77] The other principal officers, Kligrapp Harry E. Mabey, a carpenter, and Klabee Howard, a mail carrier, were lifelong residents of the city, but neither possessed significant leadership qualities.[78] Consequently, Klansmen deserted in droves. While certain Klan members on several occasions in the summer of 1927 joined law enforcement officers in raiding illegal gambling and distilling opera-tions near Salt Lake, the chapter after 1926 never reacquired sufficient strength to sponsor a public demonstration of any kind.[79] By late 1927, the Invisible Empire had expired as a viable organization in Salt Lake City.[80]

Despite two concerted recruiting drives in 1921–22 and 1924–25 and a membership that varied annually but reached approximately twenty-five hundred overall, Klankraft failed to take enduring root in Salt Lake City or even exert a significant influence on the community. The reasons for this failure are varied. One major problem was that the capital city chapter never developed effective leadership. The potential was there inasmuch as early Klan leaders and much of the rank and file were middle-class businessmen and professionals (until the chapter was taken over by working-class elements as the klavern deteriorated in 1926), but no talented individual assumed the helm. The presence of inattentive (E. T. Cain) and unscrupulous (William Cortner) national Klan representatives compounded the leadership problem. Even more important, Klan leaders failed to exploit local issues that might have enabled the order to forge a meaningful community role and counter the strong opposition of traditional leaders. This meant that Salt Lake Klankraft remained an imported commodity, receiving its primary organizational impetus from outside influences rather than indigenous community concerns.

The traditional Utah problem of the separation of church and state was the most promising issue the Klan could have used to exert influence in the community. The anger of some Mormons and of most non-Mormons at the LDS church's interference in and domination of local economic, social, and political life reached new heights after World War I during the presidency of Heber J. Grant. But before the Klan, organized initially by gentile businessmen, could politically exploit the church-state issue, it was overshadowed first by the reappearance of the old anti-Mormon American party and then by the Order of the Sevens. The American party demonstrated the danger to community relations posed by overt confrontations between religious groups, while the Sevens provided an effective behind-the-scenes political alternative to the Klan. The KKK thus was unable effectively to exploit anti-Mormon sentiment and thereby gain a political foothold in Salt Lake City.

Ultimately, however, it was the Invisible Empire's inability to overcome the hostility of community leaders that doomed the order. The negative publicity from the press and the opposition from municipal officials in the form of the antimask ordinance were important, but paled in significance to the determined attack of the LDS church. The persistent and determined opposition of the Mormon hierarchy voiced through the *Deseret News,* semiannual conferences, church literature, and local ward meetings constituted the single most important factor inhibiting the growth of Klan influence in Salt Lake and the state. Although a few Mormons joined the Klan, the church's opposition effectively mustered nearly three-quarters of the population against the Klan.

In Salt Lake City, the Invisible Empire confronted and was eventually overwhelmed by the highly visible empire that dominated Utah. First, Mormon demographic dominance meant that there was a small pool of potential recruits. Second, the KKK's ideal of restoring traditional American values possessed diminished relevance in a state that was culturally the embodiment of traditional America: overwhelmingly Anglo-Saxon, largely rural and agricultural, and morally puritanical. Most important, the LDS church effectively performed the "moral reform" function of the Klan. In addition to the essential clannishness of Mormons, the LDS ward was a homogeneous corporate community emphasizing conformity and obedience and where the governing bishopric systematically supervised the personal deportment and sumptuary habits of members. In effect, Mormonism and the functioning of the LDS church made the Klan superfluous in Salt Lake City.

In the end, the KKK could only offer the pseudofraternalism of a sub rosa organization with no ongoing purpose, program, or place in the community. The remembrance of a Salt Lake Klansman who later enjoyed a long and distinguished career as county treasurer is a fitting epitaph for the Klan in the capital city:

> The Klan was just what the organizers told us it was—a patriotic, religious organization. We'd hear talks about Americanism, sing patriotic songs and hymns, and so on. I really enjoyed it at first, but then, well, it seemed like there just wasn't any point to it anymore. You know, it's funny. One day it was all the rage and the next—nothing. It just died out. I don't know why. I was pretty active for a while, but now I really can't remember much about it. I remember buying my robe, going to meetings, a couple of parades, and that big get-together up on Ensign. Guess that's all there was to it.[81]

Such was the story of the Invisible Empire in Salt Lake City: form without substance. Yet it is important to note that the KKK did not die in the city because of popular repudiation of its principles. Largely unwilling to affiliate with the hooded order, Salt Lakers were willing to promote or acquiesce in nationwide patterns of discrimination and bigotry. The Klan's legacy was a de facto invisible empire of prejudice that would continue to haunt the city for decades.

NOTES

The author would like to express his gratitude to Utah State University Press for permission to use material from his book *Blazing Crosses in Zion: The Ku Klux Klan in Utah* (Logan, Utah, 1982).

1. For Salt Lake City, see Thomas G. Alexander and James B. Allen, *Mormons*

& Gentiles: A History of Salt Lake City (Boulder, Colorado, 1984); Chauncey D. Harris, Salt Lake City: A Regional Capital (Chicago, 1940); and Dale L. Morgan, "Salt Lake City: City of the Saints," in Ray B. West, Jr., ed., Rocky Mountain Cities (New York, 1949), 179-207. The most detailed history of Utah is Richard D. Poll, ed., Utah's History (Provo, 1978); also valuable are Dean L. May, Utah: A People's History (Salt Lake City, 1987), and Charles S. Peterson, Utah: A Bicentennial History (New York, 1977).

2. U.S. Bureau of the Census, Fourteenth Census of the United States, 1920: Population, III, 1030, 1033; Poll, ed., Utah's History, 687, 688, 692.

3. For the repeated admonitions about secret societies, see the footnote reference to 2 Nephi 10:15 in the Book of Mormon. Fifteen Mormons, at least five of whom were missionaries, were killed in the southern states between 1879 and 1900. See William W. Hatch, There is No Law... A History of Mormon Civil Relations in the Southern States, 1865-1905 (New York, 1968); Gene A. Sessions, "Myth, Mormonism, and Murder in the South," South Atlantic Quarterly 75 (Spring 1976): 212-25; Leonard J. Arrington, "Mormon Beginnings in the American South," Task Papers in LDS History No. 9 (October 1976), Historical Department, Church of Jesus Christ of Latter-day Saints, Salt Lake City.

4. Richard D. Poll, "Utah and the Mormons: A Symbiotic Relationship," second annual David E. Miller Lecture on Utah and the West, University of Utah, April 23, 1980.

5. An excellent introduction to the history of ethnic and racial minorities is Helen Z. Papanikolas, ed., The Peoples of Utah (Salt Lake City, 1976).

6. Newell G. Bringhurst, Saints, Slaves, and Blacks: The Changing Place of Black People Within Mormonism (Westport, Connecticut, 1981); Lester E. Bush, Jr., "Mormonism's Negro Doctrine: An Historical Overview," Dialogue: A Journal of Mormon Thought 8 (1973): 11-68; Margaret J. Maag, "Discrimination against the Negro and Institutional Efforts to Eliminate It" (M.A. thesis, University of Utah, 1971); and Ronald G. Coleman, "A History of Blacks in Utah, 1825-1910" (Ph.D. dissertation, University of Utah, 1979).

7. Leon L. Watters, The Pioneer Jews of Utah (New York, 1957); Juanita Brooks, The History of Jews in Utah and Idaho (Salt Lake City, 1973); Jack Goodman, "Jews in Zion," in Papanikolas, ed., Peoples of Utah, 187-220; Bernice M. Mooney and Jerome C. Stoffel, Salt of the Earth: The History of the Catholic Diocese of Salt Lake City, (Salt Lake City, 1987). The best general treatment of the Mormon-gentile split can be found in Peterson, Utah, passim.

8. See Dean L. May, "Economic Beginnings" and "Towards a Dependent Commonwealth," in Poll, ed., Utah's History, 193-241; Thomas G. Alexander, A Dependent Commonwealth: Utah's Economy from Statehood to the Great Depression (Provo, 1974); Gibbs M. Smith, Joe Hill (Salt Lake City, 1969).

9. For the urban scene, see Alexander and Allen, Mormons & Gentiles,

passim, and Richard C. Roberts and Richard W. Sadler, *Ogden: Junction City* (Northridge, California, 1985).

10. Larry E. Nelson, "Problems of Prohibition Enforcement in Utah, 1917-1933" (M.S. thesis, University of Utah, 1970), 121.

11. John Sword Hunter, "Cigarette Prohibition in Utah, 1921-23," *Utah Historical Quarterly* 41 (Fall 1973): 358-72.

12. For immigration patterns, see Papanikolas, ed., *Peoples of Utah.*

13. *Laws of Utah,* 1919, chap. 93; Leroy E. Cowles, "The Utah Educational Program of 1919 and Factors Conditioning Its Operation" (Ph.D. dissertation, University of California, 1926). For the problems and processes of acculturation, see Philip F. Nottarianni, "Utah's Ellis Island: The Difficult 'Americanization' of Carbon County," *Utah Historical Quarterly* 47 (Spring 1979): 178-93; and Helen Z. Papanikolas, "Ethnicity in Mormondom: A Comparison of Immigrant and Mormon Cultures," in Thomas G. Alexander, ed., *"Sour-Butter and Hog Wash" and Other Essays on the American West* (Provo, 1978), 91-135.

14. In particular, see Allen Kent Powell, *The Next Time We Strike: Labor Union Activity in the Utah Coal Fields* (Logan, Utah, 1985).

15. *Deseret News,* June 17, 1922; January 8, 1923.

16. *Sugar House Times* June 16, 1922; *The Citizen,* June 17, 1922.

17. For a statewide study of the Klan in Utah through the early 1980s, see Larry R. Gerlach, *Blazing Crosses in Zion: The Ku Klux Klan in Utah* (Logan, Utah, 1982).

18. Gerlach, *Blazing Crosses,* 11-15; *Deseret News,* June 21, 1921.

19. Alexander and Allen, *Mormons & Gentiles,* 163-195.

20. *Sugar House Times,* March 24, 31, 1922; *Salt Lake Tribune,* January 30, 1925.

21. *Fourteenth Census: Population,* III, 1035, 1038.

22. For an overview of Salt Lake's problems during the 1920s, see Alexander and Allen, *Mormons & Gentiles,* 163-95.

23. Ibid., 14-15, 303-7.

24. Gerlach, *Blazing Crosses in Zion,* 25-26.

25. Letter printed in the *Salt Lake Telegram,* September 20, 1923.

26. *Deseret News,* April 14, 20, 1922; *Salt Lake Telegram,* April 16, 20, 27, September 20, 1922; *Salt Lake Tribune,* April 16, 20, 1922.

27. Private journal of Charles Kelly, Charles Kelly Papers, Box I, Utah State Historical Society, Salt Lake City.

28. *Salt Lake Telegram,* September 20, 1923. See also *Deseret News,* October 31, 1926; *Salt Lake Telegram,* November 1, 1926.

29. Articles of Incorporation, File No. 16027, Office of the Secretary of State, Salt Lake City; *Salt Lake Tribune,* November 15, 1923.

30. Gerlach, *Blazing Crosses,* 29-30.

31. Journal of Charles Kelly.

32. Ibid., entries for January 8, May 21, September 23, 1922.

33. Gerlach, *Blazing Crosses*, 31–32.

34. Journal of Charles Kelly, entries for May 21, September 23, 1922.

35. *Deseret News,* March 9, 1922; *Salt Lake Telegram,* March 9, 1922; *Salt Lake Tribune,* March 10, 1922.

36. *Salt Lake Telegram,* April 14, 1922; *Salt Lake Tribune,* April 15, 1922.

37. *Deseret News,* May 10, 1922; *Salt Lake Telegram,* September 28, 29, 1923; *Salt Lake Tribune,* September 29, October 6, 1923.

38. *Deseret News,* August 23, October 5, 19, 1921; April 14, 24, 1922; April 16, August 24, 1923; *Salt Lake Telegram,* August 23, September 18, 21, 22, 26, October 2, 4, 11, 29, 1923.

39. *Salt Lake Telegram,* September 20, 1923; *Salt Lake Tribune,* September 20, 1923.

40. The speeches were published in *Improvement Era* 26 (December 1922): 97–100, 180–84.

41. *Papers Read at the Meeting of Grand Dragons, Knights of the Ku Klux Klan at Their First Annual Meeting* (Asheville, North Carolina, 1923), 112–13.

42. Letters quoted in the *Salt Lake Telegram,* September 20, 1923.

43. The gentile composition of Masonic lodges in Utah stemmed from two factors: (1) the LDS church counseled Mormons against joining the oath-bound, secret society and (2) the Masonic Order banned Mormons from membership on the grounds that LDS temple rites constituted "clandestine Masonry." The Masonic position is best explained by past grand master S. H. Goodwin, *Mormonism and Masonry* (Salt Lake City, 1925) and *Additional Studies in Mormonism and Masonry* (Salt Lake City, 1927). The Mormon rebuttal is detailed in Anthony W. Ivins, *The Relationship of "Mormonism" and Freemasonry* (Salt Lake City, 1934), and E. Cecil McGavin, *"Mormonism" and Masonry* (Salt Lake City, 1935).

44. Reuben Joseph Snow, "The American Party in Utah: A Study of Political Party Struggles during the Early Years of Statehood" (M.A. thesis, University of Utah, 1964).

45. Smith, "Cigarette Prohibition in Utah," passim.

46. Brad E. Hainsworth, "Utah State Elections, 1916–1924" (Ph.D. dissertation, University of Utah, 1968), 257–65 and Appendix II; Stanford J. Layton, "Governor Charles R. Mabey and the Utah Election of 1924" (M.A. thesis, University of Utah, 1969), 30–37; Dan E. Jones, "Utah Politics, 1926–1932" (Ph.D. dissertation, University of Utah, 1968), 42–44, 157–58; Larry R. Gerlach, "The Politics of Patronage: The Order of the Sevens," work in progress.

47. The LDS church's endorsement of Harries, which brought the constitutional issue of the separation of church and state into Utah courts, has been ignored by historians and political scientists; the author is presently working on a detailed account of the episode.

---

48. *Salt Lake Telegram,* August 29, 30, 1923.

49. Nelsen trounced Galigher by some 5,000 votes—19,804 to 14,796. Burton (19,823) and Green (17,991) were easy victors over Lawrence (16,188) and Williams (14,046). See *Salt Lake Telegram,* November 7, 14, 1923.

50. *Salt Lake Telegram,* October 31, 1923.

51. Gerlach, *Blazing Crosses,* 62–75, 87–99.

52. Ibid., 63, 85.

53. *Salt Lake Telegram,* September 17, October 20–21, 1924.

54. Gerlach, *Blazing Crosses,* 75–84.

55. *Ninety-Fifth Semi-Annual Conference,* (Salt Lake City, 1924), 44–49.

56. *Salt Lake Telegram,* November 8, 1924. The articles of incorporation are located in the Utah State Archives, Salt Lake City.

57. For more on Held and his band, see *Deseret News,* August 15, 1936; *Salt Lake Telegram,* August 16, 17, 1936. For sources describing the parade, see note 58.

58. *Deseret News,* February 24, 1925; *Citizen,* February 28, 1925; *Bingham News,* February 28, 1925. The *Salt Lake Tribune,* adhering to its policy of ignoring the KKK, made no mention of the parade.

59. *Citizen,* September 27, 1924; February 14, 1925.

60. *Western Recorder* (Payette, Idaho), April 15, 1925; *National Kourier* (Western and Pacific edition), April 24, 1925.

61. Gerlach, *Blazing Crosses,* 107–108.

62. On the collapse of the Klan in Carbon, Utah, and Weber counties, see ibid., 108–15.

63. *Salt Lake Telegram,* June 2, 1925.

64. Salt Lake Corporation, Ordinance No. 1, Ordinance Book for 1925; Records of Salt Lake City Board of Commissioners (1925), 350; *Salt Lake Telegram,* June 18–19, 1925.

65. *Deseret News,* August 29, 30, 1925; *Salt Lake Telegram* August 29, 30, 31, 1925; *Salt Lake Tribune,* August 29, 30, 31, 1925; *Citizen,* August 29, 1925.

66. Interview with Henry E. Mabey, Salt Lake City, August 15, 1980; *Deseret News,* September 23, 1925; *Salt Lake Telegram,* September 23, 1925; *Salt Lake Tribune,* September 24, 1925.

67. There is no record of the deliberations in city commission minutes. See *Deseret News,* September 23, 1925; *Salt Lake Telegram,* September 23, 1925; *Salt Lake Tribune,* September 24, 1925.

68. *Deseret News,* October 6, 1925; *Salt Lake Telegram,* October 6, 1925; *National Klan Kourier,* October 22, 1925.

69. A Klan advertisement disavowing support for Olson and Moran appeared in the *Deseret News,* October 16, 1925.

70. *Deseret News,* November 2, 1925; *Ogden Standard Examiner,* November 2,

1925; *Salt Lake Telegram,* November 2, 1925. The final tabulations were Finch, 12,236; Moran, 10,140; Barnes, 8,342; and Olson, 6,407.

71. *Salt Lake Telegram,* December 23, 1925; *Salt Lake Tribune,* December 24, 1925; *New York Times,* December 24, 1925.

72. For more on the Minute Men, see Robert A. Goldberg, *Hooded Empire: The Ku Klux Klan in Colorado* (Urbana, 1981), 106–112.

73. *Deseret News,* January 26, 1926; *Denver Post,* January 27, 1926.

74. Harry E. Mabey interview.

75. For coverage of the 1926 elections, see Jones, "Utah Politics," 37–44, and Gerlach, *Blazing Crosses,* 123–26.

76. *Deseret News,* October 30, 1926; *Salt Lake Telegram,* October 31, November 1, 1926.

77. Patten appears in the *Salt Lake City Directory* only for 1926.

78. Howard's rather checkered personal life came to a tragic end: in May 1939 he was tossed into the drunk tank of the Salt Lake City jail, where he died as a result of a fistfight with another prisoner. *Deseret News,* May 30, 31, 1939.

79. *Kourier Magazine* (June 1927): 32; Harry E. Mabey interview.

80. The charter of incorporation filed by Cortner in November 1924 had a legal life of twenty years; nonpayment of fees resulted in the expiration of the charter on November 8, 1944.

81. Interview with Sid Lambourne, Salt Lake City, July 25, 1980.

6

Robe and Gown: The Ku Klux Klan in Eugene, Oregon, during the 1920s

ECKARD V. TOY

As two white-robed Klansmen on horseback rode down Willamette Street on January 7, 1922, a flaming cross on nearby Skinner's Butte suddenly brightened the gloomy evening sky above Eugene.[1] This public display of Klan symbols in the center of town signaled the beginning of the second phase of recruiting for Eugene Klan No. 3. The next day, an advertisement in the *Eugene Morning Register* announced a lecture, "The Truth About the Ku Klux Klan," by "Dr. R[euben] H. Sawyer, formerly pastor of the Christian Church of Portland, and for several years Masonic lecturer in England, Canada, and the United States."[2] For fifty cents admission to the Eugene Theatre, Klansmen and the curious could hear Sawyer's lecture and then watch an accompanying motion picture double feature, *The Face at Your Window* and *The Ku Klux Klan Rides Again,* which the advertisement described as "Eight Reels of Thrilling Pictures with a Message of Warning to American Manhood and Womanhood."[3]

The Rev. Sawyer spoke from a stage decorated with a sword, a Bible, an American flag, and a replica of a burning cross. After telling an attentive capacity audience that the Klan "is not 'Anti-Catholic' or 'Anti-Jewish' . . . , but is simply non-Catholic and non-Jewish," Sawyer outlined the corrupting influences of aliens on American society and morals and expressed his suspicions about Japan's goals in Asia and his fear of the "rising flood of color" throughout the world.[4] Although race was not a dominant social issue in Eugene, racism was deeply rooted in Oregon, and Sawyer appealed to the ingrained prejudices of his listeners. "We control Madmen, mad dogs and other mad beasts," he exclaimed. "The negro [*sic*] in whose blood flows the mad desire for race amalgamation is more dangerous than a maddened wild beast and he *must* and *will* be controlled."[5]

Having done his best to stir local passions, Sawyer remained at the Hotel Osburn for several days, conferring with Klansmen and recruiting "prominent men" for the hooded order. But these missionary efforts were not rewarded immediately. In March, after two months had passed with little additional notice of their organization, members of the Eugene Klan publicly donated money to the Salvation Army.[6] This charitable act revived curiosity about the KKK, but the local klavern's membership drive remained stagnant until the elections of 1922 provided controversial social issues and an opportunity for Klansmen to unite in a statewide crusade against private and parochial schools.

It had taken nearly a year for Eugene Klan No. 3 to reach this stage of organizational development and political maturity. The first kleagle had arrived in Oregon from California in early 1921. Shortly after Major Luther I. Powell swore in the first Oregon Klansmen at Medford in southwestern Oregon, other kleagles, newly arrived from California, Texas, and Louisiana, worked their way by train and automobile to isolated communities on the coast and in eastern Oregon and to the numerous small towns of the fertile Willamette Valley where most of the state's population of about eight hundred thousand lived. While Texan Bragg Calloway sought recruits among policemen, firemen, and fraternal groups in Portland, C. N. Jones contacted Masons, Odd Fellows, Elks, and American Legionnaires in Eugene, the largest community in the southern part of the Willamette Valley. When the publicity-minded Powell met with curious and wary public officials in Portland on August 1, 1921, to proclaim the Klansmen's "respect for the law" and to introduce some new converts, he boasted that the provisional Portland Klan had nearly one thousand members and that Klans were organizing rapidly in Astoria, Salem, Tillamook, Ashland, Medford, and Hood River.[7] Several days later, it was "reliably reported" in the *Morning Register* that the Ku Klux Klan had been secretly organizing in Eugene for several weeks.[8]

At first, the editor of the *Eugene Morning Register,* whose newspaper was aligned with the Republican party, sarcastically responded to this intrusion. The Klan, he explained, satisfied the "tribal fondness for mummery not met by other lodges," but he expressed "grave doubts" about Klansmen "parading the streets attired like a cheap ghost in a home talent melodrama," and concluded: "We have a cynical notion that such pillow coverings as are used in this way will be chiefly useful for concealing the lack of furnishings in the wearer's attic."[9] But such public ridicule failed to blunt the Klan's recruiting drive, and by early 1923 Eugene would be described as one of the "thoroughly Ku-Kluxed cities of Oregon."[10] Here and elsewhere in Oregon, the editorial tone generally softened and concern for advertising revenues heightened when the Klan demonstrated its strength in politics and its growing influence in service and fraternal organizations and in many churches.[11]

The Ku Klux Klan may have been new to Oregon, but many of the attitudes and issues it exploited during the 1920s were not.[12] The twentieth century inherited the historical residues of racism, nativism, and anti-Catholicism that were primary components of the social practices and cultural traditions of the early settlers in Oregon, who were overwhelmingly native-born, white, and Protestant.[13] This narrow population base reinforced a moralistic determinism about the cultural imperatives of a chosen people in a promised land and explained, at least in part, the violence directed at Indians and Chinese-Americans in the nineteenth century and the negative attitudes toward Japanese-Americans in the twentieth century.[14] These assumptions about race and society also help to explain why the laws and constitution of Oregon initially banned not only slavery but also free blacks.[15]

Historically, there had been few black residents in Oregon, and most of the state's black population of approximately two thousand in 1920 lived in Portland, a few railroad towns, and some small milltowns. Blacks had seldom been victims of organized violence, but social segregation and racial discrimination were accepted practices in most communities, and segregated neighborhoods and business districts became increasingly common in Portland after World War I. Eugene's few dozen black families, whose men were predominantly railroad employees and women domestic servants, lived in small residential pockets near the Ferry Street Bridge and in west Eugene.

Although the predominantly male Chinese-American population had decreased by one-half since early in the century, there were still several thousand Chinese-Americans in Oregon in 1920, most of them clustered in Portland, which, at one time, had the second largest Chinatown on the Pacific coast. The Japanese-American population in Oregon, though similar in size, was growing and differed from the Chinese-Americans in other significant ways. Because more Japanese-Americans were married, there was a higher proportion of women and children, and these families generally lived in a few milltowns, some urban locations, and in rural areas like the Hood River Valley, where they had begun to purchase land and plant orchards.[16]

Despite Oregon's legacy of racism and the significance of race in Klan dogma, racial issues were less significant than political, educational, and religious issues in the 1920s. Moreover, the racial and moralistic attitudes of Klansmen were not significantly different from those of other Oregonians. While Klansmen accepted a popular and coarse version of racial supremacy as their cultural standard, many reformers embraced a refined form of racial prejudice that blended Anglo-Saxonism and nationalism with concerns about the social and cultural consequences of racial amalgamation and unrestricted immigration. There were also other similarities in attitudes and ideology. Many Oregonians, not just Klansmen, believed that the state should be kept free of alien influences, whether papal or Bolshevik, and that meant using whatever means were necessary to promote patriotism and protect the sanctity of Oregon's public schools and private morals.[17]

While these attitudes send confusing signals to historians, there were other equally confusing contrasts in Oregon's political culture in the 1920s. Agrarianism and vestiges of a small-town past persisted against the inroads of urbanization and rapid technological change, while cosmopolitanism shared an uneasy coexistence with a staid social conformity and a powerful desire to preserve traditional moral values. These social and cultural dichotomies were revealed in full measure in Eugene, where the state university and the local lumber mills stood in stark contrast to one another and to the agricultural heritage of the Willamette Valley. Bootleggers and prostitutes, the camp followers of the rugged army of loggers, trainmen, and millworkers, added another dimension to the contrasting social images in Eugene and multiplied the worries of political conservatives and social reformers alike.

But apprehensions about "the world's oldest profession" had a modern counterpart in fears about the fate of a younger generation, since movie theaters and automobiles, those twin scourges of *Middletown*'s Muncie, Indiana, had also invaded Eugene. In early 1922, following a series of editorials advocating internationalism, disarmament, and the disbanding of the R.O.T.C. unit on campus, the student newspaper, the *Oregon Daily Emerald,* published an editorial about student morals entitled "The Mid-Victorian or the Modern." The editor asked: "Have we not departed too far from the 'mid-Victorian'?"[18] His answer in the affirmative reflected the paradoxes of a generation in flux.

Early in the 1920s, a roving band of evangelists responded to these social and moral problems by conducting revivals and harassing sinners throughout Oregon. That era's premiere evangelist, the Reverend Billy Sunday, who owned a farm in Oregon's Hood River Valley; the Reverend Virgil K. "Bearcat" Allison of the Christian church in Lebanon, Oregon; and Dr. E. J. Bulgin, whose circuit ranged from the Middle West to the Pacific coast, preached to thousands of Oregonians about the sinful nature of modern society and the threats posed by cultural and political radicals. Perhaps it was not planned, but Bulgin's revival in Medford, Oregon, in 1921, and some he conducted in other states coincided with the arrival of Klan kleagles and "escaped nuns" and apostate priests, who repeated old tales of priestly immorality and revived a latent anti-Catholicism. Not to be outdone by itinerant soul-savers, many local ministers and newspaper editors added their jeremiads to this chorus of concerns.[19]

While these social and moral issues provided stimuli for the Klan, there were numerous other reasons for the hooded order's success in Oregon. The transcontinental railroads, the well-developed interurban rail system around Portland and in the Willamette Valley, the rapidly expanding telephone network, and the automobile aided Klan recruiting, contributed to the rapid exchange of information, and boosted attendance at Klan initiations and rallies. Klansmen were also fortunate in their timing, as political parties in the state had reached a critical stage of internal realignment about 1920. Tax issues, the good roads movement, and economic stagnation in agriculture and the timber industry pitted worker against owner, city and town against countryside, and different parts of the state against one another.[20] In addition, the Red Scare of 1919–20 revived prewar memories and wartime fears about the Industrial Workers of the World–the Wobblies–and heightened concerns about unrestricted immigration. In 1921, the KKK thrust itself into this volatile social atmosphere and challenged the direction and mood of conventional politics in Oregon. The Klan, as Luther I. Powell explained to Portland officials, was militantly "devoted" to "one-hundred per cent Americanism" and moral uplift.[21]

The social reservoir from which the Klan drew its members in Oregon represented, in Earl Pomeroy's words, "a collaboration of older and newer strains of population, of advocates and enemies of change."[22] In communities like Eugene, where descendants of pioneer families had long dominated politics and the local economy, the Klan became a countervailing political force, but Klansmen in Eugene also appealed to defenders of traditional culture and gained the support of some social reformers on issues of prohibition, education, and sexual morality.

Opponents of the Klan were also a varied lot. Labor leaders, ministers of mainline churches, and conservative politicians joined Catholics, Jews, and other minorities in resisting the Klan, and William S. U'Ren, the elderly Populist and progressive who was the father of "the Oregon System" of the initiative and referendum, denounced Klansmen as "anarchists."[23] But these categories of opposition fail to explain an even more complex ideological problem, since demands for cultural conformity and racial uniformity were not confined to Klansmen or conservatives. Many social reformers and old progressives, who fought vigorously against the Klan in Oregon, advocated restrictions on immigration and supported the sterilization and educational psychology movements that shaped the scientific racism of the 1920s.

If Oregonians were justifiably disturbed about economic problems and moral issues in the early 1920s, there were few reasons to fear labor radicals, Jews, Catholics, or racial minorities. The Wobblies were few and in disarray in the aftermath of the deportations and political repression of the Red Scare and the adoption of antisyndicalism laws by the state legislature in 1917 and 1919. There were only a few thousand Jews in Oregon, and Roman Catholics comprised only 8 percent of the population. And in a state where native-born citizens were by far in the majority, where blacks totaled only about two thousand in 1920, and where the number of persons of Asian ancestry, other than Japanese-Americans, decreased with each census after 1910, there seemed to be little cause for the formation of an overtly racist and nativist organization.[24] Nevertheless, the KKK grew remarkably fast and became a potent political force between 1921 and 1924. How did this happen and why did so many men join the Ku Klux Klan?

Few Oregonians believed the KKK posed any threat to Oregon's political establishment in 1921. Replying to an inquiry from the *New York World* shortly before opening his reelection campaign, Republican Governor Ben Olcott explained that the Klan had made "practically no impression on our people."[25] He changed his mind after Klansmen engaged in a series of night-riding episodes near Medford in the spring of 1922 and endorsed his political opponents in the primary and general elections. Journalists also vacillated. At first, many of them ridiculed the secrecy and rituals of the hooded order, but, by 1922, as the Oregon Klan grew in numbers and political influence, the majority of newspaper editors adopted a more ambivalent stance. Some small-town newspapers supported the Klan; others maintained a benevolent neutrality. Only a few journalists risked their careers and revenues by crusading against the Klan.[26]

These contradictory reactions were not uncommon, since the Invisible Empire in Oregon was much more than a secret fraternal society. The KKK rapidly emerged as a statewide social movement with a specific political agenda, and, under the aggressive leadership of King Kleagle Luther I. Powell and Grand Dragon Fred L. Gifford, the Oregon Klan achieved greater political success than any other state Klan on the Pacific Slope.[27] Powell, who was from Shreveport, Louisiana, was the most powerful Klansman in the state until early 1922, when Gifford, his Portland protégé, wrested control of the state organization from him and became Grand Dragon of the Realm of Oregon.[28] A former union business agent and supervisor for the Northwestern Electric Company in Portland, Gifford was not a member of the "pioneer" generation in Oregon, but, unlike Powell, he was not an outsider and had long been active in Portland Masonic circles.[29]

Gifford accelerated the Klan's pace of recruitment and strengthened its role in politics. His critics portrayed him as duplicitous and amoral and charged that he intended to establish a Klan political machine with himself as boss. But the Grand Dragon was an enigma. C. C. Chapman, editor of the *Oregon Voter,* interviewed Gifford in early 1922 and wrote that "he radiates a spirit of sincerity, and evidently is very much in earnest, believing he is performing a high patriotic duty . . . in promoting the Ku Klux idea." The Klan, Gifford told Chapman, was "opposed to control of American public affairs by aliens or by so-called Americans whose primary allegiance is to a foreign power." He confirmed that the Klan was "in entire accordance" with the antialien land bill sponsored by the American Legion and the state Grange, and asserted that the Klan was "for compulsory education in the public schools in a real sense. By that I mean that no child should be permitted to be educated in the primary grades at any private school." After outlining the organization's political goals, Gifford told Chapman that "after a few years you will not regard the Klan as a menace."[30]

Despite Gifford's reassuring tone, the Klan had already become a disruptive influence in Oregon. But the KKK was not an aberration. The

Klan adapted easily to Oregon's social and political environment because its doctrines resembled the nativist attitudes and cultural values held by a majority of Oregonians in the years after World War I. The political campaigns of the immediate postwar period reflected the widespread appeal of patriotic and nativist ideas. During a special legislative session called in 1920 to consider economic and tax issues, Oregon legislators unanimously adopted a joint resolution asking Congress to restrict ownership of land by aliens and passed a bill requiring foreign language periodicals, pamphlets, and circulars to print an accompanying literal translation in English. Its American Legion sponsors argued that the bill was necessary to "combat German and Bolshevik propaganda."[31]

At its regular session in 1921, the legislature set an agenda that its allegedly Klan-dominated successor in 1923 would largely complete. Using patriotic arguments, legislators in 1921 introduced bills aimed at regulating the curriculum of private and parochial schools and sectarian colleges, prohibiting the wearing of religious garb by teachers in the public schools, and requiring a loyalty oath for teachers and college professors. Legislative opponents united to defeat these bills by narrow margins in 1921. But many of these legislators then voted for a bill championed by Dr. Bethenia Owens-Adair to permit the sterilization of the socially unfit, and they also voted for an amendment strengthening the state's antisyndicalism law. The state senate briefly reversed that pattern. Governor Olcott, the Oregon State Grange, and the American Legion had endorsed a bill aimed at preventing Japanese-American farmers from purchasing land. While the Oregon House of Representatives passed the bill, senators rejected it. In explaining their vote against the alien land bill many of the senators said that they simply preferred a more comprehensive federal law.[32] Thus, the stage was set for the Klan to enter Oregon politics.

Although taxes and economic reconstruction would be the decisive issues in the elections of 1922, the Klan's endorsement of Democrat Walter Pierce for governor demonstrated the opportunism and shrewdness of its leaders, and Pierce's victory in November appeared to confirm the organization's political influence. The Klan had suddenly become an important factor in both major parties. It helped to elect a Democratic governor, and many members of the Republican-dominated state legislature were Klansmen or had received the organization's endorsement. Once in session, the 1923 legislature quickly and easily passed an alien land law, a law prohibiting teachers in public schools from wearing religious garb, and a law requiring "the teaching of the Constitution of the United States in the public and private schools of the state."[33]

Oregon Klansmen also gained national notoriety in 1922 by campaigning for an initiative measure introduced by the Southern Jurisdiction of Scottish Rite Masons that would abolish private and parochial schools for children between the ages of eight and sixteen. Klansmen and their allies argued that they were on the side of democracy and that the will of the majority would prevail. The Reverend E. V. Stivers of the First Christian Church of Eugene explained that its "proponents" believed the school bill would "provide that the coming generation in this state should be taught as to insure its becoming an all-American generation." Arguing that the bill was "constructive" and "not factional," Stivers concluded: "The home, the school, and the church are the three pillars upon which this nation rests."[34] In an "Introduction" to *The Old Cedar School,* a polemical pamphlet distributed during the campaign, King Kleagle Luther I. Powell described the school issue as "a battle of the mass of humanity against sects, classes, combinations and rings; against entrenched privilege and secret machinations of the favored few to control the less favored many."[35] Voters narrowly approved this controversial measure in the general election of 1922. But after a series of bitterly contested court battles, the United States Supreme Court declared the law unconstitutional in January 1925, eighteen months before it was scheduled to take effect.[36]

Despite these successes, the strength of the Klan vote in the 1923 legislature is difficult to measure. The new laws were not simply products of Klan sponsorship; rather, they reflected the popular appeal of efforts to reinforce conformity in a state with a predominantly white, native-born, and Protestant population. Yet, the surprisingly close vote on the school issue suggests that ethnicity and religious affiliation did not always determine how people would vote. Moreover, the Oregon Klan began to decline long before the Supreme Court decision in 1925.

Although its opponents often insisted that the Klan was monolithic, its unity was fragile from the beginning. Klaverns outside Portland, including Eugene Klan No. 3, periodically and sometimes successfully challenged Gifford's attempts to force or entice them into submission.[37] There were numerous minor controversies, but dissension about which Republican candidate to endorse in the senatorial election of 1924 widened existing fissures between the Portland leaders and those in other communities. Faced with mounting opposition, Gifford resigned as Grand Dragon in early 1925, and the Oregon Klan rapidly disintegrated into small and competing factions.

While the activities of the Klan at the state level are important, the differing perspectives about the motivations and actions of its members can be examined most clearly in their local context. In December 1923, the *Oregon Voter* reported that there were fifty-eight chartered and seven provisionally chartered klaverns in Oregon.[38] Portland had the largest klavern, and the network of Klan political and promotional activities radiated from Gifford's Portland headquarters to nearly every section of the state from 1922 through 1924. But several other klaverns in Oregon, including Eugene, enrolled a larger proportion of the local population and had more and longer lasting political successes. It is this local context that reveals the reasons for the successes and underlines the failures of the Ku Klux Klan in the 1920s, and Eugene, Oregon, provides a social laboratory where issues and leadership can be brought into sharper focus.

Although its population barely exceeded ten thousand in 1920, Eugene ranked as Oregon's fourth-largest city and had many economic advantages over nearby towns. It was centrally located in Lane County, a large and sparsely populated county that extended eastward to scattered logging camps and milltowns in the Cascade Mountains and westward to small fishing villages at Siuslaw Bay on the Pacific Ocean.[39] Officially, Eugene was barely fifty years old by World War I, having been incorporated in 1862, twelve years after Eugene F. Skinner built a cabin on the site. Skinner, who was born in Essex County, New York, had arrived in Oregon from California with his family in 1846, the year Great Britain and the United States signed the treaty partitioning the Oregon Country. Skinner's claim was at the foot of a small hill on the west bank of the Willamette River and near the old Indian trail and the fur trade route linking the Hudson's Bay Company post at Ft. Vancouver with California. The first Willamette River steamboat arrived at the new townsite on March 3, 1857, but the steamboat era was brief, as construction crews for the Oregon and California Railway extended the tracks from Portland to Eugene in 1871. Two decades later, the Southern Pacific Railway completed a direct rail connection with California.

But the local transportation revolution was just beginning. An enterprising businessman introduced mule-powered streetcars to Eugene in

1891, and by 1906 four automobiles competed with the streetcars, other horse-drawn vehicles, and pedestrians. Early in the century, an electric interurban rail system connected Eugene with Portland, slightly more than one-hundred miles distant, and, in 1919, the city constructed an airport.[40] By the mid-1920s, the "good roads" movement had expanded Eugene's hinterland by stimulating the construction of a network of paved highways throughout the Willamette Valley. Automobiles and buses soon became the dominant modes of local transportation, forcing the rapid decline of the interurban system and, by 1927, displacing the last streetcar line in town.[41]

Eugene grew slowly but steadily in the last decades of the nineteenth century, with its population increasing from 861 in 1870 to 3,236 in 1900. As the emerging city entered the twentieth century, it shared a decade of accelerating economic growth with many other towns in the Willamette Valley. By 1910, diversification in agriculture, expansion of grain milling, and shifts in the timber industry nearly tripled Eugene's population to 9,009. But this growth abruptly ceased. Despite the added stimulus of World War I, the decade after 1910 ended in relative economic and social stagnation. The city's population increased only to 10,593 in 1920, as a postwar economic slump slowed the rates of growth in agriculture and the timber industry.[42]

But Eugene quickly regained its economic momentum. In the 1920s, the city's "strategic location on the Pacific Highway" and the Southern Pacific Railroad connected it with the major markets and shipping outlets of San Francisco and Portland and reinforced its economic and political dominance over Lane County. As the county seat, Eugene was the focal point for local politics and for state and federal courts. The city also served as the county's financial and "retail center," with several banks, "nearly half of . . . the retail outlets," and "three-fourths of all sales" in the county. Although it was described as "a town of small stores and specialty shops," four department stores accounted for 11 percent of the retail sales. Its location and resources also made Eugene the medical and cultural center for the southern end of the Willamette Valley. Eugene had a large hospital run by the Catholic Sisters of Mercy, boasted vaudeville and motion picture theaters and two daily newspapers, the *Evening Guard* and the *Morning Register,* which had a combined circulation of nearly sixteen thousand, and it was also the home of the University of Oregon and Eugene Bible University.[43]

Lane County's economy was heavily dependent on agriculture and timber. In 1922, 5,800 of the county's 9,900 workers were employed in farming and agricultural enterprises and another 2,000 worked in the timber industry, with most of the manufacturing enterprises located outside Eugene. The Eugene Fruit Growers Association cannery, the Eugene Woolen Mills, and sawmills and lumber products firms were the principal industrial plants within the city, and the Southern Pacific Railroad yards and the University of Oregon were its largest employers. Although they differed in size and product, each of these employers had seasonal employment patterns that required numerous part-time and migrant laborers.[44] Typically, agriculture and logging attracted large numbers of single men, and towns where they roomed or spent their leisure hours had a disproportionate number of saloons and prostitutes. Neighboring Springfield, even more than Eugene, reflected the uneasy social and political tensions between settled families and migratory loggers. But Eugene also had its share of social outcasts and social radicals, and they mixed uneasily with persons of more conventional mind and behavior.

Oregon's economy recovered rapidly between 1922 and 1927, when timber would again join agriculture as ailing industries. During the years of the Klan's greatest growth from 1921 through 1924, building permits for residential and commercial construction in Eugene increased "by 650%" and Eugeneans in 1925 proudly boasted of the completion of their newest landmark, the Eugene Hotel. The city nearly doubled its population between 1920 and 1930, and by the end of the decade, Eugene's 18,901 residents comprised nearly one-third of the total population of Lane County.[45] Only a few hundred members of racial minorities, a few dozen Jewish families, and several hundred Roman Catholics resided there.[46]

Until the 1890s, Eugene had been essentially a small farming town with virtually no ethnic, religious, or racial diversity. Nevertheless, this outward appearance of uniformity and stability was deceiving. Eugene sat precariously balanced on the geographical edge of political conflict in the 1850s, when antislavery sentiments in the northern part of Oregon clashed with the more traditional Democratic party alignment of southwestern Oregon. Both parts of the state shared anti-Catholic attitudes, which dated back to the missionary period of the 1830s and 1840s. These attitudes revived briefly in later decades with the Know-Nothing party and the American Protective Association, and in the

1890s readers in Eugene even "found populism mixed with anti-Catholicism in the *Eugene Broad-Axe.*"[47]

Despite these underlying social and religious tensions, politics in Eugene and Lane County in the early twentieth century had few distinctive characteristics. After giving Democratic candidate William Jennings Bryan a narrow margin of victory in 1896, Lane County voters usually followed national trends in presidential elections, deviating only in 1916 by favoring Republican Charles Evans Hughes over President Woodrow Wilson. That vote illustrated what would become the most distinguishing characteristic of politics in Lane County–the Republican presidential vote exceeded the national average throughout the 1920s.[48] Although the victory margins were typically smaller, state and local elections revealed a similar tilt toward the Republicans.

But local politics also displayed other characteristics in the early 1920s. "Bigotry and prejudice, suspicion and discord, strife and hate," Salem reporter Harry N. Crain wrote in 1922, "are the returns Eugene and Lane county people have realized on their investment in the Ku Klux Klan."[49] By the time the *Morning Register* first reported that the Klan was organizing in Eugene, more than eighty men had already joined the provisional chapter that would become Eugene Klan No. 3.[50] Shortly after arriving in Eugene, Kleagle C. N. Jones convinced several dozen war veterans and younger members of local fraternal organizations and service clubs to join the hooded order. Once organized and under the leadership of Exalted Cyclops Frederick S. Dunn, the head of the Latin Department in the University of Oregon, these Eugene Klansmen equated their "One-Hundred Per Cent Americanism" with anti-Catholic agitation. They sought to remove Catholics from public offices and Catholic teachers from the public schools. They also opposed Mercy Hospital and vigorously resisted the effort to establish a Newman House for Catholic students at the University of Oregon.[51]

Of 140 identifiable members of Klan No. 3 in 1922, slightly more than 60 percent held middle-class occupations and 10 percent were skilled and semiskilled laborers (Table 6.1). Nearly 80 percent of these Eugene Klansmen were married, and, whether they were homeowners or renters, a majority lived in the most exclusive or most stable neighborhoods. They ranged in age from about twenty to sixty, with the majority between thirty and fifty-five. Approximately one-quarter of the Klansmen were business owners or managers, but the membership included a cross section of occupations in Eugene: the owner and the manager of the Ford agency and a half-dozen of their automobile salesmen and mechanics; a local agent, foreman, and several employees of the Southern Pacific Railroad; two attorneys; the owner of an insurance agency and his salesmen; a shoe store owner and his clerks; several independent businessmen; a newspaper publisher; a dentist; a surgeon; two city officials; a county commissioner; the local commander of the National Guard; the rector of the Episcopal church; a Latin professor, and the university football coach. Several Klansmen were members of the local American Legion post and most of them belonged to one or more fraternal organizations.

TABLE 6.1

Occupational Distribution of Eugene Klansmen, 1921–22

Occupational Status Group	Number	Percent of Members Identified
High nonmanual	12	8.6
Middle nonmanual	44	31.4
Low nonmanual	34	24.3
Skilled	7	5.0
Semiskilled and Service	13	9.3
Unskilled	3	2.0
Unknown	27	19.3
	140	99.9

Occupational status group categories conform to the status group classification used in Robert A. Goldberg, *Hooded Empire: The Ku Klux Klan in Colorado* (Urbana: University of Illinois Press, 1981), 183–86.

If kleagles initially tended to contact members of fraternal organizations and social clubs, the work place was also an important source of new members. Although the Eugene Klan enrolled a larger proportion of blue-collar members after 1923, recruiting techniques differed only slightly. A Eugene Klansman in 1923 advised an Albany Klansman to pick names from the city directory of "men who were known to be on the right side."[52] During its first two years, the Eugene Klan enrolled many younger businessmen and aspiring politicians, who intended to use the secrecy and unity of the KKK to frighten moral reprobates and to mobilize opposition to entrenched economic and political leaders.

Several Klansmen were among the new officers elected by the Eugene Chamber of Commerce and the Elks Club in 1922, and Klansmen led the local American Legion post for several years. Reporter Harry Crain, who wrote a series of articles about the Klan for the *Salem Capital Journal,* described the Eugene Elks Club in 1922 as "little more than a meeting place for Klansmen," since its new directors, Benjamin F. Dorris, Clyde Fisk, and Major William G. White, the local commander of the National Guard, and Joseph E. Turnbull, the club's secretary, were all prominent members of the KKK.[53] The Klan went beyond notoriety to a degree of respectability and longevity with a listing for its headquarters in the Beckwith Building and for its secretary, Michael J. Thompson, in *Polk's Eugene Directory* in 1925.[54]

Eugene Klansmen eagerly jumped into the political arena in 1922, campaigning for a slate of candidates for state and federal offices recommended by Grand Dragon Gifford. Although several of their candidates, including a Eugene school principal running for state superintendent of public education, suffered defeat, Klansmen found allies among Protestant ministers, nativists, public schoolteachers, and social reformers during the campaign for the Oregon School Bill.[55] Lark Bilyeau, the president of the Eugene Compulsory Education League and no Klansman, expressed widely held sentiments in arguing that the school bill would guarantee that "our people will become knit into one common bond of peace, harmony, and brotherly love . . . "[56] Sixty-nine percent of Lane County voters, the highest percentage in any county in the state, approved the measure. Lane was one of fourteen counties where voters favored the school bill; Charles Hall, the Republican gubernatorial candidate endorsed by the Klan who lost in the primary election; and Walter Pierce, the Democratic gubernatorial candidate endorsed by the Klan who won the general election.[57]

Since they had only a few months to mobilize their political forces, Eugene Klansmen could not take full credit for this outcome. But they were beneficiaries of this political realignment, and they displayed a pragmatic approach to local politics. After failing to displace the Republican Old Guard in Lane County, Klansman tried briefly to create a slate of independents, but had more success working within the Democratic party. Local Democrats, who had eagerly sought Klan support, discovered, too late, that support could quickly turn into domination. Klansmen proved so effective in infiltrating the county's Democratic Central Committee in 1922 that the *Eugene Evening Guard* chided:

The Bourbon ship comes 'round the bend,
Good-bye, old party, good-bye.
All loaded down with Ku Klux men,
Good-bye, old party, good-bye.[58]

This flirtation between Klan No. 3 and the local Democratic party initially caused some businessmen to defect from Klan ranks. It also attracted "new faces and new issues," and the relationship did not end abruptly.[59] In 1924, Alta King, an attorney, the city recorder, and a Klansman, was elected chairman of the Lane County Democratic Central Committee.[60]

The drive for moral purification of the community went beyond opposition to prostitution, support for prohibition, and the school bill initiative. Although only two city and county officials and only 3 percent of the teachers in Eugene's public school system were Catholics, Eugene Klansmen vigorously campaigned to purge Catholic teachers from the public schools. Klansmen John B. Patterson and A. E. Brigham lobbied the school board to dismiss three women whose teaching contracts were under review. All were Roman Catholics and, though Klansmen denied that they had singled out the teachers because of their faith, critics charged that religion, not competence, was the only reason behind the ouster attempt. Despite widespread criticism and opposition from two of its members, a majority of the school board voted to dismiss the teachers. The controversy erupted again in the next school board election. L. L. Ray, a board member who had vigorously opposed the Oregon School Bill and defended the teachers, lost his bid for reelection to a woman, sponsored by the Klan, who pledged to dismiss all Catholic teachers from the public school system. In an interview nearly fifty years later, Ray recalled that he "was soundly defeated" in one of the largest school election voter turnouts in memory.[61]

Mercy Hospital came under attack on several fronts in the early 1920s. Some Eugeneans opposed the hospital simply because it was run by Catholics. But the battle took on a new dimension when hospital administrators, facing tax delinquency charges, argued that the hospital was a charitable institution and therefore exempt from taxation. Critics countered by arguing that such a status would give Mercy Hospital an unfair advantage in competition with other private hospitals. Klansmen joined the campaign against granting the tax exemption and were allegedly involved in an attempt to purchase delinquent tax receipts in order to foreclose on the hospital. Mercy Hospital survived these assaults, but its foes carried the fight to the state legislature, and, in the 1923 session, state representative Ben F. Kenny of Eugene introduced a bill to tax "literary, benevolent, charitable and scientific institutions . . . operated for compensation."[62] Although Kenny admitted that the hospital was his primary target, he had no record of a Klan affiliation, and in 1922 the KKK had apparently opposed his election. Despite the success of other Klan-sponsored legislation in 1923, Kenny's bill lost by a narrow margin. This became a moot issue a few years later when the Oregon Supreme Court ruled in favor of the hospital.

Just as these controversies began to disrupt Eugene's political calm, Klan No. 3 found itself under attack. Following a shooting incident between Klansmen and alleged bootleggers in Inglewood, California, in the spring of 1922, officers in Los Angeles confiscated Klan membership lists from the office of Grand Goblin William S. Coburn, who was in charge of recruiting for California, Nevada, Oregon, Washington, and Idaho. The names of several dozen Eugene Klansmen were on the lists that Los Angeles District Attorney Lee Woolwine released to the press.[63] This public exposure of its membership pierced the Klan's protective veil of secrecy, and several members of Klan No. 3 suddenly lost interest in the organization. Fearing additional defections, local Klan leaders launched a new recruiting campaign that featured initiations and cross-burning ceremonies on the hills overlooking Eugene and Springfield. Much to their chagrin, the *Salem Capital Journal* published a second set of names after three young girls, who had witnessed one of these fiery initiation rites on Emerald Heights, found a list of eighty Eugene Klansmen.[64]

This second incident caused additional members to quit attending meetings, but none of them publicly repudiated the Klan and several new candidates joined Klan No. 3 after recognizing the names of prominent citizens among its members.[65] The elections of 1922 gave additional momentum to Klan No. 3, which would grow to an estimated 400 to 450 members by the fall of 1922.[66] In June, shortly after the primary election, a one-half page advertisement in the *Morning Register* announced that the Reverend Mr. Sawyer would return to Eugene to lecture and show Klan motion pictures at the Eugene Theatre on June 29 and 30. But Sawyer had to cancel his appearance, having become enmeshed in the nasty factionalism that resulted in Hiram Wesley Evans replacing Klan founder, William Joseph Simmons, at the helm of the national Klan in Atlanta.[67] L. E. Burger lectured in Sawyer's place. Burger could not match Sawyer's flamboyant style, but he displayed ample evidence of motivational salesmanship. Claiming that Klan membership in Oregon exceeded thirty-five thousand men in thirty-one klaverns, Burger boldly proposed that Klansmen build in Portland a three-million-dollar auditorium to seat fifteen-thousand persons.[68] Oregon Klansmen never achieved this goal, but the fact Burger even advanced this grandiose scheme demonstrated the confidence of Klan leaders as their organization approached the peak of its power.

During this period of expanding membership and increasing political activity, many klaverns planned local projects that were intended to improve the Klan's image and expand its public role. Some Eugene Klansmen, for example, wanted to draw the University of Oregon into their orbit, thus gaining legitimacy for the Klan program and also providing a constantly renewable source of members. But university administrators and the student newspaper discouraged faculty and students from joining the Klan, and graduates of the university were among the most outspoken opponents of the Klan in Eugene and elsewhere in the state. "The University campus is no more a place for the white robed Ku Klux Klan, than is the great state of Oregon," the *Oregon Daily Emerald* editorialized. "Such an organization as this," the editor concluded, "must never be countenanced on a college campus."[69]

When Eugene Klansmen finally recognized that their effort to influence the university had no chance, they turned their wrath against the school, spreading rumors of Catholic influence on campus and contributing to the erosion of the previously positive town/gown relationships. These actions had ramifications beyond the town and the campus, since the University of Oregon had a unique position in Eugene. It was a community within a community, and it had a statewide educational and political constituency. Since its founding in 1876, the university had grown steadily, if slowly, and Eugene businessmen had an economic stake in it. After a brief period of readjustment following World War I, the university "entered a new era of rich productivity." A statewide property tax adopted in 1920 momentarily eased the university's fiscal problems and contributed to a "minor building boom" on campus.[70] Other significant changes accompanied this physical expansion. "The 1920's," explained historian James H. Hitchman, "proved to be a time of administrative reorganization, improved quality of faculty, expansion of the student body to over three thousand, increase in research funds, growth of graduate work, new facilities, and numerous additions to the curriculum."[71] Another feature of that decade was visible in the transformation of the social atmosphere on campus, as intercollegiate athletics and fraternities and sororities often resembled the stereotype of student life in the "Roaring Twenties."[72]

These changes on campus created new problems. While the growth of the university pleased many businessmen, some faculty members deplored and resisted the changes in administration and curriculum and were apprehensive about the dominance of the "Greek system." Off campus, the rapid increase in Eugene's nonstudent blue-collar population matched the increases in enrollment and contributed to town/gown tensions. The university also faced challenges outside Eugene. Aside from athletic rivalry and periodic fights between students, the university had to compete for state funds with Oregon Agricultural College, the state's land grant institution located less than fifty miles away in Corvallis. William Jasper Kerr, the ambitious president of O.A.C., "had bested his university counterpart in session after session of the state legislature" and wanted to establish administrative hegemony over the university in Eugene by creating a combined educational establishment under his leadership.[73] In the midst of these challenges, the university's popular and successful president, Prince Lucien Campbell, resigned because of ill health, and a committee of three administrators governed the university from 1924 to 1926.

The full extent of Klan influence among faculty and students is impossible to determine. Klansmen were cloaked in secrecy, and they had few targets on campus. Although there were many rumors about pro-Catholic sympathies on campus, only 7 percent of the students and 5 percent of faculty members were Roman Catholics. There were few faculty members from other minority groups and almost no black or Asian students during the 1920s. And there was no need for a Klan to promote racial segregation when university administrators had already "refused to allow black women to room in the college dorms with white women."[74] Unlike Rice University and a few other colleges, the University of Oregon never had a separate student klavern, but the Eugene Klansmen initially enjoyed success on campus. The head of the university's Latin Department was Exalted Cyclops of Klan No. 3 during its early years, and many other members of the local klavern had ties with the university. Some Klansmen owned businesses that catered to students, several of them were alumni, a few were faculty members, and a half-dozen were students, including at least two members of Kappa Sigma fraternity. In addition, the university football coach, C. A. "Shy" Huntington, and the graduate manager, Jack Benefiel, were members of Klan No. 3, while student Maurice L. Willcox delivered such a convincing pro-Klan monologue in his extempore speech class in 1923 that Klansmen printed and distributed copies of his "Klan Americanism" speech throughout the state.[75]

Shortly after the primary election in the spring of 1922, Dean Henry D. Sheldon of the university's school of education confided to historian Joseph Schafer, a former University of Oregon faculty member who had become Director of the Wisconsin State Historical Society:

> We are having the hottest campaign you ever heard of here over the Ku Klux Klan. Ben Olcott, the governor, is out against the Klan. One of the other candidates is supposed to be backing it. Several of the members of our august faculty have joined its ranks. In fact the president of it is said to be our old friend, the head of the Latin Department. As is usual in such cases the wildest rumors are afloat. A large number of faculty members are supposed to be Jesuits in disguise. The whole thing is very silly and yet is likely to have considerable influence in the next year or so.

In his reply to Sheldon, Schafer noted that he had recently seen an article about the Oregon Klan in a Madison newspaper. "I personally feel," he concluded, "that men who participate in a movement of that kind have forgotten a good deal of fairly recent history."[76]

But Professor Frederick S. Dunn, the focal point of these letters, was a teacher of Latin, not history, and he was an early and ardent member of Klan No. 3. Despite his academic credentials, including an M.A. in classical languages from Harvard University, Dunn was a typical Eugene Klansman. He was not an outsider. He was born in Eugene in 1872, educated in its public schools, and graduated from the University of Oregon in 1892. Dunn earned a second bachelor's degree from Harvard University in 1894, and began graduate studies on the Ivy League campus the following year. In 1896, Dunn interrupted his graduate work to accept a position at Willamette University in Salem, Oregon, and taught at this staunchly Methodist school until 1898, when he got the opportunity to return to his hometown and teach Latin at the University of Oregon. Dunn adapted quickly to the familiar academic and social environment of Eugene, completing the work for his M.A. degree in 1902 and taking an active part in community affairs as a member of the Methodist Episcopal Church, the Republican party, "all branches of masonry," and the Elks Club. On campus, he served for many years as faculty sponsor of the YMCA chapter.[77]

Although he was not a major participant in campus politics, by the 1920s Dunn was a member of the campus "Old Guard," upset with dilution of the classical curriculum, and disturbed by the changing character of the school, the community, and American society. Although an authority on campus affairs characterized him as "a typical Oregon primitive," Dunn was neither slavishly provincial nor obsessively prudish.[78] During the early 1920s, he continued to work on a novel about Caesar's Gallic Wars, and his lectures "to the men of the faculty on 'Solar and Phallic Religions' " in 1921 and 1922 drew appreciative audiences.[79]

Dunn made no secret of his dual roles as college professor and Exalted Cyclops of Klan No. 3, but student inertia and faculty resistance nullified attempts to expand the role of the Klan on campus. Failing in that effort, Klansmen concentrated on protecting students from subversion by radical ideas and alien influences. They opposed controversial speakers and attempted to restrict the activities of Newman Hall, the newly established religious center for Catholic students. Father Edwin V. O'Hara of St. Mary's Catholic Church in Eugene officially opened Newman Hall at 13th and Kincaid streets, barely two blocks from campus, in October 1921.[80] O'Hara stocked Newman Hall with a small library of religious books and taught short courses in English literature and religion that were open to all students. Although considered an aggressive step by critics, this practice simply followed the well-established example of the campus YMCA and YWCA clubs. The "Ys," with the blessing of the university administration, had played an active role on campus for many years. In addition to sponsoring dances and speakers, they maintained a student lounge on campus, ran the official job register for students, and also offered short courses in religion and ethics. Local Roman Catholics, Jews, and religious liberals had often and unsuccessfully criticized this apparently official sanction of these Protestant Christian Associations. Now, civil libertarians faced a dilemma about whether to side with the Klan or the Newman Club, and they divided on the issue. Klansmen did not face that dilemma. Although O'Hara did not request that the Newman Club be granted the same status on campus as the YMCA and YWCA organizations, Klansmen and other militant Protestants rejected any campus role for Newman

Hall and sought to tax it while leaving the "Y"s' exemption intact. This effort failed and, like Mercy Hospital, the Newman Club survived the ordeal.

Having gained notoriety rather than a victory, Klan No. 3 largely abandoned its attempts to influence the university. Although economic self-interest prevailed over any effort to hurt the institution, local Klansmen increasingly regarded the university as an enemy rather than a potential ally. But that attitude mattered little to most students. By the fall of 1923, an expanded athletic program, the new curriculum, and a new wave of social activities diverted their attention. For students, the Klan was rapidly becoming a historical curiosity.

But appearances were deceiving. Eugene Klansmen had never devoted their full attention to the university. The political campaigns of 1922 took most of their time and energy, and members of Klan No. 3 were eager participants in parades, rallies, and initiations, traveling by car and train to communities throughout the Willamette Valley. This mix of fraternal and political activities continued to attract new members to Klan No. 3, and the political events of 1923 drew even more attention to the local Klan. The school board conflict of 1922 was simply the beginning of a series of local political victories attributed to Klan influence. After candidates endorsed by the Klan won nearly every municipal office in Eugene in the elections of 1922, Klansmen and their allies turned their attention to incumbent Mayor O. C. Peterson and two officials he had appointed, City Attorney O. H. Foster and Chief of Police Chris Christensen, the latter a Roman Catholic. While religion may have been a factor in this dispute, complaints about an understaffed police force and their failure to enforce prohibition and stop prostitution placed the city attorney and chief of police in the center of the controversy. In the spring of 1923, after several months of heightening tensions within the city and its administration, the mayor and his two appointees abruptly resigned. Rumors circulated that the Klan had focused attention on Christensen because of his Catholic religion. Whatever the principal reason for the resignations, the *Oregon Voter* asserted that "Eugene now appears to be one of the thoroughly Ku Kluxed cities of Oregon. The resignation of the mayor, city attorney, and Catholic chief of police leaves the city administration in control of Gifford's secessionists."[81]

In fact, the Eugene Klan was less bound to Grand Dragon Gifford than C. C. Chapman of the *Oregon Voter* knew. Gifford and the Oregon Klan both reached their peak of power in 1923 as opposition, the apparent success of their legislative agenda, and the lack of new issues at the state level eroded Klan membership. But klaverns in Eugene and some other communities continued to thrive because local issues provided new stimuli. In Eugene, for example, a bizarre episode involving the Doukhobor religious sect from Canada combined with the senatorial and presidential election campaigns of 1924 to temporarily stem the decline of Klan No. 3.

Disillusioned by the treatment of his communitarian sect in Canada, Russian exile Peter Vasillevich Verigin announced a plan to move 10,000 of his followers from their farms and villages in British Columbia to the Willamette Valley, where he planned to establish a satellite community. The Doukhobors' reputation for radical forms of protest preceded them, and, in January 1924, Lane County residents reacted with shock to the news that Verigin had purchased 875 acres of farmland in three parcels located only eight miles from Eugene and that he planned to buy an additional 10,000 acres in the county. Verigin's announcement pushed local political controversies aside, and former enemies would become allies in opposing this new threat. When a small contigent of Doukhobors arrived in March 1924, the Eugene post of the American Legion, whose commander, George Love, was also a Klansman, adopted a resolution condemning the "invasion." Verigin's assurances that the Doukhobors would be law-abiding citizens failed to assuage local opinion, and opponents escalated the campaign against them. Love spoke to organizations throughout the county outlining the Legion's position on the Doukhobors and seeking to mobilize opposition against them. In his dual role as Legionnaire and Klansman, Love confirmed, as other examples have suggested, how easy it was to blend the ideas and goals of one organization with those of another.[82]

Just as this battle against the Doukhobors gained momentum, Eugene Klansmen found themselves aligned with several other klaverns in opposition to Grand Dragon Gifford, who wanted to dictate the Klan's choice of a candidate for the United States Senate seat of Republican Charles L. McNary in 1924. While the popular McNary delayed announcing that he would run for a second term, some of his potential challengers in the Republican primary traveled from klavern to klavern seeking endorsements. When Gifford hesitated to name a challenger to McNary, klaverns outside Portland supported different Republicans. Klan No. 3 endorsed Kaspar K. Kubli, a Portland printer, the Speaker of the Oregon House of Representatives, a U of O alumnus, a graduate of Harvard Law School, and a Klansman. McNary, who had little to fear from any of the potential challengers, neither sought Klan support nor rejected it. He easily won the Republican primary in May and would win a convincing victory over his Democratic opponent in the general election in November.[83] Although thousands of Klansmen, including the Grand Dragon, attended a Memorial Day rally in Tillamook in 1924, the primary election campaign demonstrated that the unified Klan of 1922 had suddenly become the disorganized Klan of 1924.

With the primary election over, the Doukhobor issue simmering, and the fall campaign months away, Eugene Klansmen had an opportunity to recapture public attention when they hosted a large parade and an initiation at the Lane County Fairgrounds on June 27, 1924. This would be one of the state Klan's last major activities, but it was also a reminder that the hooded order was not dead.[84] Hundreds of Klansmen and their families from Portland, Grants Pass, Ashland, Medford, Roseburg, Salem, Corvallis, Albany, McMinnville, and other towns drove to Eugene in car caravans, while dozens of others arrived by train. It was a festive occasion for the Klansmen, and the Saturday night parade attracted thousands of spectators, although organizers were disappointed that only about four hundred Klansmen, some Women of the Klan, and a few Royal Riders of the Red Robe marched through downtown Eugene, instead of the two to four thousand marchers they had expected.[85] The Eugene city band and the local Independent Order of Odd Fellows' band accompanied the marchers in the parade, which took place against the backdrop of a fiery cross and fireworks on Skinner's Butte. Afterward, families and friends gathered at the fairgrounds to watch an elite degree team from Grants Pass conduct an initiation ceremony for dozens of new Klansmen from Eugene and nearby towns. Bathed in the glow of a huge cross "lighted with red electric bulbs," Imperial Lecturer C. R. Mathis, in a reference to the Democratic National Convention then underway, told the large crowd: "The great question tonight is whether the Democratic party will stand for one hundred per cent Americanism or for Rome." Later that night, Klan No. 3 fed more than five hundred

Klansmen at a banquet in the National Guard armory, while more than one hundred Klan officers celebrated at the Osborn Hotel, and the degree team from Grants Pass "was entertained at the Peter Pan" restaurant.[86]

Compared to the parade, events of the summer were merely an anticlimax. During the lull before the fall election campaign, Klansmen and their allies revived the Doukhobor issue. In August 1924, Legion Commander Love, accompanied by M. J. "Mike" Thompson, the secretary of Klan No. 3, addressed an anti-Doukhobor rally in Junction City, a small town with a large Scandinavian Lutheran population about fifteen miles north of Eugene. Speaking to more than one hundred concerned citizens, Love and Thompson described the potential threat, and urged Junction City residents to oppose any attempt by the Doukhobors to purchase land in the northern part of Lane county. Some local residents expressed their willingness to take up arms against the invaders, but the conflict never reached that stage, since Verigin's murder by dissident sectarians later that year ended the abortive attempt by the Doukhobors to colonize Lane County. In fact, few Doukhobors had moved to the county, and they eventually sold their land and returned to Canada.[87]

These events of 1924 prolonged the life of Klan No. 3, but the KKK was in general retreat throughout most of Oregon by the end of 1924. The defection in that year of Lem A. Dever, the colorful and egocentric editor of the state Klan's newspaper, *The Western American,* was the final blow. Gifford abruptly resigned from his position as Grand Dragon early in 1925, leaving the Oregon Klan adrift and leaderless. Although a new recruiting campaign initiated by the Atlanta headquarters kept some klaverns alive for several years, attempts to reorganize the Realm of Oregon faltered and then failed. The indefatigable King Kleagle Luther I. Powell and a few allies tried unsuccessfully to resurrect the Klan in a slightly different form in 1926, when they incorporated an Improved Order of Klansmen in Oregon. Powell declared that the new organization would be independent of other national Klans, and he hoped to establish its headquarters in Salem or Eugene where other anti-Gifford factions still met.[88] But there was little interest in a synthetic Klan, and even an Improved Order of Klansmen did not find a hospitable environment in Eugene in 1926.

Several factors contributed to this change in attitude. Eugene Klansmen had achieved some of their principal goals, exposure in the newspapers caused some defections, and political parties entered a period of relative stability after 1924. Among the more significant factors was the resurgence of the local economy, which swept away much of the discontent that had contributed to the early growth of the Klan. As Henry Sheldon noted in early 1922: "The mills are opening again. Western Oregon is reasonably prosperous; eastern Oregon is slowly picking up out of its condition of bankruptcy."[89] A series of railroad construction projects, which brought new jobs, increased population, and money to Eugene in the mid-1920s, provided access to large stands of virgin timber and improved freight and passenger service with California. After 1926, when the Southern Pacific Railroad completed its Natron cutoff through the Cascade Mountains, Eugene became "the most important division point in Western Oregon" and community leaders celebrated with the "Trail to Rail" pageant, exchanging hoods for pioneer garb.[90]

Exactly when Klan No. 3 died is uncertain. It did not collapse suddenly, and a klavern in Cottage Grove, twenty miles south of Eugene, continued to meet until the mid-1930s. But the economic depression of that decade imposed its own limitations on the Klan, and even these vestigial remains of the Invisible Empire soon withered away. An attempt by Gifford, Dever, and iconoclastic Socialist Tom Burns to revive the Oregon Klan in 1937 failed miserably.[91]

If there is an emerging consensus about the Ku Klux Klan, it is the recognition that local issues and interests determined its success or failure in the 1920s. When judged only by its ideology, there would seem to be little reason for the KKK to thrive in Eugene, since the city's population, like that of the state, was overwhelmingly white, native-born, and Protestant. Basically, Klansmen in Eugene sought to keep things that way. But many Eugene Klansmen were salesmen or relatively young owners or managers of local businesses, who had a stake in a developing economy. Thus, in a time of political realignment, the Klan provided a means to challenge what they perceived as entrenched economic and political interests that often resisted change.

While violence was uncommon in Eugene, and in Oregon generally, Klansmen effectively used other types of social coercion and political processes to control racial and religious minorities. But these consequences of actions sometimes obscure the reasons for them. Did Oregonians, for example, simply confuse religious bigotry with patriotism? Was the attempt to purge the Catholic teachers from the public schools in Eugene merely a symbolic gesture or was it a logical extension of the compulsory school bill? Did these actions have only cultural significance or was Catholicism also perceived as a primary cause of social ills? The Catholic position on pro-hibition and social problems identified with ethnic groups in east-ern cities often triggered negative responses toward the church and its members. In "The Ku Kluxing of Oregon," which he wrote for *Outlook* magazine in 1923, journalist Waldo Roberts explained that the Klan's "appeal for 'a moral uplift' had been highly effective" in Oregon.[92]

If some questions about the Ku Klux Klan have been resolved, others remain unanswered or only partly answered. The Klan's sec-recy, discipline, and structure provided the means to mobilize public opinion and influence political parties. Historians need to trace the cross-fertilization of ideas and attitudes through the social network of parties, organizations, and communities, since fraternal ties and religious institutions reinforced economic interests and educational goals. During the first phase of organization, Klansmen in Eugene represented a cross section of the community. As the Klan declined in strength, its social composition shifted toward a larger blue-collar component and Klansmen attempted to substitute fraternalism for political activities.

What induced men to join the Klan and why did so many of them leave the organization so soon? In 1952, nearly thirty years after her late husband had served as the Exalted Cyclops of the Oregon City klavern, Mrs. Rosa E. Green explained to journalist Stewart Holbrook: "I think it was curiosity and politics as well as boredom [that] made people join" the Klan.[93] Six years later, Mrs. Green wrote to Holbrook about her recent conversation with the widow of another Oregon City Klansman. "[Mrs. Dollar] and I both agreed," Mrs. Green confided, "that most of the ex-members were ashamed they ever were members. But that was part of your Americana of the '20s, at least in Oregon."[94]

NOTES

1. *Eugene Morning Register,* January 8, 1922.
2. Sawyer served as Grand Lecturer of the Pacific Northwest Domain of the

Klan until August 1922. See Lawrence J. Saalfeld, *Forces of Prejudice in Oregon, 1920-1925* (Portland, 1984), 46.

3. *Eugene Morning Register,* January 8, 10, 1922.

4. Ibid., January 12, 1922.

5. Reuben H. Sawyer, *The Truth About the Invisible Empire of the Knights of the Ku Klux Klan* (Portland, 1922), 12.

6. *Eugene Morning Register,* March 22, 1922.

7. *Portland Oregonian,* July 31, August 2, 1921; *Eugene Morning Register,* July 8, 1921; E. Kimbark MacColl, *The Growth of a City: Power and Politics in Portland, Oregon, 1915-1950* (Portland, 1979), 160–61; Kenneth T. Jackson, *The Ku Klux Klan in the City,* (New York, 1967), 196–97.

8. *Eugene Morning Register,* August 7, 1921.

9. Ibid.

10. *Oregon Voter,* May 26, 1923.

11. Charles Fisher, the publisher and editor of the *Eugene Evening Guard,* which was aligned with the Democratic party, strongly opposed the KKK; but Joseph E. Shelton, the paper's co-owner and advertising manager, was a Klansman. See Warren C. Price, *The Eugene Register-Guard: A Citizen of the Community* (Portland, 1976), 134, 155–67.

12. Actually, the Ku Klux Klan was not completely new to Oregon. An organization opposing Chinese laborers in the Oregon City Woolen Mills adopted that name in early 1869. See Eckard V. Toy, "The Ku Klux Klan in Oregon; Its Program and Character" (M.A. thesis, University of Oregon, 1959), 22.

13. See Priscilla Knuth, "Nativism in Oregon" (M.A. thesis, Reed College, 1945), and Malcolm Clark, Jr., "The Bigot Disclosed: 90 Years of Nativism," *Oregon Historical Quarterly* 75 (June 1974): 108–90.

14. See Patricia N. Limerick, *The Legacy of Conquest: The Unbroken Past of the American West* (New York, 1987), and Eckard V. Toy, " 'Promised Land' or Armageddon? History, Survivalists, and the Aryan Nations in the Pacific Northwest," *Montana, The Magazine of Western History* 36 (Summer 1986): 80–82.

15. *Constitution of the State of Oregon,* Article I, Sections 34 and 35; Article II, Section 6.

16. See Elizabeth McLagan, *A Peculiar Paradise: A History of Blacks in Oregon, 1788-1940* (Portland, 1980); and Yuji Ichioka, *The Issei: The World of the First Generation Japanese Immigrants, 1885-1924* (New York, 1988).

17. For additional historical background, see Eckard V. Toy, "The Ku Klux Klan in Oregon," in J. Edward Thomas and Carlos Schwantes, eds., *Experiences in a Promised Land: Essays in Pacific Northwest History* (Seattle, 1986), 269–86.

18. *Oregon Daily Emerald,* January 7, 1922.

19. Toy, "The Klan in Oregon; Its Program and Character," 1–25. The controversial Dr. Bulgin, who conducted a series of revivals in Medford shortly before Luther I. Powell organized the Klan there, had close ties with Klansmen throughout Oregon, California, and Indiana, among other places on his itinerary. Billy Sunday conducted periodic revivals in Oregon while visiting his farm in the Hood River Valley.

20. James D. Ziegler, "Epilogue to Progressivism: Oregon, 1920–1924" (M.A. thesis, 1958), 10–12; Dorothy O. Johansen and Charles M. Gates, *Empire of the Columbia: A History of the Pacific Northwest* (New York, 1967), 493.

21. MacColl, *The Growth of a City,* 164–65.

22. Earl Pomeroy, *The Pacific Slope: A History of California, Oregon, Washington, Idaho, Utah, and Nevada* (New York, 1965), 226.

23. *Portland Oregonian,* August 4, 1921.

24. *Fourteenth Census of the United States, 1920: Population,* II, 46.

25. Telegram from *New York World* ,and reply, September 22, 1921, in Ben Olcott Papers, Special Collections, University of Oregon, Eugene.

26. George E. Turnbull, *An Oregon Crusader* (Portland, 1955), 106.

27. For the few studies of the Klan in Oregon communities, see Eckard V. Toy, "The Ku Klux Klan in Tillamook, Oregon," *Pacific Northwest Quarterly* 53 (April 1962): 60–64; William Toll, "Progress and Piety: The Ku Klux Klan and Social Change in Tillamook, Oregon," *Pacific Northwest Quarterly* 69 (April 1978): 75–85; Jackson, *Klan in the City,* 196–214; David A. Horowitz, "The Klansman as Outsider: Ethnocultural Solidarity and Antielitism in the Oregon Ku Klux Klan of the 1920s," *Pacific Northwest Quarterly,* 80 (January 1989): 12–20.

28. C. Easton Rothwell, "The Ku Klux Klan in Oregon" (B.A. thesis, Reed College, 1924), 126.

29. *Oregon Voter,* March 25, 1922. Gifford's parents moved from Minnesota to Portland in 1889 when he was twelve years old. He grew up in the Portland of John Reed, Louise Bryant, and C. E. S. Wood.

30. Ibid.; *Portland Telegram,* November 6, 1922.

31. *Oregon Voter,* January 24, 1920.

32. *Oregon Voter,* January 15, 22, March 5, 1921; Harry W. Stone, Jr., "Oregon Criminal Syndicalism Laws and the Suppression of Radicalism by State and Local Officials" (M.A. thesis, University of Oregon, 1933).

33. Marjorie R. Stearns, *The History of the Japanese People in Oregon* (Eugene, 1939), 51; *Laws of the State of Oregon* (1923), 17, 60, 77, 145, 232; *Oregon Voter,* March 3, 1923.

34. Stivers's comments were reprinted in *The Dawn* (Chicago), March 10, 1923.

35. Luther I. Powell in "Preface" to George Estes, *The Old Cedar School* (Troutdale, Oregon, 1923), 5–7.

36. Jane W. Bryant, "The Ku Klux Klan and the Oregon Compulsory School

Bill of 1922" (M.A. thesis, Reed College, n.d.); Donald L. Zelman, "Oregon's Compulsory Education Bill of 1922" (M.A. thesis, University of Oregon, 1964). Pierce defeated Olcott 133,392 to 99,164, while 115,506 favored the school bill and 103,685 opposed it.

37. *Oregon Voter,* March 25, 1922.

38. Ibid., December 8, 1923.

39. The county was named for Joseph Lane, Oregon's first territorial governor and, later, the vice presidential running mate of John C. Breckinridge on the proslavery Democratic ticket in 1860.

40. Lewis L. McArthur, *Oregon Geographic Names* (Portland, 1974), 260; Mike Helm, *Eugene, Oregon: A Guide, 1984-85 Edition* (Eugene, 1984), 2-5; Works Progress Administration Writers Program, *Oregon: End of the Trail* (Portland, 1940), 167-75; Randall V. Mills, *Railroads Down the Valley: Some Short Lines of the Oregon Country* (Palo Alto, 1950), 91-92; Lucia W. Moore, Nina W. McCornack, and Gladys W. McCready, *The Story of Eugene* (New York, 1949), passim; *Portland Oregonian,* September 10, 1989.

41. Helm, *Eugene,* 2-5.

42. University of Oregon Bureau of Municipal Research and Service, *Population of Oregon Cities, Counties, and Metropolitan Areas, 1850-1957: A Compilation of Census Counts and Estimates in Oregon* (Eugene, 1958), 4.

43. Paul L. Shinn, "Eugene in the Depression, 1929-1935," *Oregon Historical Quarterly* 86 (Winter 1985): 343.

44. Ibid.

45. Ibid.

46. Eugene's population increased to slightly more than a hundred thousand in 1989, but there were still only a few thousand residents of various racial minorities. Despite its more cosmopolitan campus in the 1980s, the number of minority students attending the University of Oregon was still relatively small when compared with similar schools in other states. The Eugene city council appointed its first black member in February 1989. None has ever been elected.

47. Donald L. Kinzer, *An Episode in Anti-Catholicism: The American Protective Association* (Seattle, 1964), 95.

48. Edgar E. Robinson, *The Presidential Vote* (New York, 1970), 306.

49. *Salem Capital Journal,* October 25, 1922.

50. *Eugene Morning Register,* August 7, 1921.

51. *Salem Capital Journal,* October 26, 1922.

52. W. E. Begg to F. W. Cameron, Ku Klux Klan MSS 22, Oregon Historical Society, Portland, Oregon.

53. *Salem Capital Journal,* October 27, 1922.

54. *Polk's Directory, Eugene, Oregon, 1925.*

55. David B. Tyack, "The Perils of Pluralism: The Background of the Pierce

Case," *American Historical Review* 74 (October 1968): 83. See M. Paul Holsinger, "The Oregon School Bill Controversy, 1922–1925," *Pacific Historical Review* 37 (August 1968): 327–41; and Lloyd P. Jorgenson, "The Oregon School Law of 1922: Passage and Sequel," *Catholic Historical Review* 54 (October 1968): 455–66.

56. Zelman, "Oregon's Compulsory Education Bill," 116.

57. Ibid., appendix B.

58. Turnbull, *An Oregon Crusader,* 137.

59. *Salem Capital Journal,* October 27, 1922.

60. *Eugene Morning Register,* June 11, 1924.

61. *Salem Capital Journal,* October 27, 1922; clipping circa 1962 from *Eugene Register-Guard,* in author's files.

62. Zelman, "Oregon's Compulsory Education Bill," 62.

63. David M. Chalmers, *Hooded Americanism: The History of the Ku Klux Klan* (New York, 1981), 120; *Portland Oregon Journal,* April 29, 1922.

64. *Salem Capital Journal,* July 19, 1922; *Portland Oregon Journal,* October 27, 1922. Many of the Klansmen were also on the earlier list, but several new names appeared on this roster.

65. *Salem Capital Journal,* October 17, 1922.

66. Ibid., 1, 7.

67. See Toy, "The Ku Klux Klan in Oregon; Its Program and Character," 40.

68. *Eugene Morning Register,* June 29, 30, 1922.

69. *Oregon Daily Emerald,* May 17, 1922.

70. Telephone conversation with K. Keith Richard, University Archivist, University of Oregon, July 31, 1989; Shinn, "Eugene in the Depression," 343–44.

71. James H. Hitchman, "Northwest Leadership in Education: Henry Davidson Sheldon at Oregon, 1900–1947," *Idaho Yesterdays* 24 (Spring 1980): 7.

72. See the discussion of these images in Paula S. Fass, *The Damned and the Beautiful: American Youth in the 1920's* (New York, 1977).

73. Don E. McIlvenna and Darold D. Wax, "W. J. Kerr, Land Grant President in Utah and Oregon, 1900–1908, Part II," *Oregon Historical Quarterly* 86 (Spring 1985): 22.

74. McLagan, *A Peculiar Paradise,* 144.

75. *Salem Capital Journal,* October 26, 27, 1922; Saalfeld, *Forces of Prejudice,* p. 9.

76. Henry D. Sheldon to Dr. Joseph Schafer, May 15, 1922, and Schafer to Sheldon, May 20, 1922, in Henry Davidson Sheldon Papers, Special Collections, University of Oregon, Eugene.

77. Moore, McCormack, and McCready, *The Story of Eugene,* 153; Frederick S. Dunn, "Staff Information Form," August 2, 1926, University of Oregon Archives.

78. Telephone conversation with K. Keith Richard, July 31, 1989.

79. *Oregon Daily Emerald,* January 25, 1922.

80. For more on O'Hara and his political activism, see Edwin V. O'Hara, "The School Question in Oregon," *Catholic World* 116 (January 1923): 482–90; J. G. Shaw, *Edwin Vincent O'Hara: American Prelate* (New York, 1957); Tynack, "The Perils of Pluralism," 86.

81. *Oregon Voter,* May 26, 1923.

82. *Portland Sunday Oregonian,* November 3, 1983.

83. Steve Neal, *McNary of Oregon: A Political Biography* (Portland, 1985), 77–83.

84. *Eugene Morning Register,* June 24, 25, 26, 27, 28, 29, 30, July 1, 1924. Grand Dragon Gifford missed this rally, since he was a member of the Klan delegation attending the Democratic National Convention in New York City.

85. Ibid. The Royal Riders of the Red Robe was a Klan-affiliated organization for the foreign born.

86. Ibid.

87. *Portland Sunday Oregonian,* November 3, 1983.

88. *Portland Oregonian,* January 24, 1926.

89. Sheldon to O. F. Stafford, February 27, 1922, in Sheldon Papers.

90. Moore, McCormack, and McCready, *The Story of Eugene,* 209.

91. Rothwell, "Klan in Oregon," 117; Saalfeld, *Forces of Prejudice,* 2–3; Toy, "The Klan in Oregon," 147–48.

92. Waldo Roberts, "The Ku Kluxing of Oregon," *Outlook* 133 (March 14, 1923): 490–91.

93. Rosa E. Green to Stewart H. Holbrook, October 1952, in Stewart H. Holbrook Papers, Manuscript Division, University of Washington Libraries.

94. Green to Holbrook, 1959, in Holbrook Papers.

7

Order, Solidarity, and Vigilance: The Ku Klux Klan in La Grande, Oregon

DAVID A. HOROWITZ

When Governor-elect Walter M. Pierce appeared before the La Grande Provisional Klan on November 21, 1922, the klavern secretary described the meeting as "one of the best ever held in the state of Oregon." Klavern minutes proudly recorded that 116 members of the La Grande Ku Klux Klan accepted Pierce's thanks for the support of all "100% Americans" in the recent election. "Let us bid Klansman Pierce God's speed in his new undertakings," the secretary intoned, noting that the La Grande lodge would continue to support the governor-elect "as we have done in the past."[1]

A subsequent synopsis of Klan activities reported that the visit from "Our Walter" had begun the dramatic rise in the membership of the La Grande klavern.[2] In fact, the chapter had thrived since its founding in May 1922, and its success was rooted in the economic and cultural features of the city's colorful history.

Located three hundred miles east of Portland in the Grande Ronde Valley of the Blue Mountains, Union County's La Grande was a small city of some seven thousand people in 1920. As the commercial hub and highway construction headquarters of eastern Oregon, this bustling county seat boasted a payroll second only to Portland. La Grande served as a processing center and distribution point for regional fruits, grains, and livestock. The site of twenty manufacturing facilities, the city also hosted four lumber mills employing thirteen hundred workers.[3]

Rail transportation was the most important influence on La Grande's development and culture. The town had been settled as a milling and mining center in the 1860s, but it first prospered when the Oregon-Washington Railroad and Navigation Company built a rail link to the settlement in 1884. The following year the frontier city incorporated.

Local business interests soon convinced the railroad to establish a division point on land donated by a leading townsman. By 1890, the Union Pacific system had taken control of the railroad. Bolstered by its role as a rail distribution center for Powder Mountains gold and as a processing and distribution point for cattle, wheat, fruit, and lumber, La Grande grew to three thousand strong by the turn of the century. Its main street featured cast-iron statuary and opulent Victorian homes adorned with cupolas and cornices. Voters adopted the commission form of municipal government in 1913. This Progressive innovation provided for the election of three at-large city commissioners and appointment of a professional city manager.[4]

By the 1920s, railroad logging, division maintenance shops, and booming lumber mills provided La Grande with a thriving commercial life. As the city's population grew from seven to eight thousand in the 1920s, the *La Grande Evening Observer* noted that the municipality contained the fourth largest public school enrollment in the state. The secretary of the local Chamber of Commerce boasted that La Grande's civic pride had resulted in "a clean, beautiful little city . . . an ideal place in which to live." In 1925, the Chamber of Commerce estimated that one-fourth of La Grande's homes were owned by Union Pacific employees. With 850 resident workers and an annual payroll of $1.8 million, the railroad provided important economic stability to eastern Oregon's major metropolis. Yet railroading, mining, and agriculture attracted newcomers whose social backgrounds varied from the white, native-born Americans who comprised 93 percent of Union County's 1920 population.[5] Citizens worried that the small Chinese community might spread the use of opium to the population at large. Others associated the city's blacks, Mexicans, and Italians with drunken behavior and violation of Prohibition laws.

Although 1920 Census figures showed only forty-six people of Chinese ancestry in Union County, the Chinese played a large role in the region's history. Originally coming to the valley during the gold rush and railroad boom of the 1880s, the Chinese stayed on as merchants, laundry proprietors, restaurant owners, cooks, and gardeners. But fears of job competition during the depression year of 1893 prompted a white mob to burn La Grande's Chinatown and expel its residents. Hostility resurfaced in 1917 when a dispute among Chinese tongs led to a shoot-out near the city post office, resulting in the death of a popular Chinese restauranteur. After authorities arrested six men for the murder, a citizens' panel investigated La Grande's Chinese opium dens and single house of prostitution. An agreement with tong leaders allowed the six gunmen to be tried for second-degree murder and the rest of the Chinese community to remain unharmed. Despite the lack of renewed violence, suspicion of the Chinese remained an essential part of the La Grande psyche.[6]

While census figures showed only fifteen black city residents in 1920, immigrant whites accounted for another 425 and 1154 others reported at least one foreign-born parent. By 1926, moreover, nearly half of the religiously affiliated people of the county were members of the Church of Latter-day Saints (the Mormons) and the Roman Catholic church, both outside the confines of American Protestant tradition. With adherents among the hundreds of area families of German, Irish, and Italian background, the city's Catholic community had established a solid position in commerce, politics, and cultural affairs by the 1920s.[7]

In cooperation with Portland and Pendleton Klan organizers, the La Grande Provisional Klan selected initial officers in the spring of 1922. On May 11, 1922, the secret order's first meeting, Klansmen chose James E. ("Ed") Reynolds, a substantial farmer and propertyholder, as exalted cyclops (chief officer) and Dr. J. L. McPherson, a town dentist, as klaliff (vice-president). McPherson replaced William G. Sawyer, owner of a La Grande hay and feed store, who later asked to withdraw from Klan membership. Meanwhile, Claude E. Cooper, a watchmaker at one of the downtown jewelry stores, accepted responsibilities as chapter kligrapp (secretary). Four nights after the initial meeting, nearly one hundred La Grande men converged on the Star Theater to pay 55¢ a head to listen to Portland minister Reuben H. Sawyer discuss the Klan and its mission.[8]

The former pastor of the East Side Christian Church, Sawyer had a statewide reputation as a fiery speaker. He normally attracted interest in the Klan by contrasting the secret order's "cleansed and purified Americanism" to the foreign values of Catholics, Jews, and immigrants. Such sentiments could be found in *The Truth About the Invisible Empire of the Ku Klux Klan,* a Klan pamphlet incorporating a lecture that Sawyer had delivered in Portland in December 1921. Sawyer's La Grande performance began when the minister and several Klansmen marched to the cross-lit stage in full regalia. He told the audience that the Klan had to go directly to the people in secret meetings because the nation's newspapers had been "bought up." Sawyer then discussed "one hundred percent Americanism" and delivered his customary attack on Catholics and the foreign-born.[9]

Sawyer's two-night stand at the Star theater paid dividends for the La Grande Klan. Between May 11 and May 31, the klavern inducted forty-two members and began renting the Eagles Hall for meetings. La Grande Klansmen also appointed a committee of fifteen to approve "One Hundred Per Cent" candidates for the May 19 primary. The lodge further voted to donate twenty-five dollars to the Reverend Stanton C. Lapham, a "needy" Baptist preacher. When Lapham expressed willingness to join the secret order, Klansmen volunteered to pay his ten-dollar initiation fee. Other business included payment of fourteen dollars to the construction company partly owned by Klansman Charles E. Harris for fabrication of the klavern cross. The La Grande klavern also rented a post office box in order to "avoid tempting a Catholic mail carrier." In August, the chapter completed its initial phase of organization by appointing Klaliff McPherson as exalted cyclops and Alfred J. Johnson, a Union Pacific accountant, as the new klaliff. By December 1922, the La Grande klavern boasted 207 members and anxiously awaited a formal charter from Atlanta national headquarters.[10]

Anti-Catholic agitators like Sawyer helped to attract Protestant townsmen to the Klan movement. But La Grande's klavern achieved legitimacy by portraying itself as a fraternal order of the highest moral principles. "Ten stalwart Americans were born again" in a "naturalization" ceremony, chapter minutes indicated in 1923, referring to the induction of "aliens" as "citizens" of the Invisible Empire. Such language portrayed conversion to Klan ranks as equivalent to rites of passage. Kligrapp Harold R. Fosner, a postal clerk who assumed chapter secretarial duties in October 1922, once described the secret order as "the greatest constructive and character building organization the world has ever known." Klankraft, exclaimed the exalted cyclops at the start of 1923, was "the noblest cause in all the world . . . it is the sworn duty of every Protestant to be leagued in this cause for righteousness."[11]

La Grande Klan meetings provided a rich web of ritual, symbolism, and ceremony for the rank and file. Besides the passwords, hand grips, and secret signs common throughout the Invisible Empire, chapter leaders insisted upon precision in the observance of klavern procedures and rites. "Klansmen," the kligrapp lectured in February 1923, "this is a militant organization and we ask you to perform this ceremony in a military manner." The officer reminded those entering the meeting to "approach the altar with a little pep in your step and salute the flag and not the exalted cyclops." Klansmen expressed pride in the symbolism of their costumes. A klavern discussion two weeks before Christmas of 1922 included the observation that the Catholic Knights of Columbus wore black robes while the Klan chose robes of white. Even the use of masks brought spirited defense. "'Tis but a symbol," notes of the verbal exchange recorded, "like in comparison to creeds in the different churches. We are ashamed of nothing, neither have we anything to hide, for we are proud of the fact that we have nerve enough to express in word and action our true convictions."[12]

Klan members saw the burning cross not only as a sign of Klan power but as a symbol of Christian sacrifice and service. In November 1922, the klavern voted to attach a battery and globes to the lodge cross. The following month Kligrapp Fosner pleaded that "we must place another cross upon the hillside to keep a-blaze our purpose in the hearts of all." Klankraft included fraternal references to "harmony" and "fellowship." A "100 percent orchestra" performed opening ceremony music for special meetings. Other klonklaves featured carefully prepared Klan food. The klavern secretary noted that knights at one session forgot their "crave for moonshine" and devoured hot dogs, "Ku Klux Klan Cake, . . . Thick Klanish Cream for our Niggar Soup, and apples from the Garden of Eden."[13]

Klavern leaders insisted upon standards of strict morality before accepting anyone into the secret order. After endorsement by individual Klansmen, officers read aloud the names of applicants before they were turned over to the Board of Klokans for investigation of religious background and character. In March 1923, the klokans rejected three men without explanation: a logger, a grocery clerk, and soldier Alonzo Dunn. Several weeks later, the minutes recorded that the entire chapter had turned down several men for membership. One turned out to be an Indian not eligible for acceptance under the Klan's exclusion of nonwhites. The other six faced disqualification for a year because of alleged moral problems. Among them was Dunn, cited for questionable "character and affiliations." Klan investigations showed one applicant to be vulnerable to frequent bankruptcy, another to be living with a woman not his wife, and a third to be guilty of "selfish motives." The Board of Klokans concluded that a fourth applicant had a "bad reputation" and that another had been involved in unlawful proceedings. A final petitioner was dismissed as a notorious "moonshine" drinker.[14]

Once Klansmen gained membership, they faced surveillance of their demeanor, organizational loyalty, and behavior. Understandably, dues payments provided an apt challenge for individual and collective discipline. Many Klansmen had not come forth with dues money, lodge minutes stated in December 1922. "Don't delay any longer," pleaded Kligrapp Fosner, "and remember that promptness is the keynote of industry." One week later, the visiting kligrapp from nearby Pendleton warned that once the chapter received its national charter, members would be required to attend one out of every three meetings. Two weeks after that, Exalted Cyclops McPherson complained that "very few of you" had taken the time to promote Klan affairs. "The final realization of this cause," he preached, "must mean the sacrifice of each and every individual of time, money, and devotion to your officers.... Have you given up one night's pleasure to pay your dues?" Ultimately, McPherson threatened, "you are going to account for the title you wish to defend."[15]

The demands of moral surveillance went beyond organizational discipline. Idle gossip provided a favorite target for Klan leaders. "If you've got anything on your chest," suggested the visiting Pendleton official, "get rid of it while you are here assembled and don't tell it to the wind on the streets below." In an extended addendum to the minutes of March 27, 1923, Kligrapp Fosner expanded upon the same theme. "Did you ever stop and realize," he asked, "that most of this talk you pick up on the street is all bunk. Klansmen, you should live above the rabble of the everyday clamor. Remember when you come to lodge that this is not an old maid's convention. It don't [sic] take brains to promote these little personal issues. So let's think more deeply, act more in harmony and sacrifice more for the cause we pursue and in the end we shall be better for it."[16]

La Grande Klan leaders realized that moral revitalization was an important but difficult feature of klavern management. In February 1923, the chapter postponed the naturalization ceremony of grocery store manager William Keefer at the last moment. Citing reports that Keefer had been seen drunk in the company of a Klansman's wife, lodge officers called for further investigation of the applicant's character. "We want you to practice klanishness [sic]," Kligrapp Fosner noted with some humor, "but don't pull this fraternity stuff with another man's wife." A month later, the Klan secretary inexplicably returned to the subject at the close of a personal addendum to the March 27 minutes. "If you married klansmen insist upon going out with another man's wife be awful sure she doesn't belong to a klansman," he advised. "You may have occasion to meet that gentleman in the klavern and I am sure it would be a very embarrassing position for each of you."[17]

The Ku Klux Klan portrayed itself as a fraternal order promoting solidarity among its members. For example, the La Grande klavern featured a standing committee to send flowers to sick members and assist those in need of financial support due to medical emergencies or other circumstances. When the chapter agreed to pay the sixty-dollar hospital bill of a Klansman in May 1923, it also voted to create a sinking fund to defray the future expenses of ill or financially needy knights. National Klan ritual described such unity as "klannishness" and swore initiates to uphold it as one of the Invisible Empire's four secret oaths. Klannishness referred to loyalty to family, nation, race, and the Klan itself—"true Americanism unadulterated." Klannish fidelity, wrote founder William J. Simmons, was the "One great underlying principle" of the secret order. With social, moral, and vocational applications, klannishness embodied the desire to "live and act as to safeguard and enhance" the "interest and welfare" of klansmen. It suggested a fraternity of Protestant men pledged to honor their mutual spiritual and economic interests.[18]

Klan leaders frequently felt compelled to remind the rank and file of the obligations of klannishness. "Klansmen, we have all shirked responsibility in the past and practiced our klanishness [sic], in a very loose manner," Pendleton's kligrapp admonished La Grande members a week before Christmas of 1922. When Oregon Grand Dragon Fred Gifford visited the following March, he ordered Methodist minister O. W. Jones to read the sixteenth chapter of Romans to emphasize the organization's principles ("mark them which cause divisions and offences contrary to the doctrine which ye have learned, and avoid them"). Such doctrines of exclusivity fed Klan antagonism to the Roman Catholic church and its followers. "We must ever consider ourselves engaged in battle until we or those to follow behold the downfall of Catholicism buried in the ruins of its own iniquity," Kligrapp Fosner observed following the election of November 1922. Ten weeks later, Grand Dragon Gifford told a special meeting of La Grande Klansmen that the secret order was "not against the way the Catholics worship; but we are against the Catholic machine which controls our nation." Gifford warned listeners to "expect some trouble" from a newly arrived Catholic priest in the central Oregon community of Bend, an official he described as a "big man politically" up to "no special good."[19]

Concern over Catholic influence remained a mainstay of klavern operations. Klannish loyalty depended upon "100 percent" Americanism. As leaders of a secret organization, lodge officials worried about spying. Once they avoided the problem of a Catholic mail carrier by renting a post office box, Klan officers focused upon Raymond R. Garrity (presumably an Irish-Catholic), whom they accused in November 1922 of suspiciously lurking in the hallway leading to the lodge room. Although a formal complaint against Garrity never materialized, klavern officials consistently preached caution. In December 1922, the acting lodge treasurer warned Klansmen not to make statements regarding Klan numerical strength because of a possible "leak" in the organization. Paranoia reached its most dramatic form in April 1923 when Fosner passed on a report "that all good K.C. [Knights of Columbus] carry a 32-automatic when they go out at night."[20]

As a regional service and distribution center and as the home of a diversified work force, the bustling city of La Grande featured a wide variety of shops and businesses owned by Catholics, Jews, and Chinese. Accordingly, klannishness took on explicit economic relevance for the native-born Protestant men of the Ku Klux Klan. In January 1923, Grand Dragon Gifford cautioned that "this order does not boycott anybody—we just promote klanishness [sic]." Yet, less than two weeks later, Exalted Cyclops McPherson lectured that if Klansmen were serious enough about practicing klannishness, they would know to find out if a man was "right" before purchasing goods from him. In fact, the klavern immediately followed up on McPherson's admonition by voting to require the kligrapp to make a list of "right" businesses and to read it at every meeting.[21]

Economic klannishness worked to bolster Protestant business interests in La Grande. For example, a visiting Klansman announced the availability of night work for a "100 percent man" at a local automobile agency. Yet economic solidarity was difficult to maintain. In December 1922, Kligrapp Fosner reported that Klansman and automobile salesman C. H. Tull had purchased meat from the town's Dutch butcher, that Klansman and hardware store proprietor Fred Huffman shopped at the wrong grocery, that county clerk and Klan member Kenneth McCormick still ate at the popular but German-owned Herman's Lunch Counter, and that Klansman and state senator Colon Eberhard had stayed at a Catholic-owned hotel. Tull compensated for his lapse a few weeks later by delivering a speech on klannishness. He advised "that when you go to Pendleton, you want to watch your step or the chief of police might ask you why you didn't eat your meals in an American restaurant." Tull also reminded lodge mates to insist on dealing with a Klansman when buying an automobile at the Roach dealership where he was employed.[22]

The ultimate challenge to klannishness came when lodge member J. Garfield Holm's grocery fell into bankruptcy in February 1923. "We believe our klanishness [sic] toward Klansman Holm has been very lax," noted Kligrapp Fosner, taking the occasion to ridicule knights who did their business at the Jewish-owned Hooverized grocery chain. Fosner reported the creation of a special klavern committee to aid Holm and "show this village that we are strong enough to support our members." In March, the Klan panel announced the reopening of the grocery. The following month, Holm told the klavern that business had prospered beyond expectation, but that many Klansmen still did not patronize the store. Kligrapp Fosner noted that a letter on the practice of klannishness would go out to "these half-baked klansmen" and that it would request that they observe their oath or explain their reasons for noncompliance.[23]

La Grande knights of the Invisible Empire maintained a steady campaign against the retention of Frederick L. Meyers, a Catholic, as cashier of the La Grande National Bank, the largest financial institution in town. "We still have a few klansmen who do their business at the La Grande National Bank," Kligrapp Fosner noted in November 1922. "Don't forget you are klansmen." But in January, Klansman George T. Cochran, a prominent attorney who sat on the board of directors of the rival United States National Bank of La Grande, informed the klavern that Meyers's immediate removal would bring a loss of $50,000 to the cashier's firm. Cochran asked lodge members to hold off their attack. "We desire to force Meyers from his position," the attorney explained, "and still have that institution retain its full value in the commercial world." Two months later, the bank entertained honorary Klansman Governor Pierce, county treasurer and Klansman Hugh McCall, and two hundred other prominent guests at an anniversary banquet at a local hotel.[24]

As the failure of the Meyers campaign indicated, Klan economic power was not sufficient to impose the secret order's will when it threatened the financial stability of the community. Quantitative evidence on the occupational and class background of La Grande Klansmen lends support to this conclusion. Klavern minutes customarily listed the names and vocations of active members and new initiates. Relevant occupational data has also been related in three local directories of the period. As a result, it has been possible to construct a list of 326 La Grande Klansmen and to identify the vocational background of 264. Using the system of occupational classification employed in Robert Goldberg's study of Colorado Klans, an economic and class profile of the klavern has been constructed. Accordingly, 25 percent of identifiable La Grande Klansmen turn out to be of middle nonmanual status (30 percent of those with listed occupations), 18 percent of low nonmanual status (22 percent of those with listed occupations), 17 percent of skilled status (21 percent of those with listed occupations), and 13 percent of semiskilled and service status (16 percent of those with listed occupations). Altogether, over 90 percent of identifiable La Grande Klansmen with listed occupations came from these four status groups (see Table 7.1).[25]

Nearly 37 percent (ninety-seven) of identifiable La Grande Klansmen with listed occupations worked for the Union Pacific Railroad. More than 41 percent of these men were skilled manual workers, including fourteen locomotive firemen, thirteen locomotive and equipment engineers, and twelve machinists and other shop employees. Another 28 percent of Klan railroad workers were in the low nonmanual category, including nine clerks, four foremen and shop supervisors, and three conductors. Nearly 25 percent turned out to be semiskilled and service workers, including seventeen brakemen and switchmen. Over 93 percent of Klan railroad employees were either low nonmanual, skilled manual, or semiskilled workers. The klavern's rail workers, then, fell somewhere between working class and lower middle class in status.[26]

La Grande's Invisible Empire served as a job protection association for Protestant workers in a corporation managed by Roman Catholics. Klan leaders found it easy to accuse the company of religious favoritism in hiring. When a railroad crane engineer submitted his name for Klan membership in February 1923, Kligrapp Fosner commented: "Don't tell this man the Pope is O.K. unless you want to get licked." Four

TABLE 7.1

Occupational Distribution of La Grande Klansmen, 1922–23

Occupational Status Group	Klavern		Leaders	
	Number	Percent of total	Number	Percent of leaders
High nonmanual	14	4.3	8	18.2
Middle nonmanual	80	24.5	14	31.8
Low nonmanual	59	18.1	13	29.5
Skilled	56	17.2	2	4.5
Semiskilled and Service	43	13.2	4	9.1
Unskilled	8	2.5	0	0.0
Retired	4	1.2	0	0.0
Unknown	62	19.0	3	6.8
	326	100.0	44	99.9

Occupational status group categories conform to the status group classification used in Robert A. Goldberg, *Hooded Empire: The Ku Klux Klan in Colorado* (Urbana: University of Illinois Press, 1981), 183–86.

months later, Dr. R. P. Landis told the klavern that the Union Pacific had fired him as local railroad physician. "As we naturally expected," noted Fosner without explanation, "there was a Catholic in the woodpile."[27]

The La Grande Klan managed to build up substantial strength among railroad workers not usually recruited by fraternal and civic associations. At least seven klavern officers worked as clerical and nonmanual employees of the Union Pacific. Beyond job protection and Protestant solidarity, the Invisible Empire offered railroad workers a sense of dignity in an industry often beset by insecurity. Such support became particularly important during the nationwide strike of four hundred thousand railroad shopcraft and maintenance workers in the summer of 1922. In La Grande, six hundred workers walked off their jobs, precipitating a major community crisis. Although most Klan rail employees belonged to the nonstriking railroad brotherhoods, local Klansmen played a substantial role in supporting the strikers. Klansman Glenn H. Forwood, a shopcraft blacksmith, served as vice-chairman of the strikers' committee. When a strikebreaker pulled a gun on a picket,

Forwood testified against the offender to a packed court of between 250 and 300 onlookers. Forwood later filed a $100,000 suit for defamation of character against the Union Pacific. As late as September 1922, concern with strikebreaking led the La Grande klavern to create a committee to investigate "four klansmen who are strikebreakers and who are teaching negroes and japs to take places of strikers."[28]

Klan leaders insisted that organizational solidarity be extended to unity in support of community officeholders and "100 percent" political candidates. In the fall of 1922, the Invisible Empire managed to use its influence with the La Grande school board to fire Evelyn Newlin, a Catholic schoolteacher married to insurance agent Chester Newlin. But in November, Klan secretary Fosner announced that Chester Newlin had drawn up a petition to induce the board to reinstate his wife. Fosner denounced the ploy as "thoroughly un-American . . . , something that the Klan will not under any consideration tolerate if in their power to do otherwise." The kligrapp noted that Newlin sent her own children to parochial school and that "her influence with the pupils in her charge is not born of Old Glory; neither is it symbolic of the fiery cross." Fosner bitterly attacked the Newlin family, which also operated a book and stationary shop and a pharmacy.[29]

Despite her husband's petition, the school board voted 3-2 against reinstating Newlin. But the Klan's only staunch ally on the panel was former state senator Colon R. Eberhard, a member of the La Grande klavern and law partner with Klansman George Cochran. In January 1923, Cochran spoke to the Klan about forcing the release of school clerk and board member Charles H. Reynolds, an insurance man who worked out of the La Grande National Bank building with Chester Newlin. But Cochran warned that the sudden dismissal of Reynolds would disrupt the running of the school system and advised Klansmen to wait for the June elections. In March, Kligrapp Fosner reported that Reynolds had taken his first communion in the Catholic church. Later in the month, Fosner noted that a committee of Klansmen had met at Cochran's law office to select two school board candidates. Meanwhile, board member Eberhard advised that the Catholics had won over school director James Russell, president of a local meat company, and that the panel now intended to reinstate Newlin. In response, the Klan appointed a committee to meet with Russell. In May 1923, the panel reported that Russell had promised to stay away from school board meetings until the Newlin issue blew over.[30]

The June 18 school board election erased the need for concern about Russell. La Grande's Klan printed separate tickets in support of the order's two candidates and distributed them across the city the day before the contest. Klan activity may have contributed to a turnout 50 percent greater than that of any previous school board election. The results thrilled KKK organizers. Eberhard, the lone Klansman on the panel, now found himself with two Klan partners, assuring a majority of three. The leading vote getter turned out to be Dr. R. P. Landis, the recently dismissed railroad physician. Lyman W. Weeks, a local insurance man and newly elected chief of klavern investigators, took second place. The two Klan candidates gathered a 3-1 plurality over former school board chairman C. J. Black and another candidate. Klan organizational solidarity had produced a major victory in an area of civic life the Invisible Empire considered essential to its interests.[31]

In January 1923, Klansman and prominent attorney Cochran advised members of the order on the proper strategy for asserting organizational influence on the public schools. "First of all," he cautioned, "we must establish a reputation in this community and prove to these natives that we are behind the laws to the fullest extent and that we are the only truly patriotic organization existing in this community today." Ten days later, Kligrapp Fosner recounted an incident in which an Irish-American schoolteacher had refused to read the essays that two students had written on the Klan. "We will someday give her an education on Americanism," noted Fosner. The Klan secretary also observed that the Invisible Empire's interests in the schools could best be promoted through a cooperative Parent-Teachers Association (PTA). Weeks after the June 1923 school board election, Cochran reported that the Klan board of directors, which he chaired, had worked with the school board to select Klansman Harry Williams, a partner in the La Grande Electric Company, as school board clerk. On July 31, the *Evening Observer* announced that the board had unanimously chosen Williams for the post and that the panel would soon choose a site for a new school in southeast La Grande.[32]

Klan influence also extended to local government. In response to a petition requesting his candidacy, Klansman and railroad clerk C. M. Humphreys ran for the city commission in November 1922. Cochran urged the klavern to support both Humphreys and retired railroad worker William W. Kinzie, who was an Independent candidate for justice of the peace. But the results proved disappointing to leaders of the Invisible Empire. Humphreys finished fourth in a race for two open seats and Kinzie lost to a non-Klansman, 1043 to 924. Kinzie also lambasted the *Evening Observer* for "dragging" City Manager Oscar A. Kratz into the election. Besides bootleggers and other law violators, charged Kinzie, only the newspaper opposed Kratz, who had provided "a good clean and economical administration . . . the best city manager La Grande has ever had." Kinzie appealed to taxpayers and voters "to see that a few private interests do not use our money to fatten their own pockets." Perhaps it was significant that the local Klan processed Kratz's application for membership one month later and inducted him just before Christmas.[33]

The La Grande Klan fashioned itself as a political machine for native-born Protestants. Any public office that might affect the livelihood or interests of members was fair game. The Invisible Empire, klavern secretary and historian Fosner declared early in 1923, was "far stronger in this town than are the K. C [Knights of Columbus]. Let us take advantage of every opportunity to gain complete control of local affairs. We demand the right," he exhorted, "to place one hundred percent Americans on guard. Americans for America, Romans when all others fail." In March 1923, Fosner reported that the organization hoped to win appointment for Klansman Dr. George Vehrs as city health officer, at a salary of fifteen dollars a month ("not a very good paying position," the kligrapp acknowledged). When a vacancy occurred in the office of justice of the peace the following September, attorney Cochran headed a Klan committee of five to consult with County Judge U. G. Couch. But Couch voted for Hugh E. Brady, the Catholic candidate.[34]

In January 1923, Oregon Grand Dragon Fred Gifford spoke to the La Grande klavern at a special meeting. "Democraticism and Republicanism didn't mean anything to us," Fosner's transcript of the speech read. "Let's forget it and see that the right man gets in." The Invisible Empire worked with both Democrats and Republicans in Oregon. As the *Baker Morning Democrat* reported in March 1922, the Klan was heavily involved in Republican politics and had pushed its own candidate for Oregon's national committeeman. In La Grande, the klavern supported Klansman and Republican state senator Colon R. Eberhard. Elected to the legislature in 1918, Eberhard had a distinguished reputation as a former city commissioner and district attorney, member of the school board since 1914, and partner with George Cochran in one of the leading law firms in eastern Oregon. Despite such credentials and Klan support, the Democrats rode agrarian discontent to make major gains throughout the state in 1922. Eberhard carried Union County by about three hundred votes, but lost his seat to Democrat Henry J. Taylor by some fifty ballots. "We put up a good fight for klansmen Kinzie, Humphrey, and Eberhard," observed Kligrapp Fosner. "But Rome was not built in a day."[35]

La Grande's Klan also failed to influence the 1922 congressional races. The klavern had supported the effort of Republican James H. Gwinn of Pendleton to unseat five-time representative Nicholas J. Sinnott, a Catholic from the Dalles. "Anti-Catholic feeling is behind the opposition to the re-election of Congressman N. J. Sinnott," reported the *Oregon Voter.* When Sinnott prevailed in the primary, however, the Klan switched parties to back Democrat James Harvey Graham, a Klansman and realty operator from Baker. Yet Sinnott easily won reelection, although Graham carried Union County by a 3 to 2 margin.[36]

The La Grande klavern's support of favorite son Walter Pierce produced the most spectacular political triumph for the secret order. In the spring of 1922, the state KKK supported Charles Hall's efforts to unseat Republican governor Ben W. Olcott, who had publicly denounced the Invisible Empire six days before the Republican primary. But after Olcott prevailed in the close contest, the Klan switched parties to embrace the Democrat Pierce. During Olcott's campaign speech in La Grande, Klansmen burned a cross on nearby Table Mountain. Leaders of the Invisible Empire rejoiced when Pierce emerged with a 57 percent statewide plurality. Two weeks after his triumph, Pierce appeared with defeated Democratic congressional candidate Graham at a meeting of the La Grande Klan. When Grand Dragon Gifford made a special visit to the klavern in January 1923, he conveyed a message from the new governor that all appointments "would be given to men who are right." Gifford promised that Pierce would take a roster of patronage selections to the Grand Dragon's Portland headquarters so that the two men could "go over the list and weed out the culls." Pierce's success means our success," proclaimed Gifford. "Get behind this administration," he implored, "and let's give the people of the state of Oregon something in the line of true Americanism."[37]

Buoyed by a second Pierce visit to the klavern in June 1923, the La Grande Klan sought to use the governor's patronage power to solidify its position in the community. Pierce responded with three plums. In

May 1923, the klavern initiated a letter-writing campaign to gain support for the selection of La Grande Klansman Robert H. Baldock as state highway engineer. "Let's make it a personal issue and see that we have a one hundred percent American at the head of this very important position," Kligrapp Fosner exhorted. Two weeks later, the secretary reported that Governor Pierce had responded to queries concerning Baldock and that "all conditions look very favorably toward that end." Baldock succeeded in becoming district engineer for the state highway commission in 1923 and moved on to the post of Oregon chief highway engineer in 1932.[38]

Pierce made a second appointment to Klansman G. S. Birnie, a local optometrist and jeweler, who replaced William B. Peare on the State Board of Optometry. Peare had served 7½ years on the board and was in the midst of his third term. He also had gained endorsement from the state optometry associations. Yet as the son of Jack H. Peare, the Catholic chairman of the Union County Republican Committee, Peare was an obvious target for the Klan. "If Jack Peare would of had enough coons whom he swore to have known for thirty days," Fosner asserted in a yearly summary of events in March 1923, "our Walter [Pierce] would have to farm for many days yet to come." Pierce had accomplished a "worthy deed," concluded Fosner, "when he relieved William Peare of his title and given it to klansman Birnie."[39]

Former Exalted Cyclops James ("Ed") Reynolds also benefited from Pierce's patronage. A wealthy retired farmer from a pioneer family of the Grande Ronde Valley, Reynolds served as president of the Union County Farm Bureau. First, Pierce renamed the Klansman to the state fair board. Second, the governor appointed Reynolds to the Union County Tax Board after attorney Cochran suggested that the Klan circulate petitions in behalf of his fellow Klansman. As Kligrapp Fosner explained, the appointment was important because a new state law provided that three tax supervisors from each county decide on how state tax receipts were to be spent on public facilities. The new tax board soon elected Reynolds as chairman. Two weeks later, the La Grande klavern chose Reynolds as its representative to a Portland meeting of Oregon Klansmen designed to select a candidate for the United States Senate.[40]

Klan appeals for support went beyond the material gains of economic solidarity and political power to embrace a commitment to social and civic responsibility. "This organization was created for Protestants," Kligrapp Fosner noted in March 1923, "and if you are an honorable citizen and believe in a strict enforcement of the law then you owe your support to this Klan." Leaders of the La Grande klavern liked to emphasize the mainstream nature of their movement. Fosner claimed that most of the American Legion men in the city were Klansmen. And former senator Eberhard told a meeting that his visit to Elks lodges across the state convinced him that the large majority of that organization's members belonged to the Klan.[41]

The Invisible Empire built a direct relationship with the Protestant churches. In March 1923, Kligrapp Fosner announced that ministers would be admitted into the organization free of charge, already the case with Baptist preacher Stanton Lapham. Reverend O. W. Jones of the Methodist church, a favorite Klan spokesman, won appointment to the klavern board of directors in March 1923 and election as exalted cyclops in May. Klavern leaders urged members to organize automobile transportation to Jones's April 1923 speech about the Klan at nearby Island City, Governor Pierce's birthplace. Kligrapp Fosner also asked all Klansmen to attend the minister's special Thanksgiving address at the Methodist church. When klavern leaders learned that another Methodist minister had given an illustrated lecture before the Baker Klan, they invited him to La Grande in November 1923. The ensuing movie and inspirational talk, noted chapter secretary Fosner, showed "that we are not the only ones on the war path with the Casey's [K.C.'s].[42]

Fosner referred to the Christian church as the "Klan Church." Portland Klan ministers and speakers such as the Reverends V. K. Allison, James R. Johnson, and Reuben H. Sawyer all were erstwhile clergy in this denomination, an evangelical sect derived from the nonsectarian preachers of the American frontier. In La Grande, the klavern promoted lectures on the Ku Klux Klan by Pendleton Christian Church minister W. A. Gressman. Klavern scribe Fosner reported in April 1923 that Klansmen in neighboring Elgin had gathered at the town's Christian church and presented its pastor with a donation in behalf of the Invisible Empire. The following September, La Grande Klan leaders urged members and their wives to attend lectures by ex-nun Sister Mary Angel at the city's Christian church.[43]

Of the forty-four leaders and active members of the La Grande Klan, nine attended Christian church services or were church members.

Among them were key klavern leaders such as Klaliff Alfred J. Johnson and Exalted Cyclops Dr. J. L. McPherson. The Methodists, Episcopalians, and Presbyterians all claimed four active Klansmen each. Three klavern leaders were Baptists, while one attended the Methodist-Episcopal Church. Five La Grande Klansmen professed no religious association. Church affiliation for the remaining fourteen knights could not be ascertained.[44]

The Protestant character of the Klan accounted for the organization's attempt to fuse anti-Catholicism with civic-mindedness. In October 1922, the La Grande klavern underwrote a speech by "Sister La Precia" (Lucretia) at the city's Star Theater. The lecturer was a former nun and floor supervisor at Portland's St. Vincent's Hospital for seventeen years. Her unsubstantiated diatribes against the Catholic church confirmed the prejudices of Oregon Klansmen, who often arranged for her appearances. In La Grande, the klavern adjourned its weekly meeting so that members could attend the much-heralded lecture. The following week, the finance committee reported that the lodge had fronted the $140 rent for three nights at the Star Theater and had collected $135 in receipts. Kligrapp Fosner's subsequent account of yearly events suggested that the Lucretia event "did much to build up our membership" and elect Governor Pierce.[45]

The Oregon compulsory public school initiative of 1922 provided another boon to Klan popularity. The measure proposed to require children between the ages of eight and sixteen to attend public schools instead of private, parochial, or military academies. First introduced in Michigan and endorsed by the Scottish Rite Masons in 1920, compulsory public education won support from Republican gubernatorial candidate Charles Hall during the 1922 primaries. Once Hall publicized the idea, the Masons circulated initiative petitions to place the measure on the November ballot. When Democratic primary winner Pierce subsequently endorsed the initiative in September 1922, the Oregon Ku Klux Klan gave unofficial but open support to both Pierce and the school bill.[46]

Klan backers of the school bill hoped to defend "100 percent Americanism" by using public education to teach fundamental national values to all children. Both Grand Dragon Gifford and Pierce suggested that private and parochial schools encouraged snobbery and that all American pupils should be educated on the same basis. The initiative also fed into Klan charges that a powerful Catholic church used its schools to inculcate corruption and docility among its followers. In this context, La Grande klavern secretary Fosner described the effort to reinstate schoolteacher Margaret Newlin as "un-American, a direct insult to the school bill." Twenty La Grande Klansmen included a copy of the initiative in their election-eve sweep of town in November 1922. When Oregon voters approved the school bill, Fosner chortled that three Klansmen had defied the odds and demonstrated "nerve enough to bet" that the initiative would pass. But "even if our school bill fails to materialize as a true one," noted the kligrapp, "we well know how the majority of the people stand."[47]

Kligrapp Fosner referred to La Grande as "our village." The city's Klan frequently expressed support for community civic organizations, although it also wished to have a hand in running them. In February 1923, *Evening Observer* publisher Bruce Dennis, a Klan opponent, won election to the board of directors of the local YMCA. Dennis joined Klansman George Cochran, former Klansman and J. C. Penney manager C. E. Short, and Catholic bank official Frederick Meyers. Although the klavern appeared willing to work with some of its most bitter adversaries, the financial health of the Y deteriorated. In August, the Invisible Empire passed a resolution to "take an active interest in the progress of the local YMCA." Two weeks later, the klavern appointed a three-man committee to investigate prospects for the organization's future. But the local Y lacked sufficient capital to retire its mounting debt, and Methodist minister O. W. Jones told the klavern that the state unit might take over La Grande's ailing chapter. Despite Klan concern, however, the La Grande YMCA managed to avoid a sheriff's sale to pay off its debt and survived through 1923.[48]

The Klan also worked to support the Red Cross, despite the fact that Bruce Dennis and Catholic adversary Jack Peare served as officials of the La Grande chapter. In March 1923, Kligrapp Fosner noted with relish that the klavern had presented Dennis with fifty dollars for the local charity while Governor Pierce looked on. But the secretary also observed that the next Red Cross election would be held in October. In August, the Klan passed a resolution to work for a "100 percent executive" at the Red Cross and appointed a committee to accomplish the goal with former senator Eberhard as chairman. Yet Dennis continued to lead the organization, although the chapter dissolved three months later.[49]

La Grande's klavern showed active interest in improvement of the city water system, which had experienced periodic shortages since 1919. As chairman of the health and sanitation committee of the Chamber of Commerce, Klansman Dr. R. P. Landis brought the secret order into the water controversy. In August 1923, Landis convinced the city commission to explore development of an artesian well system. He argued that the construction and maintenance costs for artesian wells would run far below those of the alternative gravity flow system and that the resulting water would be free of bugs and germs and not need chlorination. After several discussions, the La Grande klavern approved the Landis proposal to drill four one-thousand-foot wells, assemble a pump, and build a reservoir. The Chamber of Commerce appeared to support Landis's plan as well. But when the city manager recommended the gravity flow system, the enusing $30,000 bond issue included both proposals. In the end, La Grande voters defeated the measure by a 3-1 margin.[50]

As the La Grande Klan prepared to accept its formal charter in March 1923, officers dedicated the chapter to civic and moral reform. Kligrapp Fosner promised that the secret order would soon focus on "a constructive program of real law enforcement such as has never before been seen in the Little Village God Forgot." He urged Klansmen to use the ballot and "the personal touch" to achieve the goals of the Invisible Empire. "So continue to be Progressive both in word and deed," admonished Fosner, "and what you are is what the Klan is to be." The klavern scribe already had informed fellow Klansmen that Circuit Court Judge J. W. Knowles had commended the Invisible Empire for its stand behind the law. In April 1923, Fosner vowed that the secret order would "prove to this city that the Klan is being instrumental in cleaning up this town and that we stand for the full enforcement of the law be he Catholic or klansman, gentile, alien, or Jew." One week later, Klansman and deputy sheriff Dexter McIlroy told the klavern that police officers were doing their best to enforce the law but that the district attorney was "lax...that is the man to clean up." The La Grande Klan then instructed its grievance board to appoint a committee to discuss full enforcement of the law with all city and county magistrates.[51]

Klansmen pictured themselves as knights responsible for the moral welfare of the community. At one meeting, klavern officials reported their investigation of a widow in financial distress and agreed to send a ton of alfalfa to a poor farmer about to sacrifice a cow because of insufficient feed. When Methodist minister and Klansman O. W. Jones indicated in February 1923 that a local laundry worker had a sick husband in Portland and was trying to support several small children, the klavern raised $26 to buy her a ton of coal and a coupon book for Klansman Holm's reopened grocery. On another occasion, the Klan chapter collected sums of twenty-five to fifty dollars for local families in trouble. Moreover, when the klavern received a third report that a city railroad worker was not providing support for three children from a previous marriage, chapter officials referred the case to the county health nurse.[52]

Klansmen had ample reason to be concerned with the decline of moral purity, family responsibility, and social decorum. Although the divorce rate remained low in Union County, the *Evening Observer* reported that only Nevada outpaced Oregon's state divorce ratio. When La Grande law enforcement officials learned in September 1922 that a local barber had sold liquor to five boys under the age of eighteen, the county prosecutor implored parents to exert tighter discipline on their children. Three months later, the *Evening Observer* reported that some forty boys under the age of eighteen spent their time frequenting "loafing places" such as local pool halls and card rooms. Further demoralization came with the news that former city police chief Roy Flexer had been arrested in Portland for transporting a woman across state lines for immoral purposes. Flexer told authorities that he had deserted his wife and children in order to accompany a married woman on auto trips across the country. In October 1923, the *Evening Observer* reported that La Grande's former law enforcement chief had been sentenced to fifteen months in federal prison.[53]

During the early 1920s, La Grande law enforcement focused increasingly upon Chinese opium rings operating near the railroad yards. But widespread drunken behavior and illegal use of alcohol disturbed authorities even more. Between August 1 and December 15 of 1922, city police arrested eighty-seven people and revealed that Prohibition offenses accounted for the great majority of their work. In 1923, La Grande officers apprehended 437 people, 177 for liquor-related crimes. Police targets included Mexicans, Italians, and notorious black bootleggers Dee Rogers and Pearl Fagin. As La Grande police stepped up their Prohibition campaign, the Klan rallied to their support. In January 1923, Klansmen Fields and Tull lectured the klavern on intemperance in the community. Ten members of the Invisible Empire then volunteered to be deputized and "help our local officials make a clean sweep of all unlawful proceedings that take place in our village." Ten days later, Kligrapp Fosner vowed to expel any Klansmen found guilty of bootlegging. Such concern was justified: knight Leonard J. Smith received thirty days in the county jail for a liquor conviction in December 1923, and Klan grocer Ray Cook faced arrest for a similar violation during the same month.[54]

In April 1923, the La Grande Klan conducted a spirited discussion about George Noble, who Fosner described as the "king of bootleggers," and sent two emissaries to the police department to observe him. They reported that Noble was in his cell, "seemingly not enjoying the company of his fellow companions, they being wops and coons." The following July, the klavern discussed a case in which a fifteen-year-old Union girl had been killed when a drunken driver lost control of the car in which the teenager was riding. These concerns took another form in October 1923 when the Klan appointed a ten-man committee "to take up the matter of Negroes on the North Side" with city officials. One month later, chairman Pearl Stiles reported that his panel had drawn up a petition to be presented at the November 21 meeting of the city commission. When Stiles and others delivered their demands on the appointed date, the *Evening Observer* described it as the most widely subscribed petition ever brought before a governing body in La Grande.[55]

Signed by nearly two hundred citizens, the document called for police prosecution of the "undesirable element" at and near "the colored colony" of the city. Klansman Moose Elledge told the commissioners that the district was "a nuisance" lying halfway between the north and south ends of town and that white women and children had been accosted or insulted by drunks and other disreputable individuals. Elledge and Klansmen J. K. Fitzgerald and E. C. Fields all demanded stricter punishment of law violators in the black district. When Fields pressed the issue, the commission asked the chief of police to rearrest black bootlegger Dee Rogers and require him to serve out the remainder of his sentence. In a matter of minutes, Rogers was behind bars. Altogether, twenty-one Klansmen signed the petition. When the Klan met five nights later, klavern leaders labeled the petition drive "very successful." The *Evening Observer* reported the following week that half the city's fifty arrests in November had involved liquor-related offenses.[56]

The Klan meeting following the city commission'protest attracted nearly 250 knights from Pendleton, Elgin, Baker, and La Grande. As Klansmen enjoyed their Thanksgiving turkey feed at Rex Hall, leaders of the secret order could well congratulate themselves on building a powerful political organization. La Grande Klavern No. 14 had received its formal charter on St. Patrick's Day, March 17, 1923. While more than two hundred Klansmen witnessed the charter ceremony on that Saturday night, two large crosses, one red, the other white, burned on a mountain behind the city. In a small story on page eight of the *Evening Observer,* organizers claimed that Atlanta only awarded charters when chapters reached a thousand members. The celebration marked the klavern's transition from a provisional Klan to a full-fledged entity of the national KKK.[57]

In May 1923, the fully empowered klavern held new elections and unanimously selected Methodist minister O. W. Jones as exalted cyclops. Under Jones's leadership, the La Grande Klan sought to raise its public image. Jones organized a nighttime public parade in late July. As several thousand spectators watched, about 325 robed Klansmen paraded down the La Grande business district in a procession headed by the municipal band and five horsemen clad in white robes. The lead rider carried an American flag; the second horseman conveyed a lighted cross. Masked rows of Klansmen followed. The parade culminated at the old fairgrounds where a filled grandstand heard lectures on patriotism and citizenship. Finally, the order inducted seventy-five new members in its first open-air initiation.[58]

Less than a month after the city hall protest, Oregon Grand Dragon Fred Gifford came to La Grande to organize support for a race for Republican Nicholas J. Sinnott's congressional seat by Klansman and prominent attorney George Cochran. An Episcopalian, Rotarian, Elk, state leader of the Knights Templar, and grand master of the Oregon Masons, Cochran had a long history of involvement in La Grande civic and business affairs. As defense attorney for the six Chinese defendants in the tong murder case of 1917, he had been impressed by the fact that "the tong was in duty bound to help" its members. Cochran carried such loyalty over to his Klan activities. Gifford now proposed to reward Cochran for his services and drive a Catholic out of the House "in order to have three congressmen who are white men."[59]

Cochran announced his candidacy for the Republican nomination after an old-fashioned torchlight parade in February 1924. His public supporters included Klaliff W. K. Gilbert (secretary of "Cochran for Congress"), Baker Klan officer C. T. Godwin, Klansman and school board member Dr. R. P. Landis, and Portland Klan minister V. K. Allison, who endorsed Cochran's program for "selective immigration" and a federal department of education. The *Evening Observer* referred to Klan backing for the candidate by noting that "a large element through-out the district is understood to be firm supporters." When confronted with charges of secret endorsement from the Invisible Empire, Cochran simply replied that "subtle and pernicious stories uttered and circu-lated about me are reacting in my favor . . . I expect to win." The Klan candidate did take Union County by a 4-3 margin. But the incumbent prevailed in the rest of the district and the political clout of the Invisible Empire proved insufficient.[60]

Significantly, Klan adversary and *Evening Observer* publisher Bruce Dennis faced no Republican primary opposition for his seat in the state senate. Dennis condemned the "mob rule" and secrecy of the KKK and viewed its members as "breeders of trouble." He reflected a growing view among state leaders that the Invisible Empire was a disruptive force. Oregon was "a divided state," editorialized Portland's *Evening Telegram* in March 1923. Religious warfare revived "by a commercial-ized secret order" had turned "every community into a warring camp" where "prejudice and ignorance supersede judgement and tolerance."[61]

Following the triumphant Thanksgiving turkey feed of 1923, the for-tunes of the La Grande Klan deteriorated. Divisiveness within the state organization contributed to its downfall. Although the klavern remained loyal to Grand Dragon Gifford and Governor Pierce, attacks on both men increased within the statewide Klan. As a result, the size of the state organization shrank dramatically and the secret order retreated from politics. Meanwhile, a special panel of the La Grande klavern told a dwindling membership in December 1923 that the chapter's opera-tion of Rex Hall was losing money and that "if something is not done to obtain some revenue . . . in the very near future . . . it will be necessary to circulate a petition to keep us from going broke." On December 11, 105 Klansmen showed up to hear Grand Dragon Gifford. After that, klavern minutes became extremely terse. Resignations also began to take their toll, climaxing with the loss of Exalted Cyclops Jones on April 1, 1924.[62]

Declining interest in the Klan coincided with the manslaughter trial of Dr. Ellis O. Willson, an Elgin dentist and active Klansman. Willson was charged with performing an abortion on a clerical assistant with whom he had allegedly engaged in sexual relations. As overflowing crowds attended the sensational trial in the winter of 1924, La Grande Klansman and school commissioner Dr. Landis testified for the prosecution. Upon conviction, Willson received a three-year prison sentence. On April 15, 1924, about six weeks after the close of the Willson trial, a klonklave of fifty Klansmen listened to the reading of a newspaper story concerning the removal of ornamental flags from the uniforms of American soldiers. It was the last meeting for which minutes of the La Grande klavern survive.[63]

The La Grande Ku Klux Klan provides a brief view of a western city's adjustment to the social and cultural changes of the 1920s. Amid a bustling and ethnically diverse railroad and milling town, the Klan represented both denizens of the middle class and those who aspired to its economic success and social esteem. La Grande Klansmen hoped to use their movement to restore the integration and cohesion threatened by modern life and diversity. Seeking both immediate economic advantage and a desire for prestige and validation, knights of the Invisible Empire confronted threatening change in a spirit of ethnic and social solidarity. They attempted to cushion the cold world of commerce and economic survival by resorting to the protection of family and ethnic networks. They tried to soften the impact of what appeared to be threatening new codes of hedonism and self-indulgence by returning to the disciplined values of their forebears.

La Grande's status as a western town afforded Klan followers a strong identification with an Oregon past that celebrated individual pioneer virtues, American nationalism, and Protestant supremacy. Despite their ability to intimidate opponents and use political and economic connections for their own advantage, La Grande Klansmen perceived themselves as "outsiders" under siege, ordinary citizens on the defensive. Unfortunately, Klan nativism denied the emerging pluralism of American society and violated the terms of the meritocracy slowly spreading through corporate and professional life. Because the Klan tried to fashion a unity based on an idealized and nostalgic concept of community, it brought about more disruption and divisiveness than social cohesion. In the end, the La Grande Ku Klux Klan had no reason to continue. Instead of solidarity and harmony, it promoted antagonism, social disharmony, and mindless prejudice.

NOTES

1. Minutes of Klan meeting held November 21, 1922, located in Records of the Ku Klux Klan of La Grande, Oregon, 1922-23, Oregon Historical Center, Portland, hereafter referred to as Klan Minutes. Minor errors of spelling, capitalization, and punctuation in these records have been corrected for readability. This essay's notes may refer to addenda, special reports, and other Klan documents produced on the date cited; all such sources are located in the records cited above.

2. Klan Minutes, March 13, 1923.

3. *Oregon and Washington State Gazetteer and Business Directory, 1921-1922* (Seattle, 1921), 242; *Polk's Union and Wallowa Counties Directory* (Portland, 1917), 9; F. E. Brinkman, comp., *La Grande City Directory* (La Grande, 1921), 7; Earl C. Reynolds, "La Grande, Oregon: The Industrial Capital of Eastern Oregon," *The Union Pacific Magazine* 4 (December 1925): 5.

4. Barbara Ruth Bailey, *Main Street, Northeastern Oregon: The Founding and Development of Small Towns* (Portland, 1982), 27, 87; *An Illustrated History of Union and Wallowa Counties* (n.p., 1902), 221; Bernal D. Hug, *History of Union County, Oregon* (La Grande, 1961), 194-96, 100, 129-30, 135-37; Reynolds, "La Grande," 5.

5. Dietrich Deumling, "The Roles of the Railroad on the Development of the Grande Ronde Valley" (M.A. thesis, Northern Arizona University, 1972), 83; *La Grande Evening Observer,* September 8, 1923; Reynolds, "La Grande," 31; U.S. Bureau of the Census, *Fourteenth Census of the United States, 1920: Population,* III, 842.

6. *Fourteenth Census: Population,* III, 837; *La Grande Evening Observer,* May 14, 1949; Frank M. Jasper, "The Chinese in Union County," unpublished manuscript located in the Oregon Historical Center, 4, 8, 10-15. The 1920 federal census listed a total of 95 Asians, Indians, and "others" as La Grande residents. See *Fourteenth Census: Population,* III, 844.

7. *Fourteenth Census: Population,* III, 844-45; U.S. Bureau of the Census, *Census of Religious Bodies: 1926,* I, 664-65. The religious census listed 1499 Mormons and 661 Roman Catholics in Union County. One La Grande KKK officer noted that a "good Mormon cannot be a klansman for first he owes his allegiance to his church, but if he can live up to our oath he is accepted by this organization." Yet the klavern agreed to write Oregon Grand Dragon Fred Gifford for clarification three months later. Klan Minutes, January 26, April 24, 1923.

8. Klan Minutes, May 11, December 5, 1922; March 13, 1923; *La Grande Evening Observer,* May 16, 1922. The klavern's minutes identify "Kleagle Warner" as the man who first organized the La Grande chapter. See Klan

Minutes, May 11, 1922; March 13, 1923. The Pendleton Klan's role in gaining La Grande charter privileges was acknowledged in Klan Minutes, March 17, 1923. For occupations of many La Grande Klansmen, see Brinkman, *La Grande City Directory* (1921), and *Polk's Union and Wallowa Counties Directory* (1917).

9. Lawrence J. Saalfeld, *Forces of Prejudice in Oregon, 1920–1925* (Portland, 1984), 45; R. H. Sawyer, *The Truth About the Invisible Empire of the Ku Klux Klan* (Portland, 1922); *La Grande Evening Observer,* May 16, 1922. For Sawyer's anti-Semitism, see *Oregon Voter,* April 15, 1922.

10. Klan Minutes, May 11, 18, 25, 31, June 8, 15, 22, July 7, August 17, 24, 31, December 5, 1922; March 13, 1923.

11. Ibid., October 17, 1922; January 2, 9, 23, 1923.

12. Ibid., December 12, 1922; February 6, 1923. For a sympathetic description of the symbolism of Klan robes, masks, and fiery crosses, see *Imperial Night-Hawk* 1 (March 5, 1924): 6.

13. Klan Minutes, November 21, December 12, 1922; January 16, February 20, 1923.

14. Ibid., March 27, May 8, 1923. For the application process, see Klan Minutes, February 27, 1923.

15. Ibid., December 5, 19, 1922; January 2, 1923.

16. Ibid., December 19, 1922; March 27, 1923.

17. Ibid., February 27, March 27, 1923.

18. Ibid., December 12, 1922; May 8, 1923; W. J. Simmons, *The Practice of Klanishness* (*sic*) (Atlanta, 1918), 1–6. For Klan oaths of obedience, secrecy, fidelity, and klannishness, see Ku Klux Klan miscellaneous file, Oregon Historical Center.

19. Klan Minutes, November 14, December 19, 1922; January 26, March 6, 1923. Gifford told La Grande Klansmen that the Catholic church owned $55 million of property in the state. See Klan Minutes, December 11, 1923.

20. Ibid., November 21, December 19, 1922; April 3, 1923.

21. Ibid., January 26, February 6, 1923. A list of 125 businessmen eligible for Klan membership already had been distributed among a klavern solicitation committee of fifteen knights. See Klan Minutes, November 14, 1925.

22. Ibid., December 5, 19, 1922; February 20, 1923. Tull later worked at Klansman Clarence W. Bunting's Maxwell agency. See *La Grande Evening Observer,* February 16, 1923. Highly competitive small-town auto dealers needed the commercial advantages of membership in fraternal orders. See Duncan Aikman, *The Home Town Mind* (New York, 1926), 116.

23. Klan Minutes, February 13, 20, March 13, April 3, 1923.

24. Ibid., January 16, November 14, 1923; *La Grande Evening Observer,* March 23, 1923. The La Grande National Bank reported $200,000 in capital in 1923, twice the amount of its competitor. See *Gazetteer and Business Directory, 1921–1922,* 200, and *Pictoral Oregon* (Portland, 1915), 54.

---

25. The occupational status of forty-four officers or active members of the La Grande klavern was much higher than that of the general membership: 18 percent "high nonmanual," 32 percent "middle nonmanual," and 30 percent "low nonmanual." See Table 7.1. For the methodology of occupational rankings, consult Robert Alan Goldberg, *Hooded Empire: The Ku Klux Klan in Colorado* (Urbana, 1981), 31, 46, 176, 197–98, 183–86.

26. Conductors functioned as traveling clerks and operating supervisors. In railroad towns such as La Grande, their income and status sometimes equalled that of lawyers and doctors. Conductors and engineers were known as the "aristocracy of labor." See W. Fred Cottrell, *The Railroader* (Palo Alto, 1940), 18–19, 108.

27. Klan Minutes, February 20, June 5, 1923; *Salem Capital Journal,* October 19, 1922. Although klavern minutes show only 97 confirmed Klan employees of the railroad, reporter and *Capital Journal* managing editor Harry N. Crain put the figure at 250. Crain's exposé of the KKK ran as a series during the fall election campaign of 1922. He reported that Union Pacific maintenance foreman Ed Fields held the post of kleagle for the La Grande chapter, but minutes only show Fields to be an active Klan participant without formal title.

28. For the strike in La Grande, see *La Grande Evening Observer,* July 1, 3, 6, 10, 11, 12, 14, 15, 25, August 1, December 12, 1922. The nationwide walkout is described in Robert H. Zieger, *Republicans and Labor: 1919–1929* (Lexington, Kentucky, 1969), 109, 117–19, 132–33, 138. For Klan involvement in La Grande, see Klan Minutes, September 14, 1922.

29. Klan Minutes, November 14, 1922.

30. Ibid., December 5, 1922; January 16, March 6, 20, April 24, May 15, 1923.

31. Ibid., May 29, June 12, 19, 1923. *La Grande Evening Observer,* June 19, 1923.

32. Klan Minutes, January 16, 26, July 10, 1923; *La Grande Evening Observer,* July 31, 1923.

33. Klan Minutes, October 17, December 5, 19, 1922; *La Grande Evening Observer,* October 5, 9, November 2, 11, 1922. One day after his induction, Kratz announced his resignation as city manager. He quickly assumed the same post in Astoria, Oregon. Ironically, Kratz displeased Astoria Klansmen and Oregon Grand Dragon Gifford by not cooperating on patronage appointments. See *La Grande Evening Observer,* December 21, 28, 1922; *Astoria Evening Budget,* March 15, 16, 17, 18, 19, 20, 21, 22, 1923. C. M. Humphreys became a spokesman for the Brotherhood of Railway Engineers. See *La Grande Evening Observer,* February 1, 1924.

34. Klan Minutes, January 2, March 20, September 25, October 9, 1923.

35. Ibid., November 14, 1922; January 26, 1923; *Baker Morning Democrat,*

March 14, 1922; *Eminent Judges and Lawyers of the Northwest, 1843-1955* (Palo Alto, 1954), 339; *Oregon Voter,* January 12, 1929; *La Grande Evening Observer,* November 11, 1922. For the influence of agrarian discontent on the 1922 election, see *Salem Capital Journal,* November 9, 1922.

36. *Oregon Voter,* April 15, 1922; *La Grande Evening Observer,* May 20, November 9, 1922; *Portland Oregonian,* November 24, 1922.

37. Klan Minutes, October 17, November 21, 1922; January 26, March 13, 1923. For Pierce's race for governor, see Arthur H. Bone, *Oregon Cattleman/ Governor/Congressman: Memoirs and Times of Walter M. Pierce* (Portland, 1981), 95-97, 147-49, 162-64. Klan support for Pierce implied endorsement of his economic populism. See David A. Horowitz, "The Klansman as Outsider: Ethnocultural Solidarity and Antielitism in the Oregon Ku Klux Klan of the 1920s," *Pacific Northwest Quarterly* 80 (January 1989): 12-20.

38. Klan Minutes, May 8, 22, June 5, 1923; *Portland Oregonian,* February 21, 1932; September 14, 1968. Baldock served on the Klan committee to pick a justice of the peace. See Klan Minutes, September 25, 1923.

39. *La Grande Evening Observer,* August 17, 18, 1923; Klan Minutes of March 13, June 5, August 21, 1923.

40. *La Grande Evening Observer,* February 20, 26, March 18, July 27, August 13, 1923; Klan Minutes, June 5, July 10, August 28, 1923.

41. Klan Minutes, January 23, February 6, March 6, 1923.

42. Ibid., March 6, 13, April 10, May 15, October 16, November 13, 20, 27, 1923.

43. Saalfeld, *Forces of Prejudice,* 14, 101, 102; Klan Minutes, December 5, 1922; February 20, April 10, September 18, 1923.

44. Active Klansmen were those who held klavern offices, participated in lodge committee work, or brought in substantial numbers of new members. See Klan Minutes, March 13, 1923. Information concerning religious affiliation was drawn from obituaries and other newspaper stories as well as correspondence to the author from relevant churches.

45. Saalfeld, *Forces of Prejudice,* 25; Klan Minutes, October 24, 31, 1922; March 13, 1923.

46. Saalfeld, *Forces of Prejudice,* 35-37, 66-75. See David B. Tyack, "The Perils of Pluralism: The Background of the Pierce Case," *American Historical Review* 74 (October 1968): 74-98.

47. *Oregon Voter,* March 25, 1922; *Portland Oregonian,* September 13, 1922; Klan Minutes, November 14, 1922. For analyses of the ideological and nativist components to the Oregon School Bill, see Kenneth T. Jackson, *The Ku Klux Klan in the City, 1915-1930* (New York, 1967), 205-6; M. Paul Holsinger, "The Oregon School Controversy, 1922-25," *Pacific Historical Review* 37 (August 1968): 327-41; and *Oregon Voter,* October 7, 1922.

48. Klan Minutes, March 13, August 14, 28, September 25, December 11,

1923; *La Grande Evening Observer,* February 27, October 9, November 7, December 11, 13, 1923.

49. Klan Minutes, March 6, 20, August 14, 28, September 11, 1923; *La Grande Evening Observer,* November 6, December 4, 1923.

50. Klan Minutes, October 9, November 6, 13, 1923; *La Grande Evening Observer,* August 16, 30, September 8, October 10, 1923; April 29, May 2, 1924. The bond was defeated 783 to 257.

51. Klan Minutes, January 16, March 6, April 10, April 17, 1923. Former prosecuting attorney John Hodgin told Fosner that when the Klan could prove "that they held the key to law enforcement in this town, that he would consider it a high honor to have his name placed on the roll of honor." See Klan Minutes, March 6, 1923. In another aside, Fosner blamed police corruption on low salaries. See Klan Minutes, March 20, 1923.

52. Klan Minutes, December 12, 26, 1922; February 20, April 17, 24, December 4, 1923.

53. *La Grande Evening Observer,* December 14, 1922; March 14, July 12, October 20, 1923.

54. Klan Minutes, January 16, 26, December 4, 1923; *La Grande Evening Observer,* August 19, December 19, 1922; January 5, April 10, 21, August 20, November 3, December 15, 1923; January 15, March 21, 1924.

55. Klan Minutes, April 10, 17, July 17, October 23, November 6, 13, 20, 1923; *La Grande Evening Observer,* July 11, November 22, 1923.

56. *La Grande Evening Observer,* November 22, December 4, 1923; Klan Minutes, November 27, 1923.

57. Klan Minutes, March 17, November 27, 1923; *La Grande Evening Observer,* March 19, November 28, 1923.

58. Klan Minutes, May 8, 15, July 24, 31, 1923; *La Grande Evening Observer,* July 23, 24, 26, 1923.

59. Klan Minutes, December 11, 1923; *Eminent Judges and Lawyers,* 337; Jasper, "Chinese in Union County," 13–15; *La Grande Evening Observer,* December 12, 1923.

60. *La Grande Evening Observer,* February 20, 21, May 15, 17, 22, 1924. The *Oregon Voter,* May 24, 1924, reported that Cochran had Klan support.

61. *La Grande Evening Observer,* May 20, December 27, 1922; May 22, November 5, 1924; Klan Minutes, December 12, 1922; *Portland Evening Telegram,* March 21, 1923.

62. Klan Minutes, December 4, 11, 18, 26, October 23, 30, 1923; April 1, 1924. For the fragmentation and decline of the state KKK, see Saalfeld, *Forces of Prejudice,* 26–28, 56–60; *Oregon Voter,* December 8, 1923; February 9, 1924; February 13, 1926; *Portland Oregonian,* January 24, October 31, 1926. For discussion of state Klan organizational problems, see Klan Minutes,

July 17, September 4, 11, October 9, 1923. After Kligrapp Fosner resigned to attend college in September 1923, klavern minute-recording deteriorated. See Klan Minutes, September 18, 1923.

63. *La Grande Evening Observer,* February 26, 27, 28, March 3, 1924; Klan Minutes, April 15, 1924.

Conclusion: Toward a
New Historical Appraisal of the
Ku Klux Klan of the 1920s

During the latter half of the 1920s, the Ku Klux Klan rapidly faded as a significant factor in American social and political life. Part of this decline can be attributed to the sordid revelations concerning Indiana Klan leader David C. Stephenson during his sensational murder trial in 1925, but, as we have seen, the hooded order had already lost much of its appeal in western communities. Once it was no longer viewed as a promising means of addressing local problems, westerners rapidly abandoned the KKK. Here and there, groups of ardent Klansmen continued to meet well into the 1930s, but their impact and influence were minimal.

Nearly seventy years after it spread across the nation like a prairie wildfire, the Ku Klux Klan of the 1920s largely remains a historical enigma. Only a relative handful of local klaverns (almost all in urban areas) have been closely examined, and even for these chapters many questions have not been answered. We anticipate, however, that the state of Klan studies will greatly improve in the near future, particularly as historians make use of the 1920 manuscript census. In the hope of encouraging and advancing this process, we submit the following observations and suggestions.

The rise and fall of the Ku Klux Klan constituted an exceedingly complex social and political phenomenon, involving millions of individuals in many different types of communities spread across a large nation. Although much additional research remains to be done, we have discovered that many of the accepted explanations for the growth of so-called intolerance in this period are of limited usefulness. Most notably, we have not detected a struggle between cosmopolitan urban forces and declining rural and small-town elements at the heart of western Klan experiences. No doubt, the Invisible Empire developed a considerable rural following in the West and elsewhere, but the extent and nature of the hooded order's attractiveness in nonurban areas and among country people who had recently moved to the city have yet to be adequately explored. Perhaps future Klan historians will be able to demonstrate how the KKK's social agenda reflected distinct rural influences; for the present, however, we sense that the Invisible Empire's appeal cut across urban and rural lines without much difficulty and that it would be a serious mistake for students of the KKK to be uncritically committed to the concept of urban-rural conflict in the 1920s.[1]

This volume's contributors would also advise against attempting to fit the second Invisible Empire into the ethnocultural school of political analysis that has so greatly influenced the scholarly view of nineteenth-century political behavior. If the recruiting pattern of western Klans holds true for other regions (and recent work on the KKK in Indiana and western New York suggests that it does), then it is clear that the Invisible Empire succeeded in attracting balanced support across the Protestant religious spectrum, including that of Episcopalians and German-American Lutherans—groups viewed by the ethnoculturalists as having often been at political odds with evangelical Protestants. Thus, the nature of the KKK's membership may demonstrate that by the 1920s Protestant-Catholic ethnocentrism had replaced pietist-liturgical conflict as the most important influence shaping American politics.[2] The order's widespread appeal among Protestants additionally indicates that the Klan should not be viewed as being composed largely of religious fundamentalists. Although many Klansmen paid homage to the "old-time religion" and rejected the thinking of religious "modernists" in the 1920s, the vast majority did not belong to fundamentalist sects; rather, they were members of traditional evangelical and nonevangelical Protestant denominations or did not formally affiliate with a particular church. The non-fundamentalist composition of the Klan is supported by a recent evaluation of 12,000 Klansmen in Indianapolis that discovered that a lower percentage of fundamentalist church members joined the Invisible Empire than any other Protestant group in that community.[3] The Klan is best seen, therefore, as an organization with strong and direct links to mainstream Protestant society.

If the 1920s KKK does not readily conform to explanatory schemas based on urban-rural conflict, intra-Protestant ethnocultural conflict, or religious extremism, then there are numerous other promising means for assessing this movement. Once a sufficient number of case studies from a variety of regions have been produced, the national Klan experience should be compared and contrasted with other episodes of social and political activism in American history, such as Populism, the various crusades of the Progressive era, and even the civil rights, antiwar, and woman's rights movements of the 1960s and 1970s. Through the careful exploitation of social science theory, election returns, and manuscript census data, scholars will determine to what extent the KKK represented a traditional form of grass-roots insurgency.[4] Such analysis will surely have to consider the profound organizational developments that took place in the 1920s, particularly the intensified effort of political and business elites to order communities in accordance with their desire for stability, efficiency, economic growth, and the maintenance of power. As the essays in this volume have shown, the Klan was often at odds with established community leaders and regularly attempted to pose as the champion of the "common people." Whether this indicated that the Invisible Empire largely (if indirectly) served as a means of expressing class discontent is debatable (this volume's contributor's have certainly not arrived at a consensus of opinion), but the role of social and economic divisions in fueling the order's rise should nevertheless receive close scrutiny.

Beyond its political and social activism, other aspects of the second Klan merit extensive examination. The Klan's role as a fraternal group needs additional investigation, particularly in light of the new and provocative scholarship that has been produced on secret men's societies in the nineteenth century. As Nancy K. MacLean has recently demonstrated, gender analysis can be utilized to learn more about the men and women who supported the KKK.[5] The techniques of collective biography, psychological analysis, and oral history should also be effective in uncovering the influences that led Americans into the Klan. Indeed, given the large membership, geographic expansiveness, and general complexity of the Invisible Empire, the research possibilities for political, social, intellectual, religious, and cultural historians and other scholars are practically limitless.

As they advance the state of Klan studies in coming years, we believe it may be of use for students of the KKK to consider a general appraisal of the Invisible Empire based on our examination of six western klaverns. We wish to express our hope that this appraisal will not serve as a historiographical shrine at which others will worship but rather as a launching platform for more advanced analysis of this important social movement. It is with this end in mind that we present the following general evaluation.

The Knights of the Ku Klux Klan (Inc.) was not a fanatical fringe group composed of marginal men. The order drew its membership from a generally balanced cross section of the white male Protestant population, with the exception of the extreme upper and lower tiers of the socioeconomic hierarchy. In the context of early twentieth-century American society, the great bulk of Klansmen were not aberrationally racist, religiously bigoted, or socially alienated, although they were more likely to openly express and act upon their views. With a few exceptions, members of the hooded order avoided violent vigilantism.

The Klan demonstrated a multifaceted appeal, but discontent over local issues primarily fueled the organization's spectacular rise. The immediate postwar period was a time of dramatic expansion and brought problems associated with law enforcement, social morality, political control, labor relations, and the allocation of community resources. These difficulties placed great strains upon established leaders and created sizeable blocs of discontented citizens, many of whom turned to the Klan as a means of challenging the policies of dominant decision makers. This does not mean, however, that the KKK should be viewed as a uniformly antielite movement. The precise dynamics of Klan-elite interaction varied from community to community, and, as the preceding case studies have shown, certain bankers, businessmen, government officials, doctors, lawyers, ministers, and newspaper editors were among those who donned white hoods and robes in the twenties.

Whatever their social or economic standing, a commitment to civic activism united members of the order. Through the medium of the Klan, citizens discussed local problems, formulated plans of action, and vigorously pursued their social and political agendas. Although the focus of Klan activism varied according to specific community circumstances, the KKK typically espoused stricter law enforcement (especially of the prohibition statutes), open and honest government, improved social morality, and Protestant control of the schools. This hardly constituted a novel or radical program: such goals had been advocated by mainstream Protestant elements throughout the nineteenth and early twentieth centuries. For the most part, Klansmen concentrated their efforts within the political arena, although some klaverns initiated boycotts of non-Protestant businesses and occasionally attempted to regulate social conditions.

Initially, the Ku Klux Klan functioned quite well as a medium of corrective civic action. The group's zealous Protestantism, ethnic militancy, and superpatriotism attracted a dedicated core of loyalists, and a policy of absolute secrecy hindered preemptive measures by the order's opponents. Operating largely behind the scenes, the Klan was free to exploit the electorate's concerns over community problems (concerns that most Klansmen sincerely shared) and make considerable political headway. Once it had achieved a degree of electoral success, however, the Klan typically foundered. The organization failed to establish an enduring political base, demonstrated little skill in administrative or legislative matters, and allowed its enemies to take the initiative. Probably more than anything else, the Klan suffered from its practice of hooded secrecy, which left the order and its political operatives vulnerable to charges of being part of a clandestine conspiracy against the American tradition of open and democratic government. Thus, ironically, the very secrecy that had assisted the Klan in political mobilization eventually became its Achilles' heel.

Political setbacks, the fading of the order's fraternal allure, internecine feuding, and growing public antipathy all contributed to the Invisible Empire's rapid decline. When they realized that their organization had little hope of changing or improving local society, Klansmen departed in droves, evidence of the spirit of civic activism that had guided most of the membership. In some locales, pockets of diehard Klansmen held firm, but this was often because they yet hoped to make a political comeback.

It would be a mistake to view the Klan's gradual downfall as a victory of enlightened liberalism over the forces of reaction and intolerance. Many of the KKK's most dedicated foes endorsed patently racist policies, held disparaging views of Catholics and Jews, engaged in corrupt political practices, and, like the Klan, conspired in secret. In certain communities, prominent anti-Klansmen opposed the order not so much on the basis of its ideology as its potential for challenging the dominance of entrenched political and economic interests. This is not to say, however, that a historical debt of gratitude is not owed to the anti-KKK forces. Unopposed, the Ku Klux Klan certainly possessed the potential to evolve into an agency of intolerant oppression.

We realize that our portrait of the typical Klansman as a mainstream, grass-roots community activist may not retain its validity in all communities; in fact, we anticipate that future scholars will discover remarkable variety among klaverns across the nation. Yet, it is clear that the biased stereotype of the Invisible Empire as an irrational movement that lay outside the major currents of American political and social life must for the most part be discarded. Not only does this traditional view unfairly depict the millions of average citizens who joined or supported the Klan, but it obscures the racism and bigotry that have traditionally pervaded United States society. Far from being a historical aberration, the Ku Klux Klan reflected the hopes, fears, and guiding values of much of the American public in the 1920s.

NOTES

1. For important critiques of the concept of urban-rural conflict in the 1920s, see Allan J. Lichtman, *Prejudice and the Old Politics: The Presidential Election of 1928* (Chapel Hill, 1979), 122–143, and Charles W. Eagles, "Urban-Rural Conflict in the 1920's: A Historiographic Assessment," *Historian* 49 (November 1986): 26–48.

2. For major works delineating the ethnocultural argument, see Paul Kleppner, *The Cross of Culture: A Social Analysis of Midwestern Politics* (New York, 1970) and *The Third Electoral System, 1853-1892: Parties, Voters, and Political Cultures* (Chapel Hill, 1979), and Richard J. Jensen, *The Winning of the Midwest: Social and Political Conflict, 1888-1896* (Chicago, 1971). For a brilliant work assessing the importance of Protestant-Catholic ethnocentrism in 1920s politics, see Lichtman, *Prejudice and the Old Politics.*

3. Leonard J. Moore, "Citizen Klansmen: Ku Klux Klan Populism in Indiana during the 1920's," book manuscript in the possession of the editor, 93–94.

4. An important first step in this regard has been taken in Robert A. Goldberg, *Grassroots Resistance: Social Movements in Twentieth Century America* (Belmont, California, 1990).

5. Mark C. Carnes, *Secret Ritual and Manhood in Victorian America* (New Haven, 1989); Nancy K. MacLean, "Behind the Mask of Chivalry: Gender, Race, and Class in the Making of the Ku Klux Klan of the 1920's in Georgia" (Ph.D. dissertation, University of Wisconsin, 1989).

Contributors

CHRISTOPHER N. COCOLTCHOS received his Ph.D. in history from the University of California at Los Angeles. His doctoral dissertation, "The Invisible Government and the Viable Community: The Ku Klux Klan in Orange County, California, in the 1920s" (1979), helped usher in a new era in Klan scholarship and remains one of the most comprehensive local studies of the KKK to date. In recent years, he has been employed as a computer-services consultant.

LARRY R. GERLACH received his Ph.D. in history from Rutgers University and is professor of history at the University of Utah. He is the author of many books and scholarly articles, including *Blazing Crosses in Zion: The Ku Klux Klan in Utah* (1982).

ROBERT A. GOLDBERG, professor of history at the University of Utah, received his Ph.D. in history from the University of Wisconsin at Madison. *Hooded Empire: The Ku Klux Klan in Colorado* (1981), *Barry Goldwater* (1995), and *Enemies Within: The Culture of Conspiracy in Modern America* (2001) are among his many acclaimed publications.

DAVID A. HOROWITZ received his Ph.D. from the University of Minnesota and is professor of history at Portland State University. His publications include *On the Edge: A New History of Twentieth Century America* (1990), *Beyond Right and Left: Insurgency and the Establishment* (1996), and *Inside the Klavern: The Secret History of a Ku Klux Klan of the 1920s* (1999).

SHAWN LAY, associate professor of history at Coker College, received his Ph.D. in history from Vanderbilt University. He is the author of *War, Revolution, and the Ku Klux Klan: A Study of Intolerance in a Border City* (1985) and *Hooded Knights on the Niagara: The Ku Klux Klan in Buffalo, New York* (1995).

LEONARD J. MOORE received his Ph.D. in history from the University of California at Los Angeles and is associate professor of history at McGill University. He is the author of *Citizen Klansmen: The Ku Klux Klan in Indiana, 1921–1928* (1991)

ECKARD V. TOY, the author of numerous articles on right-wing radicalism in the Pacific Northwest, received his Ph.D. in history from the University of Oregon. He has taught in the history departments at both the University of Oregon and Oregon State University.

Index

Index

Quaid, John E., 74, 86

Raab, Earle, 27–28
Randel, William P., 23
Randell, Andrew L., 73
Ray, L. L., 168
Reynolds, Charles H., 196
Reynolds, James E., 187, 200
Rhodes, John Ford, 3
Rice, Arnold S., 23
Rider, W. L., 78
Roberts, Waldo, 179
Rogers, Dee, 205, 206
Royal Riders of the Red Robe, 176
Russell, James, 196–97

Salt Lake City, Utah: population and ethnic
    groups in, 121, 126–27; social change in,
    127; Mormon-gentile conflict in, 127–28,
    131, 135–36; Klan in, 128–47; politics in,
    134–36, 142–43, 144–45; antimask ordinance
    in, 140–43 passim. *See also* Salt Lake Klan
    No. 1
Salt Lake Klan No. 1: founding and early
    development of, 125–26, 128–29; initial de-
    cline of, 129–36; membership of, 130–31,
    140; economic solidarity of, 131; Mormon
    opposition to, 126, 132–34, 137–38, 146–47;
    opposition to Mormons of, 131, 133–34;
    relationship with Masons of, 134; revival
    of, 136–37, 138; fraternal activities of, 138–
    42; recruiting of Mormons by, 138, 140;
    political activism of, 142–43, 144–45; final
    decline of, 143–45; law enforcement efforts
    of, 145; general evaluation of, 145–47
Sawyer, Harry, 138
Sawyer, Reuben H., 153–54, 169, 170, 187,
    201
Sawyer, William G., 187
Schafer, Joseph, 172
Scotten, Frank, Jr., 74, 86
Shannon, David A., 28
Sheldon, Henry D., 172, 178
Shelton, Robert M., 2
Short, C. E., 203
Simmons, William Joseph, 5–6, 8, 39, 56, 67,
    169, 191
Sinnott, Nicholas J., 199, 207
Sirmans, Clifford L., 86
Skinner, Eugene F., 162

Slaback, Arthur, 109, 110, 112
Slater, Hughes D., 78
Smith, Claud T., 75
Smith, George Albert, 137–38
Smith, Leonard J., 206
Southern Publicity Association, 7
Stapleton, Benjamin F., 47–50 passim, 57, 58
Stark, William, 100, 101, 108, 110, 111
Stewart, Ulysses S., 80
Stiles, Pearl, 206
Stivers, E. V., 161
Stock, Godfrey, 114, 115
Stoner, Jesse B., 2
Stuart, Gordon, 129
Sunday, Billy, 157
Sweeney, Joseph U., 72

Tannenbaum, Frank, 20, 22
Tavenner, L. W., 138
Thompson, Michael J., 167, 177
Tull, C. H., 192, 193, 205
Tyler, Elizabeth, 7, 8

U.S.A. Club (in Anaheim), 113, 114, 115
U.S. Klans, 2
University of Oregon: 163; Klan involvement
    with, 165, 166, 170, 171–74
Utah: population and ethnic groups in, 121–
    25; Mormons in, 121, 122–23; Klan in, 121,
    136, 137, 140; economy of, 123–24; social
    change in, 124

Van Cise, Philip, 43, 55, 56
Vehrs, George, 198
Vergin, Peter Vasillevich, 175, 177
Vowell, Charles L., 86, 89

Wade, Wyn Craig, 18
Wald, Kenneth D., 29
Ward, Charles S., 79, 90
Weaver, Norman F., 10, 25, 26
Webb, Asa R., 74, 86
Weeks, Lyman W., 197
White, William G., 167
White Citizens Councils, 2
Williams, Harry, 197
Williams, Parley L., 135
Willson, Ellis O., 208–9
Wilson, George, 134
Wilson, Woodrow, 4, 5, 165

The University of Illinois Press
is a founding member of the
Association of American University Presses.

University of Illinois Press
1325 South Oak Street
Champaign, IL 61820-6903
www.press.uillinois.edu